Truly remarkable! Engaging, yet practical, this self-help book reads like a novel, but is packed full of helpful strategies to enhance emotional, physical, spiritual and relational well-being. We found ourselves identifying with Mike in both his victories and setbacks as he struggles to make positive changes in his life. What is portrayed is a realistic, yet hopeful, sense of the gradual process of growth and change, rather than promises of quick fixes that so often end in disappointment. The helping roles of friends, pastors, physicians and counselors are woven into the story, allowing readers to explore potential options for themselves. Whether on their own, or as part of a small group, everyone could benefit from this book.

HEATHER DAVEDIUK GINGRICH, PH.D.
ASSOCIATE PROFESSOR OF COUNSELING, DENVER SEMINARY

FRED GINGRICH, D.MIN.
CHAIR OF THE COUNSELING DIVISION, ASSOCIATE PROFESSOR OF COUNSELING
DENVER SEMINARY

This book gets at the crux of healthy living, recognizing that health, and the counterpart, illness, are directly tied to our spiritual, social and physical condition. In an easy to read, interactive, engaging format, *The Rest of Health* is a superb book for anyone who wants to experience real health.

DOUGLAS PAAUW, MD
PROFESSOR OF MEDICINE, RATHMANN FAMILY FOUNDATION ENDOWED CHAIR IN
PATIENT-CENTERED CLINICAL EDUCATION
UNIVERSITY OF WASHINGTON SCHOOL OF MEDICINE

Marriage and family therapist Sonya Cameron, and her physician husband Dave Cameron, M.D., have teamed up fascinating insights from medicine and Christian counseling to bring readers practical help with their lives. Using a bio-psycho-social-spiritual holistic approach, they draw readers into their book with a clever storyline, while providing impactful observations and concrete suggestions for making changes in seven key skill areas for healthy thinking, feeling and being. I highly recommend that you read this book—and share it with others!

JOHN AUXIER, PH.D. ACTING PRESIDENT AND DEAN, TRINITY WESTERN SEMINARY
ACTS SEMINARIES | TRINITY WESTERN UNIVERSITY

THE REST OF HEALTH

Learn the 7 Vital Strategies to Optimize Your Well-being

David Cameron, M.D.
and Sonya Cameron, MC, LMFT

VMI PUBLISHERS • SISTERS, OREGON

Published by VMI Publishers
Sisters, Oregon
www.vmipublishers.com

All Scripture quotations, unless otherwise stated, are taken from the *Holy Bible: New International Version*. Copyright ©1973, 1978, 1984 by International Bible Society. Used by permission of Zondervan Publishing House. All rights reserved.

Verses marked NASB are taken from the *New American Standard Bible*, Copyright © 1960, 1962, 1963, 1968, 1971, 1972, 1973, 1975, 1977, 1995 by the Lockman Foundation. Used by permission.

DISCLAIMER

The story in this book and the case study examples within it are fictional. No real names, places or details from the lives of our patients or clients have been used. Any similarity is coincidence.

This book describes general principles for health and wellness and is not intended to take the place of medical advice and treatment from your personal physician or therapist. In the context of a book, the authors are not able to give professional medical advice that would be specifically tailored to any individual. Neither the publisher nor the authors are liable for any possible medical or psychological consequences or outcomes of readers following the information in this book and do not take any responsibility for how readers interpret and apply information to their lives. Readers are advised to consult with personal healthcare professionals to devise healthcare plans that will address their individual needs.

ISBN: 978-1-933204-96-3
ISBN: 1-933204-96-6

Library of Congress: 2009933742

Cover design by Juanita Dix, j.d. Design, www.designjd.net

Acknowledgments

Just as it takes a village to raise a child, it takes a committed community of supportive and encouraging family and friends to help write a book. We are grateful to those around us who have influenced and shaped the way that we think. In particular, we thank Barbara Sparks, Fred and Heather Gingrich, Rob and Louise McFadden, Doug Paauw, John Medina, Steve Schell and John Auxier for mentoring and inspiring us at various levels in our training.

We feel fortunate to be a part of the family at Northwest Foursquare Church. We would like to express our gratitude to several of our pastors and leaders including Curt and Sharon Lueck, Craig Kessel, Dave Norcross, Cathy Haggard, Tony and Charmaine Sierra, Don Shelby, Scott Dungan and Frank and Kathleen Greer for investing in us and providing opportunities to explore and follow the calling that God has put upon our lives.

There were many times we could have given up during this long and arduous process. God graciously brought encouragement through His creative Holy Spirit and through friends in our lives such as Victor Burgos, Oliver Graves, Julie Prince, Erin Hitchcock, Jim Williams, Arnie and Angela Walker, Baldwin Way, Stacie Anderson and Brianna Bean. They have helped us through providing helpful feedback and nudging us to keep going. We are thankful to our family and all of our friends who have supported us and continually reminded us of the merits of the topic. We have appreciated working with our publisher, VMI, and are grateful for their belief in our project. A special thanks to Laura Cowan, who through her editing made our book smoother and better to read.

While writing a book as a couple, we learned further insights about each other, how to love each other more fully and how to improve our conflict resolution skills (there were several times when we had lengthy discussions over a single word). We are grateful to God that He has drawn us together in our marriage. Both of our strengths were needed in the writing process, and neither one of us could have completed it on our own. Our marriage is stronger after going through this project together—I love you!

TABLE OF CONTENTS

FOREWORD

Dave and Sonya have written a book that makes issues of the heart understandable. We are invited inside the thoughts of a man named Mike as he moves from being a religious man to someone in relationship with a God who loves him. The images in the book are vivid and we find ourselves sharing Mike's experiences as he discovers how the Bible applies in practical ways to health, lifestyle, emotions and relationships. The process leads each of us gently to reflect on our own lives.

The Rest of Health is a great resource for small groups. The story leaves us engaged and wanting to talk about what we've read, and the discussion questions which follow each chapter make leading that discussion easy and keep the conversation on track. Practical self-assessments are provided for personal growth at the end of the book.

Though the story reads easily and is conversational in tone, it deals with deep theological matters. It leaves the reader hungry to draw closer to God. Through it all the fear of submitting to God is dispelled as we discover how much He loves us and how faithful He is to care for us.

STEVE SCHELL D.MIN.
SENIOR PASTOR OF NORTHWEST FOURSQUARE CHURCH, FEDERAL WAY, WA.
MEMBER OF FOURSQUARE DENOMINATION BOARD OF DIRECTORS

Introduction

We're glad you picked up this book. We purposefully wrote it in a creative nonfiction style in order to relay vital information woven throughout an enjoyable story that we hope will be a pleasurable way for you to learn. In addition to being beneficial to our patients and students, the skills and concepts in this book have certainly been influential in our own lives.

This book is for you if:

- You are a person who is ready for change but feels frustrated or discouraged.
- You are having a hard time selecting from the wide array of health information that's available and are unsure how to implement it practically in your life.
- You are a professional in the medical field, counseling field, church ministry, clergy, and/or a layperson assisting people to achieve better health.
- You are involved in a small group ministry through your church and are looking for some innovative material on Christian living to use in your church.
- You want sound, professional health information that's written without medical jargon, in accessible language, so it can be used by laypeople as well as professionals.

Let us introduce you to one of our typical patients. We'll call him John. Everything seemed to be normal for him. That is unless you asked him about his daily fatigue, headaches and back pain. After he had several medical tests performed, no specific medical problems were discovered. But by taking just a cursory look into his life, several clues could be found. His father passed away six months ago, his sixteen-year-old car has been in the shop every month recently, and he has been facing immense financial pressure. Besides work, he cut out his other normal activities such as playing soccer, going to church and joining his wife to go out with friends. Gradually, he became more somber, isolated and pessimistic. This showed up in his relationships, as he grew more disgruntled with family and friends.

In our medical and counseling practices, these are the kind of common issues that we see people facing. It is also the kind of story we regularly hear from people who attend our seminars. Lives are not compartmentalized. People are not unidimensional. There is a complex interplay between what is going on in everyone's physical, psychological, social and spiritual lives. All four of these elements of health need to be addressed and integrated in order to achieve a complete framework for wellness. This is the philosophy we go by whenever we teach or write.

Our views have been influenced by professors and mentors who have shared their wisdom of looking at health in a comprehensive way. We are grateful to them, and our work and ministry have benefited from their meaningful contributions to our lives.

Based on our training and clinical experience, we developed seven skills that we consistently see as the most influential for maintaining or recovering health and well-being. They have been field-tested in our practices with great results, and individually these concepts have been validated in medical and psychological literature. Developing skills in these seven critical areas equips readers to become unstuck and free to reach their goals.

Now, one of the things that brings us the greatest joy is seeing our students and patients undergo this transformation. We are blessed when students and patients tell us how their lives have changed as a result of developing these skills. Daily we see how improvement in these areas mends people's lives and relationships. Using the comprehensive model laid out in this book, they achieve the health, freedom and peace of mind that they have long desired.

To reinforce the material, discussion/reflection questions are at the end of each chapter and can used by individuals or small groups. If you can't find a small group to go through this book with, you could ask a friend to read it and discuss it with you. It's advantageous to have someone encountering these concepts and skills at the same time you are.

We hope this book will satisfy your hunger for techniques to improve the way you feel and experience life. Through the use of concrete strategies and practical tools, we want to assist you in going from good intentions to the reality of better health.

HOW TO USE THIS BOOK

This book will help you the most if you don't rush through it. Take advantage of the self-assessments and activities in this book. There are also blank worksheets and completed sample worksheets available in the appendices to assist you in applying the material to your life. Use these worksheets to get the most out of this book. Please feel free to photocopy them for use in your group or individual study.

We hope that with the help of this book you will be able to overcome barriers, attain the changes you desire for your life and become released into new possibilities. Parts of it may be hard work, but ultimately it will make life easier. It's worth it.

SKILL #1

LOOKING TO LEARN

## CHAPTER ONE

The Emergency Room

A re you still having chest pain?"

"Yes, but it's not as bad as it was."

Standing next to the gurney, the physician picked the EKG up off the machine. "Okay, Mike Forrester. Let's see here." The doctor mumbled the results of the heart exam as he read it. "Regular rate and rhythm, no Q waves or ST changes..."

Mike thought to himself, *I have no idea what he's talking about. I just need to know, am I having a heart attack or not?* He nodded as if he perfectly understood what the physician was saying.

"Looks pretty good," the physician said. "We drew some labs to make sure. They'll be back soon. Tell me about your chest pain."

Mike explained, "Well, I can't really say that it was chest pain for sure. It felt like my heart was pounding out of my chest, and I couldn't catch my breath. I was so uncomfortable I couldn't sit still. My vision went blurry, and it seemed like I was in the twilight zone. My body was acting as if I was running a marathon, even though I was just sitting on our couch. This sort of thing has happened before, but never as bad as this. That's why I came to the ER."

"Any tingling in your arms or numbness?"

"Yeah. I had some numbness in my fingertips of both hands for a few minutes."

"How about radiation of the pain or discomfort away from the chest?"

"No."

"How long have you been having these symptoms?"

"About thirty minutes."

"What seemed to cause your symptoms?"

"I have no idea."

The physician inquired about his past medical problems and family history of illness. Mike had been healthy and didn't smoke or drink much alcohol. There seemed to be no apparent reason for his symptoms until he heard the doctor's next question.

"Any major stresses going on in your life?"

There was a short pause, and Mike deliberately avoided his wife Sara's piercing green eyes as she sat in the chair beside the gurney. "Not really. Well, I guess I have the usual stress with work, and you know, with life in general," Mike lied. He had no intention of sharing with the physician his marital problems or his difficulties with Travis.

After a few more minutes of questions, the physician performed a brief physical exam and then was off to see his next patient, who happened to be in the same ER room. Mike could overhear the whole story about how the man had run out of money and stopped drinking his fifth of whiskey a couple days before. The man was now complaining about bugs crawling all over his skin. Anxiously, Mike looked around but couldn't see any bugs in the room. Still, he was afflicted with the compulsive urge to scratch all over.

RUMINATIONS

Thinking about the insects brought to mind the topic of Travis again. Work was becoming rather unpleasant because of this co-worker. Mike used to love his job. For a while, work had been a refuge, a place of mutual respect with only a few exceptions. One of these exceptions was Travis. While Travis seemed to keep busy, his work needed constant revision to work out the kinks. As a result, the whole team was held back. Mike couldn't stand having a project delayed. Being somewhat of a perfectionist, his internal drive compelled him to produce the highest quality work. The problem began when Travis started seeking out Mike for help. The job needed to be done properly, and unless Mike intervened the project was not going to be done correctly.

Mike had considered his options. *I could let the design flaws be discovered by the testing team, but that would just create more work for others later. Or, I could help everybody out by catching the errors early.* He had the skills to rework the code, so Mike agreed to help. But it came with a price—his time.

After a while, Mike began to rationalize that helping Travis was a decision driven by compassion. His church upbringing taught him that he was supposed to help people in need. Travis sure seemed to be in need. As a result, Mike would put in the extra time to compensate for Travis' inadequacies in performance. This extra work began to wear on Mike, and he could tell that there was something wrong. Bitterness had crept in.

For all his busyness, he doesn't produce much. How can he make so many mistakes? I feel bad for him, because he can't think things through and he hasn't been improving. Why doesn't our boss tell him how to do a better job? There's no way that I'd tell him. It would be insulting to him if I showed him how to improve, since he has been here longer than I have. Mike's imagination had begun to consider amusing possibilities. *Maybe he is preoccupied in some on-line candle-lit chat room on a hot, romantic cyber date.* It would probably never last. It would be over once the girl met Travis and discovered his unkempt black hair, disheveled clothes and potent body odor.

I wonder if anyone else at work has a problem with Travis. Maybe I'm making a bigger deal of this than it really is.

This pattern of donating more of his time to Travis at work became more onerous for Mike. He was enjoying work less and becoming more irritable. For most of his life, Mike had been quite patient with others, but he knew that he was becoming more cantankerous. He felt guilty for this change.

This is not me, Mike thought, I'm usually an easy-going guy. Plus, as a good church-going person, I'm not supposed to be irritable all the time. What happened to me? I need to work harder at not being so annoyed. I'll just ignore it and hope it goes away on its own.

Insidiously, Mike's work hours stretched longer and longer, to the point where Sara was questioning where he was going after work.

THE TEST RESULTS

While Mike was wrapped up in his thoughts about work, Sara was becoming impatient with how long things were taking in the ER. She was also getting upset that Mike wasn't paying attention to her. Instead of bringing it up at that moment, she decided to wait until she knew that he didn't have a heart attack. Casually, she opened a magazine and tried to read.

Both were startled when the physician slipped through the curtain and loudly declared, "All the labs are fine. I'm not exactly sure what caused your chest pain, but it doesn't appear to be coronary artery disease. You have a very low probability of having had a heart attack, because you're so young and your story was atypical for angina. You could benefit by losing a few pounds, though. What happened could be related to stress in your life. Regardless, I recommend that you see your primary care physician within the next couple of days for follow-up. Any questions?"

Considering it was now one in the morning, Mike and Sara were both exhausted and their questions forgotten. Mike was still thinking about the doctor's comment for him to lose a few pounds.

"Okay, my nurse will be in to get you checked out soon. I'm glad that you're feeling better."

As they were leaving the emergency room, Sara murmured under her breath, "I'm going to be so tired at work tomorrow." Too drained to reply to the veiled snub, Mike said nothing.

Questions for Group Discussion or
Individual Reflection

1) Why did you decide to read this book or join a small group studying this book? What do you hope to get out of it? Looking at this book's Table of Contents, is there a certain one of the seven skills that you most want to learn, or is there a certain area of your health in which you are especially looking for improvement?

2) Stress from people's work or personal lives has a way of impacting the way they behave in their relationships and how they communicate with others. We see some of these dynamics in the relationship between Mike and his wife, Sara. In general, how would you describe the various ways that people act or communicate when they are stressed out compared to when they feel life is more manageable and peaceful?

3) Without mentioning anyone's name, do you know someone who is having health problems that you suspect are due to stress in his/her life or other types of problems that are not physical in nature? In what ways have you seen the connection between this person's physical health and fluctuations in his/her psychological, relational or spiritual health and well-being?

4) What stresses are you currently facing in life? How is that stress affecting you? For instance, is it impacting your health, sleep, mood, relationships or work? You can expect each of the skills taught in this book to help you to deal with the various types of pressures and strains you experience.

## CHAPTER TWO

Unrestrained

Morning came much too quickly. Mike hoisted himself up on the café stool. Engrossed in thought, he waited for his Americano. The early morning sunlight came through the window and lit up his furrowed brow. He was a good-looking man with shortly trimmed brown hair. His face exhibited the expression of both confidence and competence. His prominent cheekbones and dimples displayed his charm, and others could not help but find him to be jovial and unassuming. The last few years, however, had taken their toll. Mike's athletic frame now held an additional twenty pounds, which made him look like a football player that had gone into retirement. Darkness was painted under his lower eyelids, and the valleys had deepened between his eyebrows.

Maybe it was too much caffeine. That might have caused the heart palpitations. But there's no way that I can cut down right now, not in the middle of our project. I hope these attacks go away.

Mike liked stopping by the café Wholly Grounds on the way to work. It was very convenient, just down the street from his house.

"Good morning, Mike," welcomed Isaiah, the café owner. "You're right on time, 5:30 A.M." As the only customer there that early in the morning, he was now on a first-name basis with the barista.

"How are you today, Isaiah?" Mike asked.

"Couldn't be better. What'll it be? The usual?"

"That'd be great."

The scent of freshly ground coffee beans filled the room as Isaiah went about his business and started making the Americano. Mike stood patiently while his mind raced. There were more important issues to consider than a heart beating fast every now and again. His mind reflected back to the problems with his wife and job.

WHAT WENT WRONG?

Ordinarily, Mike got along with other people easily and was esteemed by his colleagues and friends. One of the main problems Mike faced was that his wife did not join in the ranks of those who respected him.

What's wrong with her? Mike pondered. *Sara never used to act this way.* Mike went on to re-live in his mind the experiences that had been causing him distress. Things had been going so well in his marriage in the beginning. They had enjoyed the normal day-to-day activities such as grocery shopping, working on their house and playing sports together. They used to not want to be apart.

At some point, they began arguing more frequently, and Sara buried her normal light-hearted behavior. Even Mike's self-effacing attempts at humor were met with a lukewarm, half-hearted smile. *Why was she like this? What's wrong with our relationship?*

Mike grimaced as he remembered their argument a few nights ago. The continual replay of the event perpetuated the torment. He had been in a great mood when he got home. Work had gone well, and his boss had complimented his excellence in performance and morale-building on their recent project. Mike's excitement to tell Sara the news of what had happened at work imploded right from the beginning of their conversation.

"Hey, I'm home!" Mike exclaimed as he met her in the kitchen.

"I see that. Once again it's an hour after you said you'd be home and oh—so surprising—no phone call from you," Sara said sarcastically. Turning her back to him, she stepped up on the stool and stretched to reach the top shelf of the cupboards. This left Mike staring at the back of her short brown hair that suited her feisty personality.

"When I'm going to be late from work," Sara emphasized, "I always call to let you know that I'm fine, so that you won't be worried. Why is that so hard for you?"

Mike hated conflict and looked for an escape. It was time to stealthily move into "defuse the situation mode." He was now pretty good at deflecting the arrows from Sara's emotional outbursts, but timing was critical. One wrong slip of his shield could be disastrous.

All I need to do is to get her venting about something else, and I should be off the hook, he thought. *I see it work on reality TV shows all the time. Maybe I could get her upset about her family and then she would forget about me.*

"I guess I've been hanging out with your father and it's starting to rub off a little," Mike said with a playful smile.

Sara took the bait. "Don't even bring up my dad right now. Do you know what he did? He called my work 'cute,' as if I worked at a little plastic Fischer-Price school. I didn't train to be a professional childcare worker to hear his condescending mockery of my career."

Mike took a deep breath and let down his guard, realizing that he had survived the attack. She was no longer focused on his lack of punctuality. All Mike wanted was to come home, have a place to relax and share what had happened at work that day. Setting his laptop on the kitchen table, he informed her, "I have some good news from work."

"I need some good news," Sara replied with a sigh.

"My boss recognized my achievements at work today for the successful completion of the last project."

"Finally. You spend all of your time at the office, so you should be honored."

He knew that she was probably trying to be supportive by this statement; however, he was hoping that she would have been more excited about the compliment that he had received. He also wished that she didn't complain about how much he worked. Unpleasant conversations about the quantity of his workload regularly surfaced and stirred the waters. They never reached unity on this matter, and any mention of the topic tended to quickly irritate him. He had incorrectly assumed Sara would have been a bit happier with the recognition. His unmet expectation made her comment strike harder than he anticipated.

Normally, Mike could contain his emotions and pretend that he was not angry. Today, Mike couldn't stop himself. This was one of those few occasions where he could not fully restrain himself. He turned and muttered, "At least I don't spend all my time trying to please an insatiable father."

He regretted the statement even as it was coming out of his mouth and knew what would come next. Like a fool, he had returned her criticism by reopening her most painful issue. *Uh-oh, this is going to set her off. I should probably apologize to prevent this from escalating, but that would put her in the one-up position, and that would legitimize all of her arguments. It would admit defeat, and then she would think that I am fully to blame. An apology would mean that I would have to do all of the changing and she would be fully innocent.*

If Sara was angry just minutes before, she was now furious. "How can you bring that up again? I'm not the problem. You're the one who has the problem. Have you looked in the mirror and seen the workaholic staring back at you?"

She was talented at turning the tables towards his issues. He had always respected her verbal skills, unless they were aimed against him. They were a challenge to argue against. This skill of hers occasionally came back to dissect him with the swift precision of a scalpel blade.

Sara continued, "You seem to make it so much harder on yourself. If only you'd listen to my suggestions then you wouldn't always be angry about work. You agreed to stay late even though you wanted to play basketball and get some exercise. Why do you do it?"

Having an uncanny ability to pinpoint the real source of the problem, she was right on target as usual. Mike tried to buy some time. He replied, "I'm not sure." This was not entirely true, since he was often recognized at work for staying late and going the extra mile. He was highly esteemed at the office, and he had a reputation to uphold. However, mentioning that right now would open a new topic that he was leery to discuss. *If I brought that up, then Sara would question my allegiance. She'll ask if I care more about her or the office. As it is, she makes comments about my long hours and her suspicion of an affair. She'll also probe into why I care so much what other people think. This would lead to her bringing up my need to get others' approval and my need to make sure that everyone at the office is getting along.*

Mike was indeed the peacemaker. Ever since he was a kid, he had been the peacemaker. When the family fought, he would step up the humor to break the ice and change the topic. This strategy had worked for him in the past. He hated it when strong emotion was expressed. Anger, jealousy and disappointment were the hardest to be around. These emotions were time-consuming and draining. He concentrated his efforts to avoid these emotions at all cost. Deflect, derail and defend. He believed that there was no purpose to these outbursts, so it was best to avoid them as much as possible. He'd seen some families where their typical form of communication was heated arguments. Their lives seemed so turbulent and war-torn; he wanted no part of that.

Mike was convinced that steering clear of arguments was in everyone's best interest, and there wasn't much that could persuade him any differently. He felt that it was best to only focus on the positive things and to ignore problems.

Why submit to this barrage of attacks, he thought, as he was disengaging from the dispute. There was an awkward pause.

Sara took the opportunity to state what was completely obvious to her. "I'll tell you why. You complain about your co-worker and your job—the same job that you used to love. You tell me these things and do nothing about it. You're all talk and no action."

Mike was indeed stuck in a rut.

Now Mike was riled by his wife's disrespectful insults. *If I become emotional that'll give her the upper hand, and she'll win once again*, he thought. Mike had had enough. He took the nearest escape route by shutting her out.

"Fine, Sara. I'm sorry, but I have things to do." Mike was resigned to retreat, or else the pain would continue. He grabbed the newspaper and exited the kitchen.

Similar to several of their previous fights, there was an ending but no resolution. Afterwards, the tension displayed itself as a palpable coolness. They spoke to each other about the events of the week, the weather, but nothing of real substance. Vulnerability was gone, and trust was broken. Mike expected that they would be annoyed with each other for a while.

Unexpected Hope

Engrossed in the flashback, Mike lost his awareness that he was in a café and soon to be on his way to work. While he was contemplating the recent events, the barista noticed his glazed look.

Isaiah waved a hand in front of Mike's stare with a sweeping gesture to break the reverie, then handed him his drink. "Have a good day, Mike. I hope that you get it figured out."

"Thanks." Ever since Mike had started to come to work so early, he had become a more frequent customer to get his morning dose of caffeine. Mike did wonder how Isaiah could be so awake in the morning. *Oh yes, of course, he owns a café and is a patron of his own trade. However, even if he is sucking down a dozen cappuccinos, why does he take the time to bother with what's going on in my life? His questions are usually right on—how does he do that? It's a good thing that I don't tell him the whole truth; otherwise he would know what I'm really like.* Mike grabbed his drink and headed for the door.

Isaiah set down the bag of roasted coffee beans and hollered, "Looks like you got a lot on your plate there, buddy. You almost left your laptop. Better watch it. If you aren't careful, I'll hack into your system and download some of my bluegrass music onto it."

"Whoa, don't contaminate it. Okay, I'll be more careful. You're right, I've had a lot on my mind."

"You know, it usually takes just a little tweak here and there, and not a major overhaul," Isaiah said with a smile.

"What do you mean?" Mike said quizzically, knowing that Isaiah was no longer talking about bluegrass and laptops.

"Don't pay any attention to me. I have no idea what I am talking about. It's just speculation," said the barista, luring him in.

"Speculation about what?" Mike asked with curiosity.

Isaiah paused a second before responding. "On first appearance, you look like you have it all together. I've seen that picture in your wallet of your beautiful wife. You have a great job, family in the area, and lo and behold, a good sense of humor, unsurpassed only by my own."

Mike's curiosity now exceeded his normal inclination to change topics. "What are you saying?" he asked.

"Most people would think that you have everything you want. Let me make a disclaimer here: I am no Dr. Phil, nor would I want you to think that I am psychoanalyzing you. However, I like to people-watch. It comes with the job." Isaiah planted both hands on the counter and leaned closer, poised for overly dramatic sarcasm. Putting on a falsely intense whisper, he said, "It's gotta be, when you offer the wonderful brown elixir that makes the world go round."

Isaiah stood up and returned to his normal relaxed self. "Actually, I think our society does depend too much on caffeine. It makes a statement of how much efficiency and productivity are esteemed in our society. The caffeine keeps the engine going, but is that really what's most important?"

Mike liked the sassy yet philosophical turn that the conversation was taking. He used to stay up late in the night talking with Sara like this.

Mike replied in pragmatic fashion, "I guess it depends on if you want to keep your job. By the way, how can you stay in business trying to convince the world about the ills of caffeine? Maybe I need a refund." Mike smiled.

"Are you kidding me? You oughta tip me extra."

Mike was quickly feeling more comfortable around the wiry, say-it-like-it-is barista. It was as if he knew how much to pry and when to back off. *Who cares how much this guy knows about my life?* Mike began to think. *He doesn't know anyone else that I know. So what if I tell him what's really going on? I doubt that he'd broadcast my problems to other people. He seems to know that something is wrong, and maybe he could help. What did he mean anyway that it takes just a few tweaks and not a major overhaul?*

Mike sighed and said, "I'm still curious about the little tweak that you mentioned. I think I could use some in my marriage."

"Ah yes, just as I thought." Isaiah leaned against the cupboards behind him, with one hand in his pocket. "You sold your car, bought a Harley, and you want your wife to join you on your road trip to Sturgis. Wait, no, that's my life." At first, Mike was beginning to believe Isaiah, until he noticed the glint in his eyes.

The barista's countenance changed. "No really Mike, how are things going for you?"

Constrained by the clock, Mike briefly outlined the issues that had been going on in his marriage and his work recently. It felt very odd and unnerving to be exposing his life to someone that he had only known casually for a short while. Regret overcame him. *I'm being foolish. I've displayed all of my trash out there for him to see. That was a dumb mistake, he thought.*

Mike abruptly halted the story of his life and said, "I shouldn't be unloading on you like this. I'm sorry. I should be getting to work."

Isaiah responded, "No worries, I am a lot less expensive than a psychiatrist. Anyway, I appreciate your honesty, and I think you have a lot going for you."

"Really? That's good to hear." Mike was surprised that Isaiah seemed unflappable and that he had responded to him without a hint of condemnation.

"Plus, you gotta start somewhere. I think that you're already off and running."

"How can you say that?" Mike inquired.

"Well, you're ready to ask for help."

"Are you saying that I need help?"

Isaiah's playful grin also portrayed compassion and revealed the intricate wrinkles on his dark, leathered skin. "Well, you have listed your problems and told me how they haven't gone away by themselves. It's the wise person who's willing to listen to others who can help. So you've come to the right place."

"Oh wise sage, teach me more," Mike replied sarcastically.

"Now, I don't want you to think that I'm cocky. I do like to banter a bit. My confidence is that I have learned from a very good source."

"What's that?" Mike asked.

"I wish I could say I figured it out all on my own. But I've made some of the same mistakes over and over again. This head can be pretty thick sometimes," Isaiah answered.

"I can relate. Sara and I have been through some of the same problems repetitively, too. What I need is some advice from someone who knows what they're talking about. What's been helpful for you?"

Isaiah replied, "I don't know if this will sound foreign to you or not, but for me, the difference came when I began deepening my spiritual life. I found that when I started asking God for help and reading the Bible, I discovered the wisdom that I needed."

"Really?" Mike said with surprise. "I didn't think the Bible would have much to say about everyday life, or what's going on in my marriage or at my work.

Although, I can't truly say that I've read much of the Bible."

"That's an easy fix. You might be surprised how God can transform situations and perspectives. I'm amazed that God longs to be close to me and to heal the damaged parts of my life. He's been beckoning me to listen and to follow His guidance. Yet He has never forced me to do anything that I didn't want to do."

"I think my problem is just that. I wish someone would take over for a while and fix everything. Afterwards, I could take over the helm again," Mike said.

"That would be nice, wouldn't it? Most of the time, though, we need to step up and take care of business. That doesn't mean we're alone; we have a great business partner. Yet, we still have work to do ourselves."

"That's all I need. More work to do," Mike replied.

"This is a different kind of work than you may be used to. The Bible instructs us to pursue God and go with His suggestions. After that, things begin to fall into place. Our job is to be open to learn and grow."

"Do you mean that I'm in a rut? Because that's what I've been hearing lately from Sara," Mike said.

"I think that it's a tendency for all of us to get in patterns that may not be very healthy. Many things can be going well while we have some definite things to work on. I think you'd be amazed to see how some small changes can help a marriage and job.

"You may be wondering how I know," Isaiah continued. "I've been through some similar experiences in my life and marriage. I can't imagine what it would have been like for God to watch me make the same mistakes over and over again. God was very patient with me, and He waited until I was ready. Until I had a desire to learn, history repeated itself. The task of learning was difficult, but it was worth it in the end. My wife and I have a much better marriage as a result. I look forward to time with her."

Feeling more comfortable sharing with Isaiah, Mike replied, "It's good to know that I'm not the only one with problems in my marriage. At times, I'm not sure we're going to make it. I figured that we were both intelligent people and we would work it out ourselves. The thing is that I have started to get more pessimistic about our relationship. We're going in circles, and I am sick of it."

"Like I thought earlier, you're already on your way," Isaiah said, patting him on the shoulder. "You may find that it'd be beneficial to talk with a professional about this. My wife and I saw a counselor, and it made a big difference."

"Some other day I'd be interested in hearing a little more from you, but I'm not so sure about a counselor. Right now, I gotta head out," Mike said.

"Sure. It was good to get to know you more, Mike. To me, it seems that you and your wife have primarily been fighting against each other. I'm looking forward to hearing how you start fighting for her."

Mike wasn't sure what he meant by that last statement. Isaiah tended to make cryptic comments. Mike realized he was almost late for work. "Alright. I'll keep you posted. See ya."

"You know where to find me."

QUESTIONS FOR GROUP DISCUSSION OR
INDIVIDUAL REFLECTION

1) Do you have someone in your life that listens well to you and gives good advice? If so, who is it and how did the relationship develop? How has it made a difference for you? If you don't have a mentor or someone like this in your life, is there anyone you think may be able to fill this role?

2) When you're going through tough times, do you tend to reach out or withdraw? What do you like and not like about this reaction of yours?

3) Mike and Sara were unrestrained in their argument. What is your argument style or conflict style? For example, do you tend to be quiet, animated, competitive, accommodating, aggressive, compromising, defensive, collaborative or stubborn? What led up to you taking on this style?

4) How do your fights or disagreements with people usually end? Is it with a stony silence, a door slamming, an emotional meltdown, a compromise, or an apology with resolution? In coming chapters, we will see how Mike and Sara learn how to end fights well. Describe an experience where a fight of yours has ended well.

## CHAPTER THREE

The Pentagon
of Change

It was time for Mike's doctor's visit. The ER doctor had told him that he needed to follow up with his normal physician in the next couple days. It had now been six weeks. *Does anyone like going to the doctor?* Unconsciously, Mike had been putting off this visit because of the nature of what had brought him to the emergency room. He had never had chest pain like that before, so finally he had agreed to be taken to the ER. Overall, he thought he was fairly healthy. The once lean body had expanded in the past few years. His busy schedule had him eating on the run, and as a result he ate fast food more frequently and had little time to exercise.

Over the past several weeks, Isaiah's words, "fighting for her," had echoed through Mike's head. *What does it mean to fight for my wife?* he wondered. *It wasn't like she was having difficulty being faithful. There's no competitor that I need to fend off. Or is there?*

Mike wanted things to improve, but he wasn't sure where to begin. The safer route had always been to ignore the problems—and so he did. He had this nagging thought in the back of his mind, questioning whether he really wanted to live life by choosing the most comfortable route. Ironically, avoiding the problems wasn't the safest way to go. In reality, it meant he was heading towards a cliff with his eyes closed instead of open.

Mike's self-confident persona normally masked inner pain and confusion. It had reached a point now where his concerns were starting to make their mark on his physical appearance. Battle scars were beginning to show.

"Mike Forrester." The sound of his name reverberated through the waiting room. It was his turn to get up and follow the medical assistant into the exam room. He didn't think he should be nervous, but he could feel his heart throbbing in his chest. She obtained his vital signs and gathered other pertinent information. What took him off guard was what she asked next. "What is the reason for your visit to the doctor today, Mr. Forrester?" He rarely visited the doctor, so he was unprepared to answer.

I don't want to tell her the reason for my visit, he thought. *I am here to talk to the doctor about this, not her.* He paused and calculated his next evasive move. Mike came up with another reason for the visit. "I need to get checked out since my aunt has diabetes." It was truthful even, though it wasn't the main reason for the appointment.

"Alrighty," she chirped. "Here's a cup for you to leave a urine sample, and I'll be back to poke your finger to check your blood sugar. Have you eaten anything yet this morning?"

He replied, "No, I'm not into breakfast." Like most people, Mike hated needles, but thought that it would be worth it to get checked out just in case there was a problem.

"Great, that makes for a better test. When you're done, return to room three, and the doctor will be here in a few minutes."

THE INTRUSION

Grabbing the sample cup, Mike sauntered over to the nearest bathroom and swung the door wide open. To his astonishment, there on the toilet in the single occupancy bathroom sat an elderly Mrs. Johnson, his fourth grade teacher. Unfazed by the intrusion, she declared, "Well if it isn't Mikey Forrester! How are you doing?"

This was not the ideal time for catching up with an old teacher. *How can I get out of this situation?* he thought.

"Uh, I've been really busy. It's great to see you. You're looking good." *Oops, I hope that she doesn't take that the wrong way.* "I mean, it's great to run into you, I just hope that next time it's somewhere else." He quickly closed the door. Fortunately, Mrs. Johnson didn't seem to care about the location of their meeting, or getting caught with her pants down. She could have chatted there all day. Mike found a vacant bathroom and made sure to lock the door.

UNEXPECTED NEWS

Back in the examining room, not surprisingly, he waited more than a few minutes. However, Dr. Chang changed his perception of the office visit. He guessed that she was no more than thirty-five. *I bet I am older than she is.* Her short, dark hair rested just above her collar and contrasted with her white coat. Mike was surprised that she was so petite. *Aren't doctors supposed to be tall and imposing?*

Sitting down, she smiled, shook his hand and greeted him. Her pleasant demeanor accompanied the thorough and efficient approach of her investigation. After a brief introduction, she asked about his life, health, job and family, before discussing the alleged topic of the visit. "It appears that your blood sugar is a bit elevated," she said.

His jaw dropped with the unanticipated test result, and immediately thoughts of his aunt giving herself daily injections of insulin flooded his mind. *I can't give myself shots like that,* he thought.

"Your blood sugar is not in the diabetic range, but it is higher than normal. I recommend that we do a repeat fasting blood draw from your arm in a week or so."

Focusing on his own thoughts, Mike only heard distorted snippets of her explanation. *Blood sugar, diabetic range, blood draw.* His perception of what she was saying returned him to his internal worst-case scenario.

What if I my kidneys stop working and I need dialysis? That's expensive. Will my insurance cover it? How many times a week will I need to go? My aunt also lost some of her toes. Maybe I'll need to have an amputation. Would I still be able to work?

Mike noticed it coming on again. It was similar to the last episode that had brought him to the emergency room six weeks ago—the real reason for his visit today. He noticed that he was breathing fast and his heart was pounding. He began to feel pressure in his chest. Last time this happened he had thought he was having a heart attack. It was embarrassing when all the tests had come back normal and the doctor had said his symptoms were brought on by stress.

This episode presented itself in like fashion, but was a little less severe than the previous attack. Several dark spots obscured Mike's vision, and all he could focus on was Dr. Chang's shiny stethoscope. Even that seemed far away. He remembered that if he took several deep breaths sometimes he would start to feel better. Consciously and forcefully, he inhaled deeply a few times and noticed that his symptoms were starting to resolve. His thoughts were clearing—the attack was waning.

Meanwhile, Dr. Chang was busy typing at the computer. Viewing the screen, she informed the patient that he also had mildly elevated blood pressure. Then she noticed his irregular breathing. She looked over and noticed his pale face and unfocused gaze. "Are you alright?" she asked with a quizzical look. Mike attempted to appear calm and collected but was not very convincing.

No more games. Mike couldn't deny that he had his share of stresses. The sum of all of the challenges going on in his life obviously expressed themselves through his physical symptoms. He thought, *I'm sick of this. I can't keep having these attacks.* "To tell you the truth," he said, "I have been under quite a bit of stress lately. My wife and I argue a lot, and it's taking its toll on me. Plus, work is wearing me out. I have this annoying co-worker who ends up dumping his work on me. I landed in the hospital recently, because I thought I was having a heart attack. The ER doctor told me it was from stress. I'm having some of the same symptoms again now. And now you're telling me that I have high blood sugar and blood pressure. This is a bit much to handle."

"I hear what you are saying. It's amazing how many things can hit us all at once sometimes. I am not surprised that you have been having these symptoms. How are you doing now?"

"I'm feeling better. Thanks," Mike said.

"I'm glad. I need to get to the bottom of what's going on, so I'll need to ask a bunch of questions." She went on with the typical questions for his condition. He was ready for some change, so didn't mind that she inquired about his chest pain, cardiac risk factors, diet, tobacco use, sleep, concentration, and even his mood.

He did his best to be honest. However, when she asked about his sex life, he shut down. *That's off limits. I'm not going to talk to her about that.* Mike lied and told her that everything was fine in that department. He was very glad that Sara was not there at the appointment as she would be sure to inform the doctor about the mutually dwindling interest.

She noted his response and moved on. "Mike, how's the rest of your social support?" Dr. Chang asked.

"What do you mean?"

"Do you have people that you can talk to?"

"Sure. The guys that I used to be roommates with are great to hang out with. We mainly talk about sports. I'm not sure what they'd say if I told them what was going on in my personal life. I do have a few friends that I chat with on a deeper level and one that I actually told what is going on in my life. However, my wife and I don't seem to connect as we once did in the past."

"What changed?"

"We haven't been putting much effort into our relationship, and we're starting to drift away from each other."

She nodded, and Mike sensed that she truly cared about what was going on in his life.

"Do you have a religious preference?" she inquired.

"Yeah, I am a Christian. We've attended a church on and off for the past couple years. We both like it, and we have meant to go more frequently, but you know how life gets hectic. We don't know many people that go there yet. It's a large church."

"I see." Dr. Chang was switching modes to share her conclusions. Relieved that the last question was over, Mike listened intently as she spoke. "I reviewed the records from your emergency room visit. From what we have discussed today, I agree with the ER physician. Fortunately, I think that it is very unlikely that you have a problem with your heart.

"Like I said before, with all that's on your plate right now, I'm not surprised that you're having the symptoms you described. I also think that unless some of these things change in your relationship with your wife and problems at work, you're going to have a hard time taking care of your medical problems. You'll be hard-pressed making healthy lifestyle changes until your marriage and work situation are in better shape. For most people, improvement in these areas decreases their level of stress in life so that they can then tackle their medical problems head on."

"That's for sure," Mike replied. "I've been trying to force myself to eat right and exercise for ages, and it just doesn't seem to work. I can keep it up for a little while, but I can't stick to it. Too many other things seem to come up."

Dr. Chang nodded her head. "For many of my patients, the problem is not that they don't know what to do; it's that they have difficulty implementing the changes and sustaining them. That's why it's important to identify the things that keep getting in the way of being healthy. You mentioned nutrition and exercise. I've found that some of the most common barriers to eating right and exercising are being overly stressed, over-committed, fatigued, bored and depressed."

Mike thought about this for a moment. "I wouldn't say that I have been bored or depressed, but I have experienced the other things. Sometimes I am too tired to exercise or to take the time to eat healthy food. It is so much easier to pick up some fast food on the run."

"Not enough time to take care of your health. That's a problem," she said with a look of concern. She explained, "It's pretty common to consume more calories during times of stress. Unfortunately, it's not a very effective coping mechanism. When all the food is eaten, the stress is still there," she said earnestly. "What's important is finding out the obstacles and tackling them head on instead of using an ineffective coping mechanism. Those obstacles can come from various sources. The different areas in our lives are highly interconnected, and they affect each other. I have a good handout that illustrates this. Would you like to know more about it?"

"Yeah, sure."

Dr. Chang rifled through a cabinet and pulled out a single sheet of paper. "Here. Take a look at this."

THE PENTAGON OF CHANGE

Let us consider that each person is made up of four main components. This is referred to as the four-part Bio-Psycho-Social-Spiritual Model, and encompasses a person's physical condition, social connections, psychological health and spiritual well-being. It is critical to pay attention to each of these four main aspects of yourself. Only then can you truly maximize your health. By utilizing this model, you can determine your level of health in each area and then evaluate how improvements can occur in each part. The good news is that positive change in one area leads to positive effects in other areas.

For our purposes, the psychological component has been divided into two sections: thoughts and feelings. Hence it is shown here as a pentagon.

The Core Aspects of a Human Being

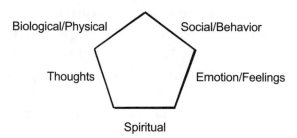

Biological/Physical   Social/Behavior

Thoughts   Emotion/Feelings

Spiritual

These different aspects of a person are interrelated. Our thoughts, feelings, behavior, social life and spirituality are closely connected. Here are some ways that these connections can occur:

- Biologically, the level of several different chemicals in our brain and certain hormones in our body affect the way we think and feel.
- Changes in the way we think cause us to modify our behavior.
- Altering the way we act impacts our social life and relationships.
- When our social life gets rearranged, this often affects our spiritual life, such as our fellowship community and peer influences.
- There isn't just one direction for the flow of change. All areas of a person can affect other areas, in any order.

EXAMPLE: Jennifer saw a couple of her friends talking at a party, and one of them glanced in her direction. Jennifer *thought* these friends were gossiping about her. She started to *act/behave* distantly toward the alleged gossipers. Jennifer *felt* angry at her friends and refused to participate in their regular prayer group (*spiritual*). After a few days of stewing about things, she decided to quit being friends with them altogether (*social*).

EXAMPLE: Paul started hanging out with some new friends who partied and got drunk every weekend. Paul joined in and drank with them. The alcohol affected his brain chemistry and functioning (*biological*). His thinking patterns became negative and cynical as he became depressed (*thoughts and feelings*). Paul started to *behave* more irritably with people around him, and he didn't want to get involved in conversations around the office. He withdrew *socially*, which others didn't mind, considering how he had been acting towards them. He felt like there must be no God, or else life wouldn't be this way for him (*spiritual*). He hoped he was wrong, though, because he wanted to go to heaven after he died.

The Good News

The good news is: If you make constructive changes in one area, it will benefit the other areas. It doesn't matter in which area you start. There will be a ripple effect of growth throughout your being.

Gaining Momentum

Consider the example of Paul's life above. If he wanted to reverse the problems in his life, all he'd have to do is begin to make changes in one area. Then the flow of health would spread to other aspects of his life.

EXAMPLE (cont.): Paul decided that enough was enough. He didn't want to bottom out any more than he had. He remembered that a friend of his was going to AA. Paul committed to trying it out (*behavior*). He heard the other AA members talking about how their Higher Power gave them the strength to overcome the temptation to drink. Paul began praying to God for this strength (*spiritual*). He noticed that he had fewer cravings for alcohol, and when he was tempted he prayed and the feeling dwindled (*emotion/biological*). From his AA group, he got to know some sober people and began hanging out with them on the weekends instead (*social*). As a result, Paul has now been clean and sober for five years.

Making the Connections

Dr. Chang finished reviewing the sheet and said, "I have found this handout to be very helpful in looking at our lives as whole people. Here's a marriage example that demonstrates this interconnectedness. You might find it to be pertinent to your life. For instance, if a husband and wife quit doing things together and stop having quality time as a couple (social/behavioral) they will start to *think* they aren't as compatible. They will believe they don't have many things in common. Over time, they will also begin to *feel* differently, like they have "fallen out of love." This may result in them doubting any divine guidance or matchmaking over their relationship (spiritual)."

"I have never considered this before." Mike reflected on his life for a moment.

Dr. Chang's pager beeped, and she quickly excused herself from the examining room, leaving time for Mike to reflect. Thinking of how this last example applied to his own life, Mike started putting together some of the pieces of the puzzle.

Mike couldn't help but notice that Sara was the only one in a crowd who didn't laugh at his jokes. She no longer seemed to appreciate him; she maybe didn't even respect him. Consequently, he had grown frustrated with trying to please her. As a result of his emotions, there had been a change in his behavior. Instead of trying to please his wife, his jovial self emerged with a more light-hearted crowd—his co-workers.

When they weren't immersed in developing software, Mike intermittently instigated practical jokes and brought the team together, adding humor to everyone's day. None laughed louder than Sylvia. Somewhat shy at first, her naivety and innocence had blossomed into full-on respect and admiration for Mike's ease at relating with people and his competence at work. Over time, she had adapted to his playful style. Lighthearted banter with Sylvia became more frequent, and some were starting to wonder if they were a little too close to work on the same team. Mike shrugged off the insinuation and would insist that they were just good friends. Yet underneath his self-protection, he himself was starting to question whether they should be so close. She was single, but he was a married man. Plus, if he admitted it, which he rarely did, he was attracted to her. He wouldn't think of admitting this to his wife, though. Sara was suspicious after seeing the familiar way her husband had with Sylvia, and had once commented on their close working relationship. Aware of being drawn to Sylvia, Mike liked the way she smiled. Oblivious to Mike's attraction to her, one day Sylvia noticed him glancing at her for a fraction of a second too long.

A New Resolve

Mike's thoughts were interrupted by Dr. Chang knocking on the door and re-entering the room.

"You know," Mike said with a thoughtful look on this face, "I used to think that there was just one answer and one way of attacking a problem. But now I see that you can approach things from several directions."

"That's right. With our health we need to broaden our perspective," Dr. Chang added. "One of the more striking examples of this is how there is a link between depression and heart attacks. Studies show that patients who are depressed are much more likely to have a heart attack, and similarly, those who have had a heart attack are more likely to be depressed. It is impossible to separate our physical and psychological health. People can't just say to someone that their problem is all in their head, because thoughts are related and interconnected to the rest of their health.

"Don't you think it's clear, Mike, that in your life you have experienced the interaction between what's been going on in your social life, your thinking and the physical symptoms that you have experienced?"

"That's for sure. I can see how my stress level with my job and marriage has risen recently. It makes sense now why I have been having these episodes of chest pain. I think in the past I've only seen the symptoms as a medical problem," Mike said.

Dr. Chang nodded her head. "Frequently people get frustrated when they try to get help from someone that sees life more narrowly. Only one area gets addressed. Some only focus on the psychological, some only on the spiritual, or some only on the physical. As in your case Mike, if we only considered the medical perspective, we'd be missing critical details. There are many causes of illness that are not biological in nature."

Dr. Chang emphasized, "Tackling the issues from a comprehensive perspective is the way to go. What's encouraging is that some small changes can make a big difference. And, like the handout says, your success in one area will pay off in the other areas. I am not going to say that those changes are easy or that everything will be perfect overnight. However, it is encouraging to find that making small steps in the right direction has a positive spiral effect. Improvement in one area crosses over to other areas. I am certain that you can have this positive momentum build in your relationships, job and physical health."

"Now that sounds good. I'm ready to do something. Where do I start?"

"Where do you want to start?" Dr. Chang returned the question right back to him.

"You're the doctor," Mike replied.

"And it's *your* life that *you're* making decisions about," she said. Dr. Chang knew that in the past Mike had difficulty implementing change with his diet and exercise. In order for him to be successful, he had to be committed and invested in his treatment.

Hesitantly, Mike formed a plan. Thinking of Isaiah, he said, "One of my friends saw a counselor in the past, and he felt that it was very helpful for him and his wife. He was encouraging me to go to counseling as well. But, I have never thought things were bad enough. I think that I have now been pushed to the point of needing to go. I can't keep going on like this."

Dr. Chang agreed with his assessment and decision. "It does sound like you need someone to come alongside and assist you during this difficult season. You know, though, you don't need to wait until impending disaster to seek counseling. You can choose it on a preventative basis too, especially if you have a lot happening at one time and you want an outside perspective."

Mike felt more convinced of his decision to see a counselor. He appreciated the fact that she was not too pushy and that she continued to ask him what he thought was the next step to improve his health. "As we've been talking, I've been realizing how great it would be to not have to worry about work or my marriage. I'd have a lot more energy and focus for getting my body in better shape. I liked how I felt when I was living an active lifestyle and eating right, but it's too hard to do right now."

"You're not alone. If you want the name of a counselor, I know someone who I think you would hit it off with. His name is Jim. Several of my patients have found him to be very helpful."

"Sure," replied Mike. "I wouldn't know where else to start."

"Here's his phone number, and I believe that he takes your insurance. I'm also concerned about your lack of friendships and spiritual vitality. I would encourage you to develop your friendships and your spiritual life. Research shows that people who have an active spiritual life tend to be happier, live longer and are better able to cope with crisis. Do you know how you might start establishing deeper friendships and spirituality?"

"Funny you should mention that. I just poured out my whole life to this guy at a café recently. I hardly know him. Yet, he seems friendly, as if he's truly interested in what's going on in my life."

"Well, if that is a budding friendship, I suggest you pursue it. I think that it's very important to have someone to talk to about the things going on in our lives.

If we don't, then we can easily lose perspective. Other people can help us to recognize when we start having a distorted view of our own lives. That's one reason why it's so important to have a vibrant community. The notion of the rugged individual is highly overrated and tends to lead to all kinds of problems like the ones that we've been discussing."

"I've been doing that at church, isolating myself. I like church, but when we do go, we tend to leave right after the service. So I don't really know people there. Sara and I have never been very involved, and as a result I can't say that we have a community that we live in. I did meet the pastor a couple times though. He seemed very welcoming. Maybe I should talk to him about some of the things that are going on in my life."

"Mike, I'm impressed that you are planning on taking these steps towards your health. You are coming up with specific plans that are reasonable to attain. That's the way to do it. These changes in life don't come automatically. You have got to want the results and make a concerted effort. I see that you are truly looking to learn, and it will pay off for you. You wouldn't believe how many people I see who ask for help but aren't willing to take the necessary steps to prioritize their health. I'm optimistic that you're going to succeed. I look forward to partnering with you."

Dr. Chang transitioned as the time for their visit was nearly up. "Since you do have mildly elevated blood sugar and blood pressure today, we will need to do some further blood tests and recheck your blood pressure at your next appointment. We've tackled a lot in one day." She stood up and shook his hand.

"Okay. Thank you. Nice to meet you, Dr. Chang."

"Nice to meet you too, Mike. See you at your next appointment."

Mike felt a strange calm that he hadn't experienced for months. Certainly it wasn't present during the first part of the doctor's appointment. The firm grasp that secrecy held over him was slowly being pried loose. The heaviness, the burden, the things unsaid had been released and uncovered to an objective person. He was reminded of the time that he worked through the night to meet a project deadline. Once the project had been completed, he had walked out in the crisp cool air of the early morning. As he forcefully exhaled, the pressure subsided. Despite his fatigue, his feet skimmed over the frost-kissed grass. The project was over. He was free. Mike now experienced a similar freedom through this doctor's visit. No longer was he shackled by solitary confinement. The world of counseling was unknown to him, but he was going to give it a try. Although he knew that the work had just begun, he had hope and fresh direction for the first time in ages.

QUESTIONS FOR GROUP DISCUSSION OR
INDIVIDUAL REFLECTION

1) The skill of Looking To Learn requires humility, acknowledging where growth is needed and seeking to learn from others. Whom do you look up to that is good at these things? What differences do you think it has made in his/her life?

2) Is there a certain area in your life in which you are Looking To Learn or make changes? What do you stand to gain? Whom do you know who has experience or wisdom in this area? Could you ask them for advice?

3) The Pentagon of Change illustrates the interplay of the main components of our lives. How have you seen this connection occur in your life? Have you ever had positive change in one area of your life produce benefits in another area? (For instance, have you had a relationship improve that in turn led to positive progress in your thinking, feeling or spiritual life?)

SKILL #2

TRANSFORMING
YOUR THINKING

## CHAPTER FOUR

Is It All in Your Head?

T he day arrived with thundering clouds and sheets of rain. Mike had had several long days to anticipate this moment. *Okay, I'm finally at the counselor's office. What's next? I'd better get ready to talk about my inner child and my mother*, he thought sarcastically. He wasn't sure if it was all the caffeine or the fear of the unknown, but he hadn't slept very well. He had never been to a counselor before, and the thought of it was daunting.

Maybe it was all of the movies that he had watched, but Mike was anticipating meeting a man who spoke with a soft, hushed voiced who spent all day asking irrelevant questions in a way that was uncomfortable and made you wish that you were anywhere but there. Mike had second thoughts about the appointment.

Isn't that what counselors do? They try and expose everything and talk about things that nobody wants to talk about. Maybe this wasn't such a good idea, coming to a counselor.

Just then, a man opened a door leading into the waiting room where Mike was sitting. The gentleman stepped aside and beckoned Mike to come in for his appointment. Even though the counselor was a little taller than Mike, he had a narrower frame. Mike thought jokingly, *I could take him.* He almost laughed out loud at the prospect of a full-on fistfight in the tranquil office. *Now that would make a good movie. It reminds me of the hilarious golf course brawl between Bob Barker and Adam Sandler in* Happy Gilmore.

The counselor's name was Jim. His head perched forward, probably from years of listening to other people's problems all day. His blue eyes made steady contact with Mike as he listened intently to what his new client had to say. The conversation was a bit awkward at first, with each one trying to figure out the other.

Jim asked Mike, "What led you to schedule an appointment?"

Mike hesitated, vacillating between whether to tell Jim that he decided to come because he was doing research for a reality TV show, or because he lost a bet in the bar. In the end, Mike said, "I'd like to give you the typical guy answer and tell you that my wife is making me come, but she doesn't even know I'm here."

"Oh, so we may be working on your openness and communication skills with your wife, huh?" Jim asked, with a lighthearted, sarcastic tone to his voice.

Mike laughed. Jim was not what he expected. The counselor was low-key and seemed like a regular guy. Initially, Mike was glad that Jim was talkative. It took the pressure off. But deep down, Mike was leery that this was all a smokescreen to make him let his guard down before Jim would strike.

On the other hand, Mike considered that Jim was a Christian counselor. Christians are supposed to be nice. But you never know. *Can I trust this guy?* Mike wondered. However, to Mike's own surprise, he was drawn insidiously towards the light but engaging conversation. He was amazed that he actually felt comfortable around the counselor. Jim leaned back in his chair, as if in agreement, and clasped his hands behind his head of wavy, sandy brown hair.

As time progressed Mike thought, *I'm not going to pay this guy to talk about sports all day. I'm going to get something for my money.* So when Jim asked Mike what he wanted to talk about, Mike dove straight in and discussed all of the issues that were going on at work. Work problems were personal, but not as personal as the issues going on in his marriage.

Mike's forthrightness made it easier for Jim to get to the heart of the matter. The frustrations poured out of the new but quickly adjusting client. "If I didn't compensate for Travis then our team would be chronically late on projects. I would hate to hear what our boss would say if we didn't meet a deadline and we lost a customer. I have a responsibility to our team." Mike's fingers alternately tapped and grasped the armrest as he spoke.

The problems were as easy to spot for Jim as they were for Sara, although Jim was more tactful in stating his observations. Feeling that it was appropriate to introduce the subject, Jim said, "Mike, it seems to me that you have beliefs and thoughts that tend to exacerbate your problems at work. What psychologists have found is that our thinking patterns can be healthy or faulty, and this correspondingly leads to either sound mental health or mental distress. Faulty thinking is like a quarterback sneak on fourth and one, without an offensive line. It's a recipe to get clobbered by the defense."

"Yeah, they get sacked," Mike commented.

"Exactly. This faulty thinking is extremely common. Everyone is prone to faulty thinking, so don't feel bad if this is a problem for you. However, some people struggle with it much more than the average person. It definitely makes it harder to win the game that way. Our job is simply to figure out how your thinking patterns tie in to what's going on. I did notice that you tend to think you have to fix everything for everyone at work. Usually in that case, people tend to be more stressed out or depressed."

Or have chest pain, Mike thought with angst.

What Jim said made sense to Mike, and it resonated with the handout that the doctor had given him. Both these professionals had described how his health was influenced by his thoughts, as well as his physical, social, emotional and spiritual life.

Jim continued, "The good news is that by changing the way you think, you can alter the way that the problems in your life affect you."

"That's great news. Then the quarterback has pass protection to get the first down."

"Right. You catch on quickly," Jim said. "Let's use an example of a man who believed that he shouldn't ask for help. This man thought that asking for help showed weakness and that people would then look down on him. It was too threatening for him to admit that he needed some assistance. At work, the fear of appearing incompetent kept him from asking questions and learning where there were gaps in his training. As a result of this belief, when he needed to learn a new skill at work, he would cover up the fact that he wasn't sure how to complete something. In effect, he wouldn't let anyone teach him how to do new things correctly."

Sounds like Travis, Mike thought.

"Due to the man's problematic thinking, his career growth and learning inevitably came to a near standstill. Over time, as things around him changed, he became increasingly less competent. He began missing the promotions and raises that his co-workers received. Ironically, this was exactly what he was trying to avoid. Near the start of his counseling with me, he was almost fired. Urgently, we discussed that it was his faulty beliefs that caused the trouble. By realizing that it is normal and important to ask for help and to be taught by others, he started to regain his competence at work. His thinking changed such that he now believes you can be strong and capable and still ask for help. In fact, it makes you stronger and more adept."

Travis needs to hear this. Mike was better as identifying others' problems than his own at this point.

Jim knew that people often have a hard time realizing the importance of healthy thought patterns. Of benefit in this situation was the fact that Mike had a Christian background. This would have already laid some of the foundation for thought management principles. By now, his client had probably gained insights from the Bible and various sermons on the subject of controlling one's thinking.

"You mentioned that you have Christian beliefs, so you may have heard these concepts before," Jim said. "All of this talk about thought patterns is not just made up by psychologists. It was written about long before the field of psychology was established. Controlling your thinking is a principle that comes straight from the Bible."

"I think I have heard in church some of what you're talking about. I know there are lots of wise proverbs in the Bible, and God tells us to meditate on things that are pure, good and wise. But can you tell me more of what you mean?" Mike asked.

"Sure. Our human nature plays a big part in our need to control our thinking. The Bible acknowledges that we can be prone to selfish motives, and our desires are not always naturally aligned with God's will and desires. Like you said, God instructs us to focus on what is good and pure. It's not our natural tendency to always be thinking that way.

"Plus, our thinking is subject to misinterpretations and flawed assumptions, either from ideas we come up with, or ideas others share with us. We can be susceptible to believing lies or falsehoods about ourselves, about others or about numerous aspects of reality. As a result, it requires effort on our part to thwart distortion and to adhere to truth. Various Bible verses emphasize our need to monitor our thoughts, take captive false ideas, actively control our thinking and renew our mind with the truths of God as He reveals them to us through Scripture and other means of revelation."

Mike slowly nodded his head, following the logic. While he had heard these ideas before, they were striking him in a new way.

"God, in His compassion," continued Jim, "wants us to be free from the problems and suffering that faulty thinking creates. He knows that we needlessly suffer sometimes, because we're believing something that isn't true. That's why He emphasizes the practice of renewing our minds and meditating on what is true and good."

Mike looked skeptical. "Is it really possible to change the way that we think?"

"Absolutely. In my job, I get to see people do it on a regular basis, in some pretty radical ways. Let's not get ahead of ourselves, though. We'll talk about how to modify our thoughts and put this into practice later on.

"First, read over this self-assessment. Don't think of it as a test. Think of it as an opportunity for you to find aspects of your thinking that are making you miserable and discover what you can do to correct it."

"I can tell you right now who's making me miserable," Mike said with a chuckle.

"Yeah, I bet you could," Jim smiled. "Okay now, why don't you take a look at these patterns that are contributing to the problems in your relationships. It won't make the annoying people in your life disappear, but it will help us to identify the barriers that prevent you from breaking out of the repetitive difficulties with those people. The first task is to pinpoint your healthy and faulty thinking habits, so we'll know where to start working. This will give us a great launching pad."

"Sounds good," Mike said. "I like your thinking—it sounds like it will save us time and me money."

"I do like to keep a good pace in counseling. I figure people wouldn't be coming to see me if they didn't want some changes quickly. Now, the chart I'm giving you lists the fifteen most common examples of faulty thinking habits. You know how people can be pessimistic and cynical? Well, they are two of the most common examples of the kind of thing I'm talking about. They're thinking habits that have been recognized and talked about for centuries. In contrast, the fifteen habits listed in this chart are rarely talked about. Because they're unfamiliar, they go undetected and unaddressed. As a result, they can wreak havoc not only in one's mind but in one's life as they permeate behavior and choices.

Jim prepared Mike for the potential results of his self-assessment. "Almost anyone going through this chart would be able to identify several of these thinking patterns in themselves. Something that's important to realize is that the more faulty thinking patterns people tend to use, the more prone and susceptible they are to feeling stressed, anxious and depressed."

"Oh, interesting. I'll have to keep an eye out for that," Mike said.

"Look for this, too—there's a connection between healthy thinking patterns and overall happiness, self-esteem and peace of mind. Plus, you tend to function and perform better. You get out of the funk of living in the confusion and discouragement that faulty thinking produces. Your mood and outlook on life will be more positive and upbeat.

"So you can see that the type of thinking patterns you use make a big impact. That's why when people correct faulty thinking they get so much relief. You can look forward to that relief, Mike."

The counselor noticed Mike's body visibly relax, and his client let out a big sigh.

Jim allowed him some time to absorb things and then said, "What this handout seeks to accomplish is to bring understanding of fifteen problematic patterns and provide fifteen favorable alternatives for each of them. Then we'll talk about how you can get good at replacing problematic thinking with healthy thinking."

"Okay, bring it on. I'm eager to get started," Mike said enthusiastically.

"Alright," said Jim. "Remember this is not a test, but an opportunity for new insights and freedom." Jim then gave his client ten minutes to fill out the handout.

NOTE TO READER: Take advantage of the self-assessment on the following page by completing it for yourself.

Healthy vs. Faulty Thinking Patterns:
Determine for Yourself What You Do

It is vital to one's mental, emotional and spiritual health to become familiar with the thinking patterns below. Which of these do you recognize within yourself? For each number, put a check in the box on the left or right column for what you mostly do, whether it be on the faulty or the healthy side.

Almost everyone, if they are honest, will have at least three to four faulty thinking patterns that they are subject to on a regular basis. If you're a person who prays, ask God to help you make good discoveries and gain valuable insights as you complete this.

#	Common *Faulty* Thinking Patterns	Alternate *Healthy* Thinking Patterns
1	☐ NEGATIVE FILTERING You let in upsetting ideas and filter out reassuring thoughts. You focus on the negative aspects of yourself, others or life, while you tend to ignore or fail to see the positive aspects. *Example*: When you receive personal feedback or constructive criticism, you tend to only remember the negative and not the positive. This is true even if you were told more positive than negative. If this describes you, then you're likely prone to Negative Filtering.	☐ CONSIDER ALL THE FACTS Try not to block out large chunks of information, whether it is what you consider positive or negative ideas. Use the bulk of all the information to come to your own conclusions. Disregard what you determine to be untrue. If you're suffering from depression, try to remember the positive thoughts about yourself or life that you had before you became depressed. Admit your imperfection, but remember that overall, God has designed you with many great traits and abilities.
2	☐ THINKING IN EXTREMES Everything is viewed as being all good or all bad. The world is seen in black or white, with no gray or in between. Things are	☐ REALIZE THE RANGE OF EXPERIENCES Begin to recognize when your thinking is becoming polarized. Things are not only great or terrible. There can be things that are mediocre, neutral,

#	Common *Faulty* Thinking Patterns	Alternate *Healthy* Thinking Patterns
	at one extreme pole/end or at the other far away pole/end. *Example*: You have great days or terrible days. Never just an okay day. Example: Today, you got a flat tire and it caused you to be late for work. You're going to appear like you're an irresponsible slacker to your co-workers. Your image is ruined.	satisfactory and livable. Much of life can be like this. It is more the exception when times or parts of life are amazing or awful. With the example of the extreme thinking to the left, you could instead be thinking, "So I got a flat tire. At least it didn't blow out and cause me to veer into oncoming traffic. I still have my health, my family, and my job." Keep the big picture in mind. Be careful not to exaggerate or minimize.
3	□ PESSIMISTIC PREDICTIONS You think that because something has been one way in the past, it will always be that way in the future. You project past negative experiences into the future. This is a habit of over-generalizing. *Example*: One person has hurt you, so you think everyone will hurt you. Example: You had one bad day, so your whole week will be bad.	□ TRUST IN A GOOD FUTURE Give up on fortunetelling and trying to predict the future. Live today the best you can and focus on what God is calling you to now. Trust God with the future as you prepare for tomorrow. You can't know what's coming, but you can be assured that God, who loves you tremendously, already has a good plan (Jeremiah 29:11). Have faith in Him.
4	□ MIND READING You believe you know what others are thinking or feeling. You think that you're so good at reading people and situations that you don't usually bother to check out your assumption. You	□ DOUBLE-CHECK YOUR ASSUMPTIONS In order to understand what's going on around us, all of us try to interpret what we see, hear and observe. However, we are bound to interpret things incorrectly from time to time. Check in with others about your assump-

#	Common *Faulty* Thinking Patterns	Alternate *Healthy* Thinking Patterns
	don't ask them if you are right. *Example*: Your boss at work mentions that money is tight in your department. You interpret this to mean that lay-offs are coming, and you start worrying about losing your job. You lie awake at night wondering about how you'll get a new job. Example: You walk into a room and the conversation dies down. You assume it's because they were talking about you.	tions and interpretations, especially if your conclusion is upsetting you. You may be wrong and are suffering needlessly. Often in our attempts to mind read, we are unaware of many possibilities. For instance with the example to the left, what really could have been happening was that the boss was mad because staff were stealing office supplies. He could have been trying to get people to stop it by mentioning the financial considerations. Jobs may not have been threatened at all.
5	☐ IMAGINING A DISASTER You imagine the most negative outcomes. You expect the worst and then get yourself worked up worrying about that happening. You fret over the what-ifs and catastrophes that may never happen. Things are blown out of proportion. *Example*: You have stomach pain and wonder, "What if I have cancer? What if my appendix is about to burst and I can't get to the hospital on time? What if I pass out while driving there and get into an accident…"	☐ STICK TO THE FACTS Don't get ahead of yourself or the situation. Most of the time, worrying over the possibilities of disaster in the future is a waste of time and energy. Plus, the chronic anxiety can lead to health problems such as panic attacks. Stay with what you know. If needed, get more information. React only to the facts, not the what-ifs. Put your creative imagination to better use. Many people imagine a disaster concerning their health or their family members' health. If this persists, see a doctor to address your concerns.

#	Common *Faulty* Thinking Patterns	Alternate *Healthy* Thinking Patterns
6	☐ TAKING THINGS TOO PERSONALLY You interpret the behavior of others as a direct reaction to you. You think others' behavior and comments are a reflection of your performance or your value as a person. *Example*: A husband has a bad day at work. He comes home grumpy, and his wife thinks he is mad at her. In return, she gets irritated with him and pulls away. She assumes it is about her.	☐ YOU ARE NOT THE CENTER OF THE UNIVERSE People make their own decisions based upon whatever goes on in their own heads. Their behavior isn't always about you. It may be about them, or something about which you know nothing. A wise saying is: "You wouldn't worry so much about what people thought of you, if you realized how little they thought of you." Remember, there can be a lot going on in a situation that you are unaware of that has nothing to do with you.
7	☐ CONFUSING RESPONSIBILITY You think that others are responsible for your problems and how you're feeling, *or* you think that you're responsible for the people around you and how they are feeling. You tend not to recognize or acknowledge people's personal choices and your own true responsibility. You may tend to blame others or yourself inaccurately. *Example*: Your teenager does something wrong. You think that if you had just been a better parent, this wouldn't have happened. You take ownership of	☐ EMPHASIZE PERSONAL RESPONSIBILITY Recognize that it is up to each person to make his/her own choices and to live with the results. Ultimately, you are not responsible for others, and they are not responsible for you. Do your best in life, and let others do the same. This is not to say people shouldn't support one another. Be loving and supportive. But don't confuse this to mean that you should make everything better for someone. Sometimes your help may actually hinder a person's growth and hurt their sense of competency. You are not to live another person's life for them, or solve their problems. If you

#	Common *Faulty* Thinking Patterns	Alternate *Healthy* Thinking Patterns
	the problem and think it's your responsibility to fix things.	feel led or inclined, you may offer to assist them as they work on solving their own problems.
8	☐ STUCK ON FAIRNESS You feel you know what is fair, but others just can't understand it or won't agree. You believe the world should operate according to what you determine is fair. You may try to demand that people adjust to the way you see things. *Example*: Family members fighting over household chores and what is fair or not. "That is not fair. I did that last time." Or, "I have this other job to do already. It's not fair that I have to do that, too." *Example*: The distribution of wealth in the world is not fair. Some people have more than they need and some are starving. While you know this is true, you have a hard time living within this reality.	☐ ACCEPT THAT LIFE IS NOT ALWAYS FAIR This world is not like what it was originally designed to be. People and their poor choices/sin make it into a difficult place to live sometimes. People will make selfish choices, and we all need to learn how to deal with this. There are things that bother us that we are not going to be able to change or control. However, there are injustices that we need to try to deal with and change, like abuse or other harmful sins. We can do our part in trying to make this earth a better place to be, by making decisions based on what's just, good and loving for us and for others. We can try to act justly and fairly. Yet it is unrealistic to expect that every other person will do the same.
9	☐ RULED BY SHOULDS You have a list of clear-cut rules about how people should act. Neither you nor anyone else should break these rules. If someone does, they are a	☐ FREEDOM WITHIN STRUCTURE Follow good principles, but don't be chained to them legalistically. The main principle God says to live by is love. God Himself says that if we love Him, ourselves and one another well,

#	Common *Faulty* Thinking Patterns	Alternate *Healthy* Thinking Patterns
	failure or a bad person. You probably try to impose your rules on other people. People ruled by "shoulds" are prone to perfectionism, often feel guilty, and have a fear of not being good enough or not getting the approval of others. *Example*: I should always be working, and I'm lazy if I am not. *Example*: I should always come up with the perfect solution. *Example*: I should be just as successful or wealthy as everyone in my family.	we will fulfill all the rules of Scripture. We have a lot of freedom and choice within this principle. Many people are ruled by shoulds because they are driven by perfectionism or pressured by others. No one on this earth is perfect. We can each aim for perfection, but recognize that we will never achieve it. When we/others fail, run out of energy or are lacking in wisdom, we need to leave room for grace, error and imperfection. We'll be a lot happier in life if we can learn to forgive ourselves and others. Meanwhile, we need to be mindful of God's continuous love for us, just as we are.
10	☐ ASSUMING EMOTION IS TRUTH Whatever you feel must be true. Sound reasoning or logic is not considered as much as feelings are. *Example*: I feel stupid; therefore I must be stupid. *Example*: I feel like I look like an idiot, so it is true that I look like an idiot. *Example*: I feel mad at that person, so they must have wronged me.	☐ CONSIDER EMOTIONS TO BE INDICATORS Our emotions are very helpful in life, as they indicate many things to us. They indicate when something is going well, going wrong, needs attention.... They inform us, guide us, motivate us and strengthen us. However, they can be confusing and multi-layered. They should not be considered as equal to truth, but as something that we can process and sort through that *can* lead us to truth.

#	Common *Faulty* Thinking Patterns	Alternate *Healthy* Thinking Patterns
11	☐ WAITING ON OTHERS TO MAKE YOU HAPPY Other people will change to suit you if you just do the right thing and work hard enough. You can change people if you speak or act precisely the right way. If you just love them enough, they'll turn around. This is a false sense of control. You think you can be happy if and only if they change. *Example*: If I love him well enough, he'll quit drinking. *Example*: If I can just teach her the value of hard work, she'll quit being so irresponsible. *Example*: If I marry this person, I'll be able to help them grow in their faith and loyalty. Then they will never have an affair or cheat on me.	☐ LET PEOPLE LIVE THEIR OWN LIVES Every person has free will and their own choices to make. When we care about someone, we want him/her to make choices that are good for himself/herself and that make us happy. We will be a lot happier if we can learn to be okay in our life, no matter what choices other people make. Everyone needs to sort his or her own way through life. If we think we can control other people's lives and make them change, we fool ourselves. Plus, we waste our time and energy, because it doesn't work. We'll end up feeling miserable and burnt out if we try. Lastly, we are not to try to be anyone's messiah or savior. We can point them to the true Messiah.
12	☐ MAKING FAST JUDGMENTS You create an overall, all-encompassing label and judgment, based on just one or two observations or characteristics. You over-generalize and jump to conclusions too quickly. *Example*: I'm not good at math, so I could never get a job in the business field. *Example*: I don't have very nice	☐ GIVE IT SOME TIME AND A CHANCE Don't limit yourself or others before you or they really have had an opportunity to try and experiment at something. Explore the possibilities and observe. You can never be successful without taking risks and dreaming a little. Those who risk little accomplish little. Don't rule things out prematurely with negative, skeptical thinking. Besides, when we limit ourselves

#	Common *Faulty* Thinking Patterns	Alternate *Healthy* Thinking Patterns

hair or clothes, so no one will ever like me or find me attractive.
Example: This person doesn't have formal education, so they can't excel in their field or job.

and what we think can happen in the future, we are often thinking God is subject to those same limits. He can do so much more than we can ever think or imagine (Ephesians 3:20–21).

13 ☐ LIVING IN THE WRONG TIME ZONE

A lot of your time and attention is focused on the past or the future. If you are past-focused, you may spend hours replaying old events or living in regret. If you are future-focused, you worry about what may or may not happen in the future. You may tend to do so much planning ahead that you miss out on today.
Example: I can't believe I made such a dumb mistake. How can I ever forgive myself?
Example: I have to prepare for every possibility.

☐ FOCUS ON THE PRESENT

Today is a gift. You only get to live today once. Make the most of it. Enjoy the moment. It's okay to spend some time reflecting on the past and considering how you can learn from it. However, if nothing can be done about the past, or you're not applying the lessons from the past to prepare for the future, then you're wasting a lot of time. Plus, you're missing out on the good things you could be experiencing in the present.

14 ☐ COMPARE AND DESPAIR

This is one of the most common downfalls in faulty thinking. It seems to be human nature to compare yourself to others. The problem is that it is easy to find a few good things in each person that you don't have. You

☐ BE YOUR PERSONAL BEST

Discover what is great about you. Sure, it's okay to get inspired by other people, but be certain to get to know your own abilities and strengths. Fulfill what you were destined to do and become. There will never be anyone exactly like you; no one else can take

#	Common *Faulty* Thinking Patterns	Alternate *Healthy* Thinking Patterns
	end up feeling discouraged, subpar or inadequate.	your place. Get comfortable with who you are and appreciate what you have to offer.
15	☐ NEED TO BE RIGHT Being wrong is unacceptable. You don't even want to think of it. You are continually on trial to prove your opinions and actions are correct. If you appear to be wrong or lose an argument, you are prone to then consider yourself weak or stupid. You fear others will view you this way and not respect you. *Example:* You want others to see that you know the best driving route to certain places. *Example:* You want the outcomes you've predicted to come true, whether that be who wins the Super bowl or how political situations play out.	☐ FOSTER AN ATTITUDE OF LEARNING It's a lot of pressure in life to always try and be right or appear right. Do you really want that pressure? Cultivate a desire to learn from others, from God and by life experience. Pride always comes before a fall. Scripture explains that the fear/respect of the Lord is the beginning of genuine wisdom. When you have a heart that is submitted to God and desires to learn from Him, you will walk in humility. You won't need to prove yourself, because your identity and confidence will be firm in Him.

Please refer to page 62 for scoring your Self-Assessment.

Scoring Your Self-Assessment
How many Unhealthy Patterns Did You Check?

0-4   Normal/Common: You probably do fine most of the time, unless your faulty   thinking pervades your thoughts frequently. Nevertheless, you can still restore more of your thinking to enjoy even more health.

5-7   Moderate Concern: People who unintentionally employ five or more Faulty Thinking Patterns on a regular basis are usually dealing with some symptoms of anxiety or depression.

8-12   Strong Concern: You are probably suffering under the weight of your faulty   thinking. You don't have to live with this burden and stress. You can be free of it. Acquire skills to interrupt and replace faulty thinking.

13-15 Seek Assistance: A decisive intervention in your thinking patterns is strongly   advised for the sake of your overall health and well-being. At this point, it is likely hard for you to focus on positive things in your life, because you are brought down so much by your thinking. Contact a professional counselor, medical doctor or pastor.

NOTE: This scoring system is a general guideline for self-assessment. There are exceptions. One such exception is that people who employ only two or three flawed thought patterns can still have significant problems with anxiety or depression. This can result when people's thoughts *frequently* follow along those few negative patterns throughout their day or week. If you have concerns about your thought life, you may want to contact a professional to assist you.

ADDITIONAL RESOURCES: For more information on truth-based thinking, visit the authors' website: www.TrueFoundation.com. There you will find an explanation of the authors' Philosophy of Ministry, which describes more of their perspective on truth-based thinking. Seminars are also offered on this subject and others.

BREAKING FAULTY THINKING

"Is it okay that I also filled out all of my wife's thinking problems?" Mike said jokingly. "Hers are easier to identify."

Jim smiled. "You've brought up a good point. It usually is easier to see the problems in other people's lives. I can say that in my own marriage, it wouldn't go over very well for me if I went home and enlightened my wife on her faulty think-ing habits. Hints usually aren't a good idea either. The real key is to get insight into our own life and make the necessary changes for ourselves. We need to let other people discover their habits for themselves. What areas did you find in your own life that you want to work on?"

"I guess that depends on how honest you want me to be," Mike replied. "Let's say hypothetically that I had all fifteen faulty thinking patterns. What would you say to that?" He wanted to see Jim's reaction.

Without a change in tone or facial expression Jim casually replied, "I would say that we have some work to do, and I'm glad you're here."

That was hardly a reaction at all. If I could have all fifteen faulty habits without shock-ing him, then I must not be too bad off, Mike thought. "I was uncertain about a few of them, but I think I've got it narrowed down. Let's see…" Mike reviewed his check-list of faulty thinking patterns. "Yes, I do my fair share of Negative Filtering, Imag-ining a Disaster.…" Mike's voice trailed off. *Yeah, it was that thinking that led to my episode of stress symptoms in the doctor's office.* He grimaced at the memory of it.

Mike went over the other items he had checked, telling Jim, "I can Confuse Responsibility at work, am guilty of Mind Reading, being Ruled By Shoulds and I Need to be Right." Mike took a deep breath, "Is that enough?" He paused in reflec-tion. "No wonder I have been having difficulties. That puts me at six faulty think-ing habits. My score places me at the 'moderate concern' level, and the scoring table says that amount usually leads to some anxiety and/or depression. Yep, that's me. Plus, I see I'm close to the 'strong concern' category. Am I your worst case this year?"

"No way!" Jim exclaimed. "The amount you listed is about par for the course. You wouldn't believe how common these habits are. It's just that these aren't top-ics you usually bring up at a cocktail party or during the meet-and-greet part of Sunday's church service, so no one else knows what is truly going on in each other's minds. Since it's part of my job, I talk to people about it every day. I help people with their faulty thinking habits all the time. It's nothing out of the ordinary.

"Today," Jim said, "The main question is where to start. The best thing to do is to identify the specific thoughts that go through your own head. Some of the examples given in the chart may be ones you have, so you could just circle those examples. But other than that, I want you to write in the margin beside each faulty thinking pattern you use what your personal example would be. Then, go over to the margin on the right side of the chart and come up with a healthy thinking substitute. Since you identified that you do mind reading, you may write in the left margin something like, "When Sara looks at me with that one expression, I know she's thinking I don't help out enough around the house." Truly, you don't know that that's what that facial expression means. So in the right margin, you could put "I don't know what that face means, but she doesn't look pleased. Maybe next time she does it I'll ask her what she's thinking."

"Okay. I see what you're saying," Mike said. "I'll fill in my personal examples before our next appointment," Mike said.

"Great," Jim replied. "That will make you well underway to improving the quality of your thinking."

MIND MONITOR

"Next," Jim said, "Let me go over some of the principles of how to change your thinking. Applying these strategies is the best method to help you to be successful. Turn to the last page of the handout."

How To Change Your Thoughts

1) If you'd like to, invite God into the process of repairing your thoughts.
2) Monitor your thoughts. Identify faulty thinking patterns. Observing mood changes will help you to recognize when you've begun to think poorly.
3) Stop the flow of your thoughts when you notice they are flawed.
4) Reject inaccurate, troublesome thoughts and replace them with accurate, truthful thoughts.
5) Develop these skills into a habit. Practice them until it gets easy and fast.

Interrupting Your Thoughts

Step three above entails recognizing your faulty thinking and interrupting the flow of it. In order to do this, choose the type of method below that suits you the best.

Physical: Put a rubber band on your wrist, and snap yourself each time you identify a faulty thinking habit.
Cognitive: Think to yourself, "Stop!" or "No!"
Audible: Say out loud or in a whisper, "Stop!" or "No!"
Visual: Imagine seeing a giant stop sign.

Jim tore off the perforated section with the five steps on it and handed it to Mike. "Here's a card with these steps on it for you to take home. People like this quick reminder of how to make the changes. Feel free to photocopy this and keep a copy at home, in your wallet or at work. You'll only need this outline available for a while. Before long, you'll have it memorized and down pat.

"In the beginning, monitoring your thoughts may be challenging," Jim explained. "Faulty thinking is often so ingrained that it often sneaks in without us having a conscious awareness of it. And many people say that their thoughts go by so fast that it's hard to have time to stop them. The key here is to do the necessary steps of identifying and interrupting those faulty thinking habits. Because you have six habits to work on, it is way too confusing to start with all six. Just start with one for now. Write on your card which habit you are trying to identify. Which one would you like to start with?"

"Let's start at the top of my list, which is Negative Filtering," Mike said.

"Okay, write, 'Negative Filtering' on your card, and keep that card in your pocket. Any time you take out your keys or anything from your pocket, it can be a reminder to you to be monitoring for those thoughts."

"I can do that," Mike said confidently.

HALTING FAULTY THOUGHTS

"Once you have identified the faulty thinking, it is important to stop the thought process. There are different ways of doing this, depending on your personality. These techniques stop the train of flawed thinking and help you get back on a better track," Jim said.

"I see the four methods listed on the handout for interrupting my thoughts," Mike said. "I'm trying to imagine myself at work yelling out, 'Stop!' They'd lock me up in the psych ward for sure."

"Yeah, you probably would get some strange looks. You might want to use a different method at work. If none of these work for you, just make up something else that does.

"After you've identified the problem and stopped your flow of thoughts, reflect on what went through your head. Write it down if you want. Separate truth from fiction. If it's something you're not sure about regarding yourself or a situation, ask a wise friend what they think. Or, you can always bring it up in your next session for us to talk about."

REPLACING THOUGHTS

Jim took a sip of his coffee and continued, "Spend some time replacing those erroneous thoughts with truth-based ones. Practice this, and it will reap great dividends. Changing your thinking habits takes dedication to monitoring your thoughts and redirecting your thoughts, but the results are liberating. Healthy thinking brings freedom from anxiety, depression, excessive burden and false guilt. It helps you to gain sound judgment and causes you to experience a more consistently peaceful, hopeful mood and state of being. I promise you the effort is worth it."

"I'm ready to start," Mike said. "How long will it take before I'm cured, Doc?"

"I've been amazed at how fast people see results. Starting with a single faulty habit has a positive cascading effect into other areas of life. Most people see improvement within one week if they focus on just one or two patterns.

"One of the first changes you will start to see," Jim said, picking up energy, "is that you'll get faster at recognizing faulty thinking. Instead of being negative in your mind set for a whole day, you might catch yourself at noon and have a great rest of the day. Eventually you can catch yourself after just a few minutes. It keeps getting easier and faster. After a while, you may notice that some of your faulty thinking patterns have disappeared altogether. They're not an issue anymore."

"I hope to get to that point," Mike said.

"I think you're very capable. In the words of Winston Churchill, 'Never give up!' It is entirely possible to change old, negative thinking habits into positive ones—even for people who have been using the unhealthy ones for sixty years."

As they were wrapping up their visit, Jim also encouraged Mike to increase how much time he was spending with friends and to get their assistance in this endeavor. This was the second time that Mike had heard this recently. It was the same message that he had received from his doctor. Hope welled up in him as he realized that these strategies could really make a difference. He was geared up to take on the challenge.

"I'll see you for your next appointment on Monday, Mike. I'll be curious to see how this affects you over the next week."

"Yeah, me too," Mike said.

QUESTIONS FOR GROUP DISCUSSION OR
INDIVIDUAL REFLECTION

Note to Readers: You can find a condensed list of the thought patterns described in this chapter in Appendix A, and a copy of this guide, How To Change Your Thoughts, in Appendix B. These are compact versions that you can tear out and carry with you for quick reference.

1) What is your reaction to how many Faulty Thinking Patterns you recognized within yourself? Was it higher or lower than you would have guessed? What did you learn by completing this self-assessment?

2) What obstacles do you think may make it hard for you to switch from faulty thinking patterns over to healthy thinking patterns?

3) What do you look forward to about getting rid of the faulty thinking you do? What benefits do you stand to gain?

4) In this chapter, Jim urged Mike to write down in the left margin of the thinking patterns chart the specific faulty thoughts that go through his head. Then he was to come up with healthy thoughts to replace the faulty ones and write those in the right margin. On your own or with a friend or small group partner, select the top three patterns you want to work on, and complete the worksheet below titled Replacing Troublesome Thoughts. This practical tool can help you to improve your thought life dramatically.

Please note that there is a completed sample of this worksheet in Appendix C to model the process, and another blank copy you can use at a later date for different troublesome thoughts you want to change. Once you've filled in this worksheet, you may want to photocopy it and carry a copy with you for review and assistance when you need it. Having a sheet like this makes it easier to retrain your thinking, but soon you won't need it because your new healthy thinking will become automatic.

Replacing Troublesome Thoughts

For this worksheet, select your own top three Faulty Thinking Patterns that you'd like to fix. On the left side, give a personal example of a specific troublesome thought of that type that goes through your head. On the right side, write the new and improved thought with which you'd like to replace it. To assist you in this, you could use the Alternate Healthy Thinking Patterns guidelines located on the right side of the Healthy vs. Faulty Thinking Patterns chart in chapter four.

SAMPLE	SAMPLE
Name of Faulty Thinking Pattern: Mind Reading	Name of Corresponding Healthy Pattern: Double-check Your Assumptions
Example: If I see someone look at me oddly, I think, "They must not like me." I tend to think that people are judging me or upset with me by how they look at me, how they talk or even by their body language.	Example: I can't know for sure what people are thinking or what their opinion is of me. If I want to know, I can ask them. I don't want to be upset over nothing.
My #1: Name of Faulty Thinking Pattern _____ My Personal Example: _____ _____ _____ _____	Name of Corresponding Healthy Pattern: _____ My Healthy Replacement: _____ _____ _____ _____

My #2: Name of Faulty Thinking Pattern	Name of Corresponding Healthy Pattern:
My Personal Example:	My Healthy Replacement:
My #3: Name of Faulty Thinking Pattern:	Name of Corresponding Healthy Pattern:
My Personal Example:	My Healthy Replacement:

Reap the Benefits

Now that you have identified your top three troublesome thought patterns and came up with specific alternatives, it will make it so much easier for you to repair your thinking. You will notice the problematic ideas in your head much more quickly. Plus, you'll be ready with a positive, truthful thought to substitute in its place.

Well done! Over the next few days, re-read this worksheet a few times to rehearse for when you're going to need to swap thoughts. Once you memorize your own specific examples, it becomes easy to exchange them. You'll soon have the relief that comes from renewed thinking that's based on truth rather than on guesswork or worry.

CHAPTER FIVE

Shrinking Faulty Thinking

Just two days after his counseling appointment, Mike received his annual evaluation from his boss. It was glowing with praise, with very little criticism.

"Well done, Mike. I'm thrilled to have you on the team. I appreciate how hard you work to draw everything together. You commit to projects, and you're well respected by your peers. I can't say enough. I need people like you to run this place."

Mike couldn't help but smile as he felt respected and esteemed for his efforts. If only his boss stopped there and had nothing else to say, then Mike would have remained in his elated mood.

The euphoria dampened as he heard his boss say, "There's only one thing that I am concerned about. Are you having difficulty getting all of your work done on time? I've noticed that you've been pulling some long hours lately. What can I do to help you get your work done so that you don't have to stay so late?"

This was painful to hear. Mike prided himself for getting things done in a timely fashion. *I'm the most efficient person on the team.* With as much positive feedback as he had received, he couldn't keep his mind off this single area of constructive criticism. *My boss doesn't know the whole story.* Mike felt misunderstood, judged and then instantly ticked off. *Here I am helping out Travis so he doesn't look so bad. Meanwhile, I'm the one getting criticized. How can our boss not realize what's going on?*

Mike was reaping the consequences of Travis' dawdling. Mike was tempted to tell his boss where the real problem resided. But by telling his boss the real issue, it would have meant admitting that covering for Travis was not such a good idea. He was held back by his need to be right. He also refrained from informing his boss about Travis, because it would stir up trouble between him and his co-worker.

I hate conflict, Mike thought. *If this gets discussed openly, then Travis will get dragged into it and we'll have a huge mess. He'll find out that I told our boss, and then he'll be upset with me. Who am I to start talking about Travis' problems? I couldn't do that; we're all adults now. I'd get blamed for creating problems at work. Think how uncomfortable it would be to work here after that.* The potential moves of social chess skimmed through Mike's mind.

Returning from his thoughts, Mike responded to his boss. "Oh, don't worry. I have everything under control. I'm just making sure that everything is done correctly."

"Okay, Mike. Keep up the good work." They shook hands and went back to their own offices.

Mike no longer believed his boss' compliments. Instead, he conjured up the image of himself working at a factory job where the items on his line were stacking up as he got further and further behind. *Do I appear that slow? Does anyone else think this? I must be a terrible employee.* Rapidly jumping from one idea to the next, Mike wasn't consciously aware of the inaccuracies in his thinking. He was thinking in extremes.

What he did notice was that he felt a forlorn look creep onto his face. A fiery gnawing sensation originating in his stomach slinked its way up to his esophagus. The turmoil in his brain sapped his energy. He felt like had just run a 10K. *I work so hard, yet I'm not appreciated. Maybe I should go work someplace else to get a fresh start.*

Triggered by the sensation of fatigue, he remembered the extra hours that he had been putting in at work to make up for Travis. This helped to break some of his harsh and unwarranted self-criticism. Suddenly, like turreted weaponry on a tank searching for its mark, his thoughts turned away from himself, and he started looking for an outward target. He could feel the anger starting to well up inside him, and he could hear his pulse at his temples. In addition to his anger, he was ashamed of the criticism that he had received and grew afraid that anyone else might find out. *If they did find out, then they would be licensed to criticize me as well. This is Travis' fault that my reputation is being questioned. He's the one that's irresponsible.*

DETECTION

In the midst of his inner turmoil, Mike fortuitously felt a card in his pocket. He touched the reminder card from Jim about faulty thinking and knew instantly that his thinking was off track. Even though he was not experienced in monitoring his thoughts, Mike knew that something wasn't right. However, it was difficult to trace what he had actually been thinking about in the past couple minutes. The more he tried to remember, the more his mind rambled on to think about other things.

I need to break the thought patterns Jim taught me about. I want to have my thoughts lined up with reality. How do I do that again? He was not used to praying at work, but he thought a quick prayer. *God, I need to change my thinking patterns to thoughts that are healthier. Will You help me?*

Now he was no longer alone in this challenge. He felt some new confidence now that he was teamed up with God. Looking down at the card, he reviewed how to stop and change faulty thinking patterns. The task at hand was to stop the chain of faulty thoughts. He internally shouted, "Stop!"

Like a youthful, untrained German shepherd, his series of thinking patterns reluctantly skidded to a halt. The canine was ready to leap back into action, and needed constant restraint from returning to thoughts of self-criticism and disastrous imaginings. Mike brought his focus to the next step of changing his thought patterns. *Where's the problem? What's wrong? Was this accurate thinking?*

He realized that when he was analyzing his thought pattern he was no longer able to think about anything else at the same time. This effectively kept the faulty thought pattern at bay. Mike was rather pleased with his success. Remembering that he had not done this alone, he silently gave a quick thanks to God. Having the card that Jim gave him was clearly useful in learning how to go about the process. Thinking more clearly now, he remembered all of the feedback that his boss had given him, and recognized that he was getting hung up on the one bit of constructive criticism. *I've got it! I was doing negative filtering.*

Now he knew that it was time for extraction. For some reason, it made him think of one of his favorite pastimes—fishing. When trout fishing, he hated catching suckerfish, since they overpopulated the lake and were no good for eating. The one consolation was that each suckerfish that he pulled out would be one fewer infesting pest in the lake. For Mike, this nuisance was similar to his faulty thoughts. The faulty thinking patterns needed to be removed so that the healthy thinking patterns could multiply.

Having detected one of his faulty thought patterns, Mike aimed towards finding other flaws in his thinking. *Was it really true that I'm not a good employee?* Mike realized he was not only doing negative filtering, he was also imagining a disaster, creating a worst-case scenario. *Plus, I couldn't let go of my need to be right about my decision to stay late to help Travis. Whoa—I'm good. It must take real talent to combine three faulty thinking patterns together so well.*

Now that his conscious mind was evaluating his thoughts, he became more aware of how ridiculous his ideas had become. *So, what do I need to do to fix this mess in my head?* He remembered that he needed to consider all the facts. In order to stop blocking out chunks of positive information, he forced himself to reiterate the encouraging feedback that he had received only a few minutes before. *How odd it is that the positive feedback went out the window so quickly and yet the one negative part stuck around to haunt me. Why did that happen?*

Recalling the handout that Jim had given him, Mike acknowledged that he would always have imperfections, yet he was created with many talents and good traits. Even if he did have a couple of things to work on, he also had a lot to contribute. Now as a warrior protecting his mental territory, he did not want to let his vision get too crowded with his shortcomings.

It's time. I need to replace the faulty thinking with healthy thinking. I am not a terrible employee. In fact, I've just heard from my boss that I'm a commendable employee that is hardworking and dedicated to our projects. God has made me a talented person. However, one area that I need to address is my working relationship with Travis. This does not mean that I'm an overall lousy employee.

This replacement seemed to work. Mike felt better. No longer was he dwelling only on the negative. After a few minutes, he was appreciating that his boss had given him favorable and supportive feedback. Plus, his boss cared enough to offer some observations about Mike working too much. Thoughts of leaving the company were history. *It is amazing how much my thinking patterns affected my mood.* Mike also noticed that his abdominal pain was subsiding and he didn't feel so tired anymore. Now he was filled with hope. *If I can make a small change in this one instance and feel so much better, imagine how I'll feel when I'm good at dealing with all of my faulty thinking habits.*

Part of Mike wanted to share with Sara what was going on, but he was still raw after the last time he had shared some good news with her. He headed off to his favorite café instead. He couldn't wait to share the news with Isaiah. The barista's off-the-cuff remark had been right on target. A small change had made a difference.

Café Celebrations

"I think that you've got a hold of something." Isaiah was his usually friendly self and particularly interested in what Mike had recently been experiencing. "At least you have a cheat sheet card to guide you in life," he jabbed.

"Yeah, it's surprising how it explicitly says to ignore all advice from you. Odd isn't it?" Mike replied.

"I like it," replied Isaiah, thinking about the Faulty Thinking Patterns.

"You like the fact that your advice should be ignored?"

"No," Isaiah said "I was busy disregarding you when you said that part. I meant I like the structured system of how to replace faulty thoughts."

"I found it very helpful for me today."

"I wish I had something straightforward like this years ago. It would have helped me out a great deal. You know, learning from others' mistakes is preferable to learning from your own. I'd rather take the preventative approach and learn how to avoid making my own mistakes."

Mike sighed, "Tell me about it."

Isaiah paused while he ground some coffee beans. "I like the fifteen healthy thinking patterns. I've heard about faulty thinking habits but never came across a set list, especially one that suggests healthy ones to do instead. I guess that my approach in the past was to avoid faulty thinking habits rather than to replace them with healthy ones. I think there is a problem with that method, though. When I just avoided unhealthy thinking patterns, I was easily drawn back to them. It's like being told not to think about a Ferris wheel. What do you naturally do? You think about a Ferris wheel. I think it's better to challenge a thought and substitute it with a new more accurate one. Yes, this information would have been very helpful for me and certainly for my marriage had I learned it earlier on in my life."

Isaiah asked to look over the sheet from Jim's counselor. "You know, the one that has particular meaning for me is the Need to Be Right. For my wife and me, this usually came up when we were in group settings. If I was telling a story and she jumped in to correct me about some of the details, it would drive me crazy."

"Give me an example," Mike inquired.

"This was a while ago now, but I distinctly remember one evening when we were with some friends talking about a *Seinfeld* episode. You know how the vignettes often apply to everyday life? Well, I was commenting on how George met a 'low-talker' and how challenging that is for me when those whisperers come into the café. With all of the racket going on in here, people need to speak up when ordering.

"Anyway, my wife jumped in mid-story and said that it was Jerry that met the 'low-talker,' not George. That wasn't my point, but I was dead certain that it was George that went on the date with the low-talker. How could I be wrong? I watched Seinfeld more often than she did. This got my wife and me off on this tangent arguing about who went on a date with the low–talker. What made it worse was that one of my friends agreed with my wife. By now, I had heartily invested in my position and couldn't give up, even though the odds were stacked against me. Plus, if I lost the argument, who'd still consider me to be the *Seinfeld* authority that I truly was?

"Looking back, I think I got a bit carried away insisting that it was George who met the low-talker. By how strongly I spoke, I cut off any more discussion on the issue. This seemed to make my wife pretty upset. Later, she was angry that I didn't listen to her and felt like I didn't value her opinion. We finally resolved the issue, and we even find it funny to talk about it now. But it was not humorous at the time. A couple weeks after the party, I watched that episode of *Seinfeld*, and in fact it was Jerry that had the date with the 'low-talker.' That was humbling."

"Man, I would have felt like an idiot," said Mike with a smile.

"Hey—watch it!" growled Isaiah.

"Alright, alright. Go on. I sure wouldn't want to interrupt your story."

"Yeah, thanks," Isaiah said sarcastically. "As I was saying, I see how needing to be right put a lot of pressure on me. It meant that I needed to be on guard at all times to defend my opinions and statements. That sure sucks the energy out of a guy. Other people would notice my defensiveness, and it hampered the way we related. By needing to be right, I often needed to prove them wrong. Some friends started to distance themselves from me because of this issue."

Mike chimed in, "I did something similar. I'm not sure if I should be helping my co-worker Travis complete his part of our projects on time. So instead of admitting possible error, I omitted telling my boss that the main reason I'm staying late at work is to help Travis. I didn't want my boss to question my judgment."

"I understand," said Isaiah.

"So how did you end up resolving things with your wife?" Mike asked. "My wife and I regularly have difficulty in this area. Maybe I can pick up a couple tips."

"What happened with my wife hit me like never before. First of all, I was clearly wrong, and secondly it hurt our marriage. Even though it was over a trivial matter, my wife felt devalued and cast aside. I think that God was showing me that I was prideful in always wanting to be right. Instead of desiring to have all the answers, my job was to desire to learn from others. At that time, I was reading the Book of Proverbs. I stumbled across a verse saying that the wise man loves those who instruct him. It's the fool who disregards instruction. As much as I hate to admit it, I was the fool and not the wise man. I finally admitted to her that I was wrong and that I was sorry. I asked her to forgive me, and she graciously did. We don't come up against that problem much anymore."

This answer made Mike visibly uncomfortable. This was what he hated—

admitting guilt. He didn't like owning up to the fact that he didn't have everything together. For some reason it was even harder when it was with his wife.

I can't remember having a conversation like this with anyone else—where someone talked about having to apologize to their spouse, Mike thought. *Isaiah and his wife are now able to laugh about their disagreement. I can't think of any of my quarrels with Sara that we can look back on and laugh.*

Isaiah continued, "I don't have a handy card that reminds me to break the cycle of needing to be right. Instead, I have repeated experiences showing me the pitfalls of that particular thinking pattern. I'm convinced now that I don't want to relive those experiences, and I'm more apt to catch myself when I'm falling into that old trap.

"The other thing I've noticed," Isaiah continued, "is that when I see other people who are less willing to admit when they are wrong, I can be pretty sure they're struggling with the same issue that I was. I find them irritating, since they won't listen to others. But I do have compassion for them."

"So, are you saying that you find me irritating?" Mike asked.

"Not so much anymore," Isaiah said, unable to control his laughter.

It made Mike cringe to think of how he had spoken to other people within the past few weeks. "Thanks for your willingness to tell me your own life example," he said. "That's very helpful. I'm wondering, how has it changed your marriage?"

"It has transformed our marriage, and this is why," Isaiah explained. "It is not that we are a perfect couple, but there is a critical element that's now in our favor."

Mike was left hanging. "What's that?"

"A willingness to grow. I'm less afraid to admit that I have things I need to work on in our marriage. I look to learn now. It's just a fact of life. Any truly honest person will agree. By the way, what you learned from Jim has reminded me of a Bible verse. Do you mind if I share it with you?"

"Please go ahead."

"It's in Isaiah. It says that God's thoughts are different than our thoughts, and God's ways are different than our ways. For me, this has meant coming up with the goal to have my way of thinking become more like God's way of thinking. I figure He's got an edge." Isaiah flashed his half-smile.

"As my mind is transformed to the way God wants me to think, I find that I am no longer a slave to the notion that I have to be right all the time. I've found freedom from trying to make myself appear perfect. It's liberating. My wife and I have been willing to change and grow, and it has made a huge difference." Isaiah's body visibly relaxed as he talked.

Mike added, "Now that I've had some experience working on my thinking patterns, I can see what you mean. Starting this process was overwhelming, but now that I have some momentum, I can tell that it's going to get easier.

"You know," Mike continued, "both my doctor and counselor encouraged me to focus on my spiritual life. Now you're bringing up spiritual things as well. I can't believe it's just a coincidence. This week, I'm going to try to meet up with my pastor."

"Really? What are you going to talk about?"

"I'm not sure. I don't know him very well, but he seems like a good guy. I know I've neglected my spiritual life, and I'm ready for that to change."

"Sounds good. I'll be interested to hear how that goes."

"I appreciate your help, Isaiah."

"That's what brothers are for."

QUESTIONS FOR GROUP DISCUSSION OR
INDIVIDUAL REFLECTION

1) What Faulty Thinking Patterns have you identified in your life? Describe any headway you've made in overcoming this troublesome way of thinking, whether it is increasing your awareness of it, interrupting your flow of thoughts, or substituting the healthy alternate way of thinking.

2) Which of the Healthy Thinking Patterns are you good at doing or getting better at doing?

3) What difference(s) do you find it makes in your life or mood once you have reduced or overcome faulty thinking?

SKILL #3

ESTABLISHING
HEALTHY BOUNDARIES

CHAPTER SIX

A World
of Possibilities

T he phone was ringing. Mike waited for Pastor Tony's assistant to answer. "Hello, you've reached Northwest Church. I'm Pam. How may I help you?" "Hi. My name is Mike Forrester. I'd like to meet with the pastor sometime this week." Anyone who knew Mike would be able to detect the apprehension in his voice.

"Okay, Mike. Let me take a look at his schedule. How does Thursday at 6 P.M. sound? He'll be here before the prayer meeting that night."

"Let's book it. Thanks, Pam."

Letting out a sigh, Mike began to think of how he would bring things up with Pastor Tony. Although it was painful to face certain realities, the rewards of his exploration into his problems were already accumulating, and that motivated Mike to dig deeper. No longer was he afraid of bringing the difficulties of his life out into the open. He saw how much easier problems were remedied once he reached out to others and revealed what was going on.

The main thing Mike was wrestling with was time-management. He was still putting in too many hours at the office, and this perpetuated conflict in his marriage.

This is really no way to live, Mike concluded. I'm showing signs of burnout, and next I know I'll be losing the gray hair I'm getting. Working till you drop is not as noble as it's portrayed to be in films and novels. I'm beginning to feel old, and I'm only in my thirties.

Thursday came. Ideas of what Mike wanted to say were still ricocheting around his brain like a pinball in an arcade machine. As he began walking up to the church office door, he noticed his pastor approaching from the other side of the parking lot. Pastor Tony reminded him of an amicable, devoted beagle with the wisdom of an owl.

Why does this man do the things that he does? How does he keep on going year after year without getting discouraged? Mike could never imagine himself being a pastor.

Tony saw Mike and gave him a hearty handshake and a pat on the shoulder. "Good to see you. It's been a few years since we've had a chance to talk, hasn't it? I've been looking forward to seeing you. Come on inside."

Mike already felt a little more at ease. Usually, he was a little uncertain what to say to his pastor, but recently he had been a little less cautious and tended to blurt out what was on his mind. "I've been anticipating talking with you as well. Thanks for making time in your schedule for me; I know that you're very busy. I can't imagine what it's like to have to put together a sermon every week on top of all your other church duties. I'd have a hard time coming up with new material every week."

Years engrossed in study had created lines across the pastor's brow. "I'm not up to it all on my own. Thankfully, the Holy Spirit guides my mind and reveals to me what topics to teach. Oftentimes, I feel like my job is to ask God what it is that He wants to say. My responsibility is to follow His lead and represent His ideas as best I can. You'd think that I'd be an expert at this after being a pastor for twenty-two years. Ironically, I feel more like a novice now than I did fifteen years ago. In the early days, more of my life and ministry was planned and carefully scripted according to my own will. It made it so much harder to try to figure things out all on my own without consulting God."

The pastor paused a moment. "Now it seems more like the adventure of riding on a roller-coaster. You know the one at Disneyland, Space Mountain, where you're in the dark and you can't see where the next turn will go. It's comforting to know that with the myriads of people that have gone on that ride before me, the wheels have always stayed on the tracks.

"Likewise, I've gained confidence that God knows what He's doing and where He's going. I have become more comfortable with this uncertainty over time. I try to focus on what God wants me to do, and I try to stay away from the things that He doesn't want me to do. Even though I can't see what is around the corner, I try to remember that there is a plan and timeline that God has in mind. It took me a while to discover that living by faith means I don't need to know what's coming and that things are still in good shape. The situation is still in control—just not by me."

The pastor gestured towards the chairs in his office. "Please have a seat, Mike, wherever you like."

"I find this fascinating," Mike said. "It seems that in my life, I get caught up in so many duties and activities that I am overwhelmed most of the time. It's hard to hold myself back, though, because I get excited about a bunch of different things."

"I'm with you, Mike. There have been several projects or different ministries I've been interested in over the years that part of me wants to jump at."

"How do you know what you're supposed to do and what you're not supposed to do?" Mike asked.

"Sometimes I don't have a choice," the pastor replied. "Urgent needs must often be addressed right away. For me, this usually entails preparing for services, funerals, weddings and meetings. However, there are many times that I can make a clear decision ahead of time on what direction to take. For example, we are considering starting up a new mentorship program in our church. Several of us have sensed God leading us in this direction. This is not an urgent decision to make, but it needs to be prioritized to make sure that it doesn't get squeezed out by things that are more pressing."

The pastor continued, "I have to make numerous decisions every day. Sometimes they're relatively easy to make, and other times they can be exasperating. Then there are other times when I have poured tremendous energy into my decision-making. I've consulted with knowledgeable people to get as much information as possible. I've prayed fervently and waited on the Lord for direction. No matter what amount of preparation goes into making a decision, or what method I use to make the choice, in the end it seems that the biggest issue is how it fits with what God is calling me to at the time. Have you ever considered, Mike, how you make decisions?"

"I guess I've never thought about that before," Mike said. "I think that I take each situation as it comes, and I try to do my best. However, I do find that I tend to get overcommitted easily and stressed out. Maybe it's because I don't understand where God is leading me."

"Many people can relate with that," the pastor pointed out. "I think what it comes down to is asking God to reveal His will to you and then waiting in faith expectantly. Most people find that over time they notice a trend in how God speaks to them. For some people, God tends to speak to them through the people in their life. For others, God shows them His will by giving them impressions or new ideas of what to do.

"One of the things I appreciate most about God is that He cares about helping us with big decisions and small ones. I've had God guide me on decisions that I thought would be insignificant to Him, but evidently they were not."

"I don't get it," Mike said. "Why would God care about our minor decisions?"

"Think about it this way: we build a track record as we make hundreds of small decisions over time. Many seemingly minor decisions are made as a reaction to the circumstances at hand. People may think, 'Oh it's just this once that I'll do this,' knowing full well that it's likely not the best decision or that it compromises their values. In reality, over time our small decisions shape our character and influence our major decisions."

Mike jumped in. "Now that's a scary thought—that my character could be changed by the small decisions that I make. I received extra change at the grocery store and kept it instead of returning it. Will this turn me into a thief?"

"Not necessarily right away. Without sticking to their principles and priorities, many people have slowly turned into someone they never imagined they'd become. I have seen this time after time. For some, lying gets to be easier over time. Ignoring their conscience or saying no to God repeatedly leads people to having a calloused heart."

It sank in for Mike. He realized that he had been making decisions on a whim, not basing them on his priorities and values. His face turned sullen.

The pastor noticed and asked, "Feel like some good news? The flip side is also true. Making good small decisions over time can turn you into the person that you do want to become. If you want to become a person of integrity, you can choose to return the change to the grocery clerk, even if no one would notice or find out. This also pertains to relationships. Those who perpetually hurt others and fail to make amends are paving the way for one lost relationship after another. But if you regularly seek to reconcile with others you've hurt, you will become trustworthy and people will be willing to work through conflict with you. You'll have stronger relationships."

This hits close to home, Mike thought. *Does he know what's going on in my relationship with Sara?*

"Take affairs for instance. They're usually the result of numerous small decisions along the way. Divorce is not usually due to one big mistake, but rather the accumulation of small decisions over time."

Affairs! Mike thought. *This is getting a bit heavy and personal. Does he think that I've had an affair? If he does, it's not true. I haven't done anything like that.* Mike's heart was racing.

"These are some of the most common problems that I tend to see," the pastor said.

Phew! Maybe he doesn't know anything about my problems with Sara. And, we're not the only ones going through problems like this. That's good to know. Even so, I'm not ready to talk about my marriage. Mike inquired, "What are good ways to go about making decisions then?"

"I've found that it's important to look at God's values and try to base your decisions on those. Do you know what some of God's values are?" Pastor Tony asked.

Mike felt a little on the spot and was unprepared for this question. After an awkward pause, he remembered the Greatest Commandments. With some pleasure in the fact that he remembered something from a sermon, Mike recounted to the pastor that the Bible says that God's greatest commandments are to love Him, and to love others as you love yourself.

"Nice work," the pastor complimented him. "You know, if everyone followed those two commandments, people would treat each other a lot better. Most sins are because of selfishness. So, if we were intent upon loving others as much or as well as we love ourselves, the numerous sins due to selfishness would be diminished."

"The Ten Commandments also reflect God's values, don't you think?" said Mike, with growing momentum and interest. "I usually try not to break those. No murdering, stealing or *adultery* here."

Mike was starting to make connections that he hadn't made before. Thinking about the recent fight with Sara, he remembered how he had brought up her issues with her dad, knowing it would enrage her, just because it took the heat off of him and deflected the attention onto her dad. *That was selfish*, Mike thought.

"I have a chart that some members of our congregation came up with in a class once. It compares society's values to God's values. The premise is that His wisdom extends far beyond our own. So basing our decisions on God's values will be the most advantageous. What do you think?" Pastor Tony handed the chart to Mike.

COMPARING SOCIETY'S VALUES TO GOD'S VALUES

Society's Highest Values

- Happiness
- Preventing Suffering
- Comfort
- Money
- Prestige and Image
- Power
- Possessions/Wealth
- Sex Appeal
- Pleasure
- Youthfulness
- Expediency or Instant Gratification
- Employment or Work
- Efficiency
- Nice House and Yard
- Entertainment

God's Highest Values

- Loving people and Loving God
- Mercy and Grace
- Prayer: Talking with God
- Honoring and Respecting Others
- The Ten Commandments
- Caring for the Poor and Vulnerable
- Good Character: e.g. Honesty
- Strong Relationships
- Justice and Taking Responsibility
- Rest and the Sabbath
- Forgiveness
- Faith and Trust in God
- Scripture Study
- Spending Resources Wisely

Some of the Values Shared by God and Society

- Freedom
- The Needs of an Individual
- Strong Work Ethic
- Education/Training
- Health and Fitness

- Family
- Equality
- Caring for Human Needs
- Environmentalism
- People Flourishing

"I don't think that I've ever thought this through," said Mike. "I thought that my main goal in life was to be happy. Many people seem concerned about preventing suffering at all cost. Maybe that's their highest value. Although, I can see how the pursuit of preventing suffering would come into competition with God's values. Just think about how many people have had to suffer for doing what was right. I know that Jesus suffered for doing what was right. If His highest value had been the pursuit of happiness at any cost, He never would've done many of the great things He did."

"I agree," the pastor added. "I was talking about this with a wealthy businessman recently. He told me that his goal in life had been to be happy and wealthy. He loved instant gratification. He had it all—or so it seemed.

"After a while, those things that once pleased him lost their sparkle. His interests would move on to something new. His tastes continued to change to the point where he had an escalating need for the bigger and better. Finally, he started to wonder what else there was to life. He could have anything that he wanted, but his heart went unfulfilled. This isn't something that many people will readily admit in a casual conversation, especially someone in his position, but I hear about it all the time doing the work I do."

Mike could see the futility of the wealthy man's efforts. He asked his pastor, "So, how could all of this help me make decisions in my life?"

The pastor did not have a chance to answer Mike's question, because someone had started knocking on his office door. "Come in," he responded.

A woman with short blonde hair and blue eyes poked her head in the door. "Sorry to interrupt you," the pastor's assistant said. "I have someone on the phone for you who says they're having a family crisis and they'd like to talk to you."

"Thanks, Pam. I'll be right there. Please tell them I have a few moments to talk to them, but then I'll have to get back to my meeting." Turning to Mike, he said, "Sorry about this. It comes with the territory in this job. I'll arrange a time to meet with them tomorrow, or I'll see if they'd like an emergency meeting with one of the other pastors. Meanwhile, here, take a shot at this," he said as he tossed Mike a handout. "I've used this worksheet myself and found it helpful. By completing this, I think you'll find answers to the question you just asked me. Oh, and that values chart we just looked at may be useful when filling it out. I should be back in a little while."

CREATE YOUR OWN PERSONAL MISSION STATEMENT

In today's fast-paced and media-saturated society, it is possible to go a long period of time without stopping to reflect on the big picture of our lives. It's easy to get distracted or overwhelmed. With the explosion of new technology, there are endless ways to waste your time under the seductive guise of entertainment.

Instead of losing sight of the big picture, take a moment to complete these sentences. In effect, you will synthesize your personal mission for each of these main areas of your life.

Relationships: I want to show the treasured people in my life that I care for them by _____

_____

_____

Character: I want to be remembered as a person who was _____

_____

_____

Being Productive: Before I die, I want to accomplish my goal(s) of _____

_____

_____

Abilities: The main skill(s) I have to offer to others is _____

_____

_____

Service: In my own way, I would like to make the world a better place for at least one person by _____

_____

_____

Identify your Passions

What things in life get you the most excited?

_____

What activities cause you to lose track of time, because you're so absorbed in what you're doing?

_____

_____

What things in life bother you the most, such that you wish you could obliterate them from the face of the earth?

_____

_____

Is there a certain group of people that you feel drawn to assist (such as the poor, single parents, the disabled, political refugees, etc.)?

_____

_____

To live a life that revolves around your purpose or calling, it is essential to recognize what you are most passionately for and against. You can promote something that you believe in, or you can oppose something you detest. For example, if you are an environmentalist, you could spend your time promoting green living by educating the public. Or, you could spend your time holding industrial companies legally accountable by opposing their wasteful and hazardous procedures.

Once you have identified your passions, you can narrow your focus, energy, talents, time and resources on what will be most satisfying to you. The rewards of your effort will become more obvious and happen at a faster rate.

Managing Your Time According To Your Mission Statement

Determining your priorities is a good way to start organizing how you manage your time. Use this worksheet to decide on an order to your priorities and to allot time accordingly. By clarifying what's most important to you in life, you'll have a springboard for making the best decisions.

You may have noticed that some of the things you value do not take a long time to fulfill. For instance, if one of your top values is honesty in relationships, you won't need to spend fifty percent of your time fulfilling this. For values such as this, the time component isn't as helpful to examine as the rank order.

Ranking Your Priorities

1) Fill in this chart by listing your core values in the first column.
2) In the second column, rank your core values as they actually are in current practice.
3) In the third column, rank your core values in the order you want to live them out.
4) Then put the percentage of time you currently spend on each core value in the fourth column.
5) Lastly, in the fifth column, write in the percentage of time you want to spend on each core value in the future.

My Core Values	Rank Order		% of Time I Now Spend on This	% of Time I Want to Spend on This
	Actual	Desired		
1) _____	_____	_____	___%	___%
2) _____	_____	_____	___%	___%
3) _____	_____	_____	___%	___%
4) _____	_____	_____	___%	___%
5) _____	_____	_____	___%	___%
6) _____	_____	_____	___%	___%
7) _____	_____	_____	___%	___%
8) _____	_____	_____	___%	___%
9) _____	_____	_____	___%	___%
10) _____	_____	_____	___%	___%
			100%	100%

Match Your Calendar with Your Priorities

The next step is to make sure these decisions are reflected in your weekly schedule. For the next three months, compare this list once every few weeks with your schedule book or calendar. See how well your rank list matches your time choices.

Leave this plan open to revision. You may get inspired later with fresh vision or take on a new role. Adapt this mission statement accordingly, as you feel led.

QUESTIONS FOR GROUP DISCUSSION OR
INDIVIDUAL REFLECTION

1) How do you make decisions? Do you tend to go by what seems to be right
at the time, or do you base decisions on your long-term values? In what
circumstances do you usually involve other people in the process of making your decisions?

2) Reflect on how you feel you are doing at living your life in accordance
with your values. If you are in a small group, discuss how this is going
with members of your group in as much detail as you feel comfortable.

3) If differences do exist between society's values and God's values, it could
explain why it is difficult to follow God's will sometimes. For instance,
God may be leading you to change to a lower paying job, which He knows
is going to bring many non-monetary rewards such as several great new
friendships. How do you think having different values than God affects
your cooperation with Him and your willingness to align your life to His
priorities? How could the differences between divine and human values
explain how some prayers seem to go unanswered (for instance, a man
praying for wealth and power when God knows that would cost him his
good character)?

4) Fill out the worksheet in Appendix D to create your Personal Mission
Statement. The appendix also includes Mike's completed Mission Statement, which may help you get started.

CHAPTER SEVEN

On a Mission

Mike was just about to put down his pen when he heard a cheerful, "How did it go?" He looked up and saw Pastor Tony coming in the door.

"Pretty good, I think. I'm just not sure what to do with it now. How do I use this practically and put it into action?"

"Well, a mission statement is meant to be used proactively—creating a strategy for your future—so it's great for planning ahead. You can also use it for the present time to assess how closely your values and ideals match your life right now."

"There were some areas where there was a difference between actual reality and my ideal," Mike said.

"What were those?" the pastor inquired.

"I realized while I was ranking my core values that I've been prioritizing my work over my wife. I couldn't help but notice it when I was doing the 'actual rank order' for how things are now. I thought I should probably put my wife above my work, but knew that if I did, it would be a lie. So, on my 'desired rank list' for the future, I put her as number one."

"I like your honesty. This chart is helpful for identifying the inconsistencies."

"I have to somehow reorder how I'm living them out," Mike said. "I feel pressure from both sides. At work, it seems I need to work faster and harder. At home, my wife tells me I should spend more time doing things with her. I feel like there's no winning."

"You mean you can't please everybody?" the pastor said with a smile.

"Yeah, don't I wish," Mike laughed. "I have a hard time telling people that I won't help them or meet their requests, including my wife and co-workers. I feel guilty when I don't do what they want. Should I feel this way?"

"You've raised a good question that comes up all the time," said Pastor Tony. "I've spoken to many people who feel that they can't say 'no' and still be the Christian they feel they ought to be. As a result, they end up doing things that they wish they weren't doing. They get worn out, and some people become bitter or resentful. This is definitely not what they wanted to become.

"I'm not sure where this mind set comes from, the notion that they need to help whoever asks them. But I can tell you it's not from the Bible. In fact, I see the opposite is true in the life of Jesus. When Jesus taught on the subject of keeping promises, He said, 'let your "yes" be "yes," and your "no," "no"' (Matthew 5:37). Implicit in this statement is the assumption that Christians can in fact say, 'No.'"

"I've never heard that taught before," said Mike.

"Yes, it's something that needs to be clarified in churches, because a lot of Christians have the same experience as you. They think the best policy is to help, help, help. Yet, setting limits is good for everybody involved.

ESCAPING THE PAPARAZZI

"Let me illustrate through the life of Jesus. He didn't work all of the time. The Bible frequently mentions how Jesus needed time alone. It says He would go up to the mountainside or the garden to be by Himself and to pray. His popularity had become a problem for Him, so He had to get away from the paparazzi."

The pastor continued: "He would take time to heal the sick, feed the hungry and teach the people. He led an active life with a full ministry. All the while, He still set clear boundaries. He didn't heal every person in the region. With so much need in the world, He could have been working non-stop if He didn't make time for other things in His life. For instance, Jesus prioritized a day of Sabbath rest and regular time with His friends Lazarus, Mary and Martha. He had other priorities that sometimes came above helping and serving others. Jesus clearly modeled setting limits on the amount work that is done. If Jesus did this and we are to follow His example, then we too must contain our workload and protect our priorities."

"I find this comforting," Mike said. "I'll need to remember this when I start to feel guilty that I may not be doing enough for the people around me. Of course, this is not to say I should neglect my responsibilities and sit on my butt all day."

The pastor smiled, appreciating Mike's candid style. He assured him, "Being clear in your priorities is also helpful for people like you who tend to be stressed out because they're overcommitted. Overcommitment is a trend that I've seen getting worse, and people can become quite anxious as a result of the choices that they have made."

"I hate saying no," Mike said frankly. I feel like I'm letting them down. I remember what my mother said when I growing up as a child. She quoted the proverb, "Lazy hands make a man poor" (Proverbs 10:4).

"Oh, I know that proverb well. Would you say that it applies to you?" the pastor asked.

"I don't think so. But, I could never be sure. So I would usually do a bit extra just to be certain. You know, as a preventative thing. Lately, the pressure comes from external sources to put in more hours at work."

"Does your boss also quote proverbs to you to make you feel guilty?" the pastor asked jokingly.

Mike laughed. "In a way, I think that I'd be able to deal with that better since I have more practice at handling guilt trips, thanks to my mom. No, the situation at work is that I have a co-worker who has difficulty with his workload. I do quite a bit of his work so that our projects will be completed on time." Mike was already coming to the conclusion that he was not doing the right thing, but he still made a last appeal to defend his past actions. He was also reluctant to stop helping Travis. "I am supposed to be giving and self-sacrificing, right?" Mike asked.

"Oh, I see." Pastor Tony had had this discussion many times before with other people. "Many people feel obligated to bend over backwards for others because they hear that they should 'walk an extra mile' and 'lay down their life' and feel that they should do anything and everything for others at the drop of a hat. Some people even think that 'turning the other cheek' means they should put up with abusive behavior. In the proper context, 'turning the other cheek' was intended to stop the practice of retaliation by those being persecuted for their faith. These verses do speak of being gracious and giving, serving one another in love, but they are not a mandate to be a doormat in daily life."

Mike looked at the pastor with confusion written on his face. "The longer that I work with this guy, the more frustrated I get. I get home late from work on a regular basis. It doesn't help that Sara is bothered by how much time I spend at work and wants more time for us together. I don't want her to be upset, but I care about getting the job done on time. I end up taking out my frustration on her, though."

"Is anyone else aware that your co-worker is having these problems?" the pastor inquired.

"Not that I'm aware of, because I tend to do all the work that he is unable to accomplish."

"Does anyone else pitch in to help out your co-worker that's having a tough time keeping up?"

After thinking a minute, Mike replied, "No not really."

"I find it interesting that you are the one who is doing all of the helping out and you are the one having a chaotic life. What would happen if you decided that you were no longer going to help him?"

It was uncomfortable for Mike to even consider the possibility. "I don't think that he would keep up. His part of the project wouldn't get done, and our team wouldn't meet our deadline."

"What would happen next?"

"Who knows? That's never happened. Our team always makes the deadlines. I make sure of that," Mike answered.

"Well, let's consider the possibility that for some reason, you don't help him on a certain project. What would happen to the team?"

"I guess our team leader would want to know what happened."

"Then what?" the pastor probed.

"It wouldn't take long to figure out where the problem was. I see where you are going. Our leader would identify Travis' inefficiencies and correct the problem. So you're saying that you want me to knowingly let my team fail?"

"Not at all," the pastor quickly responded. "What I am saying is that many people are spiritually confused when it comes to issues of responsibility and teamwork. Some Christians have a hard time because they only know the verse that says, 'Bear one another's burdens' (Galatians 6:2, NASB). They understand that they are to support one another through hard times. What they don't realize is that three verses later it also says, 'For each one will bear his own load' (Galatians 6:5, NASB). Ultimately, each person is to take responsibility for himself or herself.

"In life, there will be times when a person is overloaded and needs some help. I think that one of the most clear-cut examples is when someone is moving. Mike, you're a strong guy, and you could carry this recliner chair that you are sitting on all by yourself. Being in my fifties, I can't say the same for myself. I remember that within a month of turning thirty, my hair started turning gray, I pulled a hamstring, and I injured my neck for the first time. Life has been different ever since. For me, trying to carry my recliner by myself is asking for trouble. I might as well preemptively buy ice and ibuprofen, and cancel my schedule for the next two days while I moan and complain over every twist.

"The point I'm making is that the burden of moving all this furniture is too great for me to do by myself. Everyone will occasionally need help for burdens that are too great for them to handle alone. Yet the vast majority of the time, each person needs to do their own work and take care of their own responsibilities.

HELPING CAN HURT

"Something that comes as a surprise to many people is that by helping others you can actually be a hindrance to them. For instance, by helping out your co-worker to get his work done on time, you may be getting in the way of his professional growth. You're probably preventing him from learning better and faster ways of completing his tasks."

"Ironic, isn't it?" Mike agreed. "I had felt like the Christian thing for me to do was to help him out. This whole time I may have been prolonging problems for both him and myself."

"Welcome to the world of 'enabling.' That's when you enable people to continue in their dysfunction, while you try to make up for it. You have lots of company. It's a world where you take care of others' responsibilities. And as a result, other people don't improve, and you become bitter and irritated."

"I must say, I can relate to that," Mike said. "Not only have I been perpetuating the problem, but I have been reaping the consequences that Travis should have faced. Something needs to change so that Travis suffers his own consequences. Then he might smarten up." Mike could feel his temperature rising as he realized how he had allowed himself to be taken advantage of for such a long time.

"I guess that's one way of putting it," Pastor Tony replied. "It's normal to feel angry when you realize that you haven't set very healthy limits. It's because you're recognizing that your situation has been unjust.

"A crucial thing to remember is that God doesn't want us to burn out. Hey, have you checked out Rick Warren's most popular book? It's a book called *The Purpose Driven Life*."

"I've heard of that," Mike said. "It was on *The New York Times* bestseller list."

"Yeah, well Rick Warren got me right where it matters," said Pastor Tony. "In chapter three of that book, he says that if a person is running around stressed out, scurrying endlessly, then that person is most likely doing more than what God wants him or her to be doing. The chapter goes on to explain how that's not the kind of life God plans for us to lead.

"His comments stopped me in my tracks. When I read that I had just had an unusually busy week. It made me reconsider all that I had put on my plate. After some thought, I decided it would be best to hire an associate pastor to help me cover all that needed to be done here at the church. I've never regretted it."

"I believe that," Mike said. "I bet most people never regret lessening their work-load when they can. You must mean that's when you hired Pastor Jack. He's a good guy. I'm glad you brought him on staff, too."

"The longer I work as a pastor, the more I see how God tries to help people pre-vent burnout. I think that's why He wants us to have a Sabbath, so that we don't wear out. If we're dragging ourselves out of bed and dreading another day, that's not a good sign."

"I often dread going to work," Mike said. "I see now how most of the problem is what I bring upon myself. You're right: when it comes down to it the decision-making process is what I need to get lined up. I have some ideas on what changes I can make to alleviate things. I'm not entirely sure how to implement them yet. One thing is for sure: instead of stumbling through my decisions, I'd rather make them based on my values."

"That sounds good," said Pastor Tony.

"Thanks," Mike said pensively. "I need to look over my mission statement and see where it leads me in terms of modifications I need to make. How do you decide what work to take on or not, Pastor Tony?"

"I have many interests, so there are a lot of attractive ministries I consider. My passion could easily get me to take on far too much. But the end result would be that I'd do them poorly, or at least below my capabilities, because I'd be spread too thin.

"Instead, I consider how well a certain ministry fits in with my mission state-ment and job description here at the church. I pray and search the Scriptures to try to sense what God's will is for me. Sometimes I'll talk the decision over with some-one else. I may do any or all of these. Then, I make a decision based on the con-clusions that came out of that process."

Mike was surprised to hear how the Bible could have input or give direction to a real-life decision. He had never considered it that relevant or informative to modern life. He had mostly considered the Bible to be historical and good for moral teaching. Mike's curiosity was now piqued. He wanted to see for himself if the Bible or God could be so specific and closely involved with the details of his current life. He wondered if God only did that sort of thing for pastors. For most of Mike's life, God had seemed far off and impersonal. But that was beginning to change.

"Alright, I'll think that over," Mike said to his pastor. "I appreciate your time and help with what's going on in my life."

"You're very welcome, Mike. Over this next while, I think it'd be good if you spent some time observing your decisions and seeing if they reflect the values that you highlighted today. I'd be curious to hear what you notice. In fact, I'd like to meet up again if you're interested."

Whoa! I thought this was a one-time deal. Meet again? That would mean I'd have to really follow through on this stuff. It has been great to get to know my pastor, though. And it sure seems like he has a lot to teach me. Mike smiled. "Sure. I'll give you a call."

"If it's okay with you, Mike, I'd like to pray for you as you consider all of the things that we talked about today."

Mike was not used to people praying for him, but he thought, *What could it hurt?* He bowed his head, doing what he thought to be the international sign of accepting prayer. As the pastor prayed a blessing over him, Mike felt encouraged and somehow charged up to make some changes. What stood out most to Mike was that the pastor prayed Mike would sense what God wanted for him in his life and decisions.

Can I really detect that sort of thing? Mike questioned what he was hearing. *I always thought that prayer was just asking God for things that I needed and saying sorry over and over again. Could it ever be like how it was in the stories of the Bible, in which God apparently spoke directly to Isaiah or Moses? That sure would make it easier to know God's will for me. But does God really do that nowadays?*

They said their good-byes, and Mike was happy at the thought of seeing some more of his pastor in the future.

QUESTIONS FOR GROUP DISCUSSION OR
INDIVIDUAL REFLECTION

1) How do you decide what tasks or responsibilities to take on and what would be best left for someone else?

2) Have you ever felt like you were close to burnout? How could you tell? What did you do to rectify the situation?

3) Are there ways you'd like to simplify your life now by cutting out nonessentials? If so, what would you like to cut?

4) Have you had an experience where you believe you sensed God leading you? Describe the situation. How did things turn out?

## CHAPTER EIGHT

The Therapist's Couch

H ey Jim, no chest pain this week," Mike said brightly as he entered the counselor's office.

"Why not? Maybe you haven't been pushing yourself hard enough," Jim quipped.

"That's no way for a counselor to treat a client," Mike retorted as he kicked his feet up on the couch, assuming the traditional patient-on-the-couch stance. "I've always wanted to lie down, stretch out and let Freud do his work."

"I see you're feeling comfortable in counseling now."

Mike agreed by nodding, but he didn't want to admit that he was starting to enjoy the counseling process—at least not yet. "I specialize in making the best of a difficult situation."

Jim laughed, "You mean like being here in a counseling office with me? Yeah okay, I'll let you get away with that. I admit it. You get along with people well—even with the dubious counselor types like me." He complimented Mike but wasn't going to allow that comment to go unchallenged, especially since Mike responded well to playful banter. "Now you just need to overcome using sarcasm as your only line of defense."

Surprised by the counselor's feisty response, Mike replied, "Let's see. I can use my new skills here. This is not a time for me use Negative Filtering. So I shouldn't just focus on this one criticism you gave me. I need to keep the big picture in mind—like the fact that I'm the best client you've ever had."

Jim smiled. He was pleased at how fast Mike recognized a potential faulty thinking pattern. It was so familiar now he could turn it into a joke. "Nice work! You get an A."

"Yeah, not bad. I must say, though, that sometimes it's tricky to identify the thought pattern and change it," Mike said.

"How did the week go overall?" Jim asked.

Mike brought Jim up to speed on how things had gone with his boss and how he had caught himself using three faulty thinking patterns: Negative Filter, Imagining a Disaster and Needing to be Right. Jim was excited to hear the progress. Mike told Jim about the conversation he had had with his pastor, which started the counseling session off with discussing setting limits at work.

"Clients often talk to me about this sort of thing," Jim said. "I appreciate your pastor's perspective on this issue. I think that he had some wise advice for you."

"Yeah, me too. I was starting to think that he should be my counselor instead of you," Mike playfully jabbed.

"Hey now, watch it! I may have to start charging you double for having to put up with you." Both were now enjoying the process.

Jim continued, "Seriously, your pastor was right on. Setting limits is clearly important for making life less hectic. It allows you to stay on track and focus on your top priorities. It can be challenging in the early stages, though."

Mike did not need to be told about the difficulty of setting boundaries. He informed Jim that while growing up he had been taught to be polite and considerate. He wasn't supposed to risk offending or hurting others. The old unwritten rule had been that conflict was too messy. This led him to continuously go down the path of least resistance, the path that led to inaction in times of conflict. This coping mechanism worked for him—at least at first. It had an appearance like that of a sparkling painted finish on a vehicle. Even if the whole underside was rusting, the car still looked impressive on the outside. However at some point, the persistent neglect and rusting away of his own needs had left Mike a weathered frame. It weakened his resiliency to future collisions. By not speaking up to protect his interests, he ended up looking good but not getting what he wanted. He couldn't focus on the tasks at hand because he was busy stewing over past arguments in which he had held back.

Questioning the old family motto, Mike had decided he wanted to handle things differently. The old set of beliefs was a barrier to fulfillment for him. He wanted to set up the limits necessary for establishing his priorities at home and at work.

Applying that scenario to work, Jim explained, "Many people keep quiet about their own desires for the sake of avoiding conflict. They continue to help others to the point of neglecting their own health. Often they become ineffective in their own jobs, families and ministry because they are over-focused on others. Numerous clients have told me, 'Even though I'm not very happy, at least I am helping others.'"

Mike immediately identified with Jim's statement. He had said that to himself many times. Mike could tell that the counselor understood what was going on in his life and could probably help him implement the needed changes. Hope was rising. *Maybe this counseling stuff really works*, Mike mused.

Sensing that his client was ready to move forward, Jim asked him, "Would you like to take a look at some handouts I have on establishing boundaries and limits? They've proven useful to others for setting and sustaining boundaries."

"Sure, that would be great."

"I have a few handouts to give you today. Let's start with the one on different kinds of limits. This ties in nicely with the information you were getting from your pastor on making decisions based on your values. Some of the ideas in these handouts were initially inspired by a book you may want to pick up. It's called *Boundaries: When to Say Yes, When to Say No*. It's written by Henry Cloud and John Townsend.

Finding Your Bottom Line

What Is a Boundary?

A boundary can be defined as:

- A decision you make or a limit you set
- Anything that you agree to do or decide not to do
- A clarification of who is responsible for what
- A distinction of what belongs to you and what doesn't
- A rule of what is acceptable to you or not in relationships

Core Categories of Boundaries

Once we determine what we want, we establish boundaries to help us achieve our desires and maintain our decisions. The following are central categories or areas of boundaries:

A. Time: How you spend it
B. Money: What you buy and what you don't
C. Work/Responsibilities: Who does what and who is responsible for what
D. Relationships: How you treat others and how you ask to be treated
E. Morals & Ethics: What you care about, and how you go about getting it
F. Emotion: Taking ownership over what you feel; not absorbing other people's emotion or forcing onto others what you feel
G. Beliefs: Researching what is true and coming to your own conclusions
H. Health: Choosing to take care of yourself, such as ensuring you get proper sleep, nutrition and exercise

Oftentimes, people find it is easier to set limits in certain areas more than others. For instance, some people have no trouble setting boundaries for time-management, but have great difficulty controlling their spending and finances.

One of the prime factors for health in the area of boundaries is freely and thoughtfully making decisions for yourself and then not being too easily swayed or influenced by others to change your mind.

That's true for me, Mike thought. *I have no difficulty sticking to a budget, but I have difficulty setting limits at work with Travis, and maybe with my co-worker Sylvia, too. As a married man, I may be allowing myself to get too close to her.*

Not wanting to reveal too much about Sylvia to Jim, Mike blurted out, "I should make changes in several of these areas. Wait—I did it again. I said, 'should.' That's one of my Faulty Thinking Patterns. Here I go feeling compelled and pressured by unnecessary obligation. I'm not very good yet at making decisions based on what I most want and need. I'm rushing things, and I can feel my stress rising."

"I'm impressed that you caught your faulty thinking pattern so easily right there," Jim exclaimed. "Being 'Ruled By Shoulds' is a major reason why people get overwhelmed and burned out. It's better to select one or two things to work on at a time and leave the rest for a later date. Grow in your ability to tolerate the imperfections remaining until you can give them their due attention. Remember that improvement in one area brings positive effects to other areas in our lives."

SPOTTING BOUNDARY PROBLEMS
BY WAY OF YOUR EMOTIONS

Mike was already making major changes in his way of thinking and making decisions. He felt that this new information he was getting was going to make his life a lot easier. He felt like he could breathe easier and deeper.

Ready to move ahead, Jim said, "I have some good news for you, Mike. The way that we're created, we have a built-in system for spotting where a boundary is needed. God arranged it so that when a boundary needs to be put in place, or when an existing boundary is being violated, we tend to feel certain emotions.

"Let me give you an example. When people are being exploited, the typical response is feeling hurt, then angry, and if the situation is not dealt with properly, they begin to feel resentful and bitter. Though these emotions are not pleasant, they are helpful indicators of what is going on at the time. It's actually advantageous that these emotions are unpleasant to experience because it gives you the incentive to change things. So, one way of looking at your problem with Travis at work is that you are experiencing all kinds of warnings that something is wrong and needs to change. You feel used, angry and worn out. Aren't you grateful for how you feel?" Jim asked with a smile.

"I'm thrilled," Mike said with a tone that was anything but thrilled. "I still want these emotions to go away, but I see your point that they have a purpose."

"That's what I'm talking about," Jim said. "You're feeling more motivated. It's key to identify your emotions, and anger is one of the most influential of all. Anger is a signal that lets you know something wrong is going on, like injustice or someone being harmed. Ignoring anger is like trying to ignore appendicitis."

Mike replied, "Yeah, I guess denial doesn't work very well with appendicitis. I've been disregarding those warning lights going off, and now I feel like things are about to burst."

"Yes, you could keep ignoring the signals, but they won't go away. If anything, the pain tends to increase. The only way to make the pain or emotion subside is to respond to how you're feeling and do something about it."

"Pastor Tony helped me to realize that I could start by changing how I handle the situation at work. I think this is a good time to start making decisions by my values. I want to properly prioritize my relationships more than I have in the past. I need to stop covering for Travis. After helping him for so long, though, I'm not sure how to break the cycle. Should I all of a sudden refuse to help him one day? How's that going to make me look?"

"I can see how that would be concerning to you," Jim empathized. "That leads into the next handout. This is a self-assessment that addresses things in your personal background that influence your boundary setting. It explains certain factors that put us at risk for having difficulty setting limits."

Mike was a little hesitant to find out more than he wanted to know, but his curiosity won over. "Okay, you've got me hooked. Show me the goods."

SELF-ASSESSMENT

What Influences My Boundary-Setting?
Risk Factors

There are specific factors in people's personal backgrounds that make them prone to having low or non-existent boundaries. Put a check mark in the boxes according to your past experiences. Have you:

☐ Tended to accommodate others and sacrifice things you care about to make others happy?

☐ Made it a pattern of stepping down in a disagreement?

☐ Been in a close relationship with a person who was very manipulative?

☐ Been bullied into submission in the past?

☐ Generally been a conflict avoider?

☐ Typically kept quiet due to a fear of hurting someone's feelings?

☐ Been taught somewhere that you can't say no and still be a loving person?

☐ Taken on the role of a peacemaker?

- ☐ Had people in your life who were unreceptive or hostile to your boundaries?
- ☐ Been allowed to get away with behavior you should have had consequences for?
- ☐ Had people emotionally withdraw from you after you've set a limit?
- ☐ Had over-controlling parents who always set the rules and never let you set your own boundaries?
- ☐ Not been allowed to disagree with important people in your life (e.g. spouse, parent)?
- ☐ Grown up in a home without much structure or rules?
- ☐ Lived in an environment where the rules kept changing and were inconsistent?

Current Tendencies

Do you tend to:
- ☐ Feel selfish or guilty if you decide not to help someone when they ask you?
- ☐ Be overcommitted and feel like your life is chaotic and rushed?
- ☐ Overspend and blow through budgets?
- ☐ Disregard your own needs or neglect your own health?
- ☐ Absorb what others around you are feeling, whether you want to or not?
- ☐ Rescue other people from the consequences from their actions?
- ☐ Feel like you are the only one helping and get mad at others for not being as responsible as you are?
- ☐ Discipline children inconsistently?
- ☐ Allow people to take advantage of you or repeatedly treat you badly?
- ☐ Allow others to touch you, although you don't like it?
- ☐ Touch others without asking?
- ☐ Alter your opinions or beliefs to match others people's?
- ☐ Give of yourself, your time and your energy to the point of feeling resentful?
- ☐ Tell too much about yourself, or get close to others too fast?
- ☐ Feel used?
- ☐ Overcompensate for others?
- ☐ Try to protect others from pain, discomfort or suffering?
- ☐ Expect others to meet your needs, without you having to ask?
- ☐ Not think about or prioritize your own rights or personal choices?

- ☐   Get preoccupied with others' lives?
- ☐   Be unclear about your needs or preferences?
- ☐   Alter your behavior to fit others' moods or plans?
- ☐   Lay aside your own hobbies, goals and dreams?
- ☐   Trust others' intuition and opinions and not your own?
- ☐   Let others define who you are and are not?

If you've answered yes to several of these questions, then you likely have a problem with limits. If you worked on setting limits, you would experience significant benefits. You would probably feel more rested, organized, light-hearted and confident.

If you've answered yes to most of these questions, you have definite obstacles to setting boundaries. But there is hope. Gradually, you can learn to be assertive. Over time, you can gain more respect from others as you demonstrate respecting yourself. Improving boundaries can advance you from trying to merely survive and stay afloat to thriving and experiencing peaceful fulfillment.

After reviewing the handout, Mike said sarcastically, "Sorry, I can't relate to any of this."

Jim laughed. "Yeah, yeah. Me either."

"You already know the results of this for me, don't you?" Mike asked.

"I have some ideas based on our previous conversations. I believe it's most helpful, though, for you to see for yourself."

Not really wanting to admit that Jim could see through him so easily, Mike lowered his chin and squinted his eyes in defiance. He wasn't sure if he was crossing the counselor-client line, but he couldn't resist. He put on his falsely tough tone, "Man, you counselors think you know everything about everybody. See if you can figure out when I'm telling you the truth about which boxes I checked."

"Sure, you're on!" Jim replied through laughter.

"Alright, let's get on with it," Mike said. Mike and Jim went over the self-assessment sheet, discussing the items Mike could relate to. The conscientious client took it easy on his counselor and was honest about what boxes he had checked.

Mike had noticed that he had numerous risk factors, and he identified quite a few of the current tendencies in himself, which implied that he had questionable boundaries. He was eager for this to be different and wished his changes were already in place.

Jim said, "Now, it's time to start thinking about what it might look like to set some new boundaries in your life. To begin to practice healthy boundaries, you need to keep some important tips in mind. Start with gentle, respectful people."

Mike interrupted Jim, "Well, I know what that means. I shouldn't start with my company's regional manager. That guy doesn't respect anything others say, unless it reinforces his own opinions."

"Good idea," said Jim. "Gradually, you can work towards the harder and more manipulative people in your life. Save those pushy people for later. This will pave the way for you to build confidence and skill from other situations first. The rationale behind this is that several people in your life are not going to like you setting up limits. They may try to sabotage your efforts and resist you establishing boundaries."

"Sabotage my efforts? Why would anyone want to do that?" Mike asked.

"Selfishness. It doesn't take long for people to figure out that once you become more assertive, they won't be able to get as much out of you. You won't always be at their beck and call."

"Oh, I see. That is very self-centered." As a giving person, it was hard for Mike to imagine thinking that way. Mike considered his possibilities and decided that he'd like to set his first new limit with Travis.

"Make sure that you have an adequate support system," Jim said. "You need to have people that understand your situation and will give you honest feedback. It's important to know how you're doing, and to get encouraged by others when you feel that you're an uncaring or terrible person for setting limits. Self-doubt can creep in when you don't have people in your life backing you up.

Maybe I could talk to Isaiah about this. I bet he'd be interested and supportive, Mike thought.

"Lastly, you could rely on your spiritual resources. You could choose to pray and read Scripture during this process, to give you strength and wisdom for how to go about things. I've noticed that when people ask Him for help, God comes through for them. He guides, encourages and blesses people through the difficult challenges involved in setting up new boundaries.

"Okay now," Jim said. "Since you want to start on a limit at work, let's look at a handout I have specifically on that subject. Here it is."

HOW TO CLARIFY AND ESTABLISH BOUNDARIES
IN RESPONSIBILITIES

Once we gain an understanding of the purpose and role of boundaries in our lives, it is time to examine how we can put them to good use. This is a worksheet to help you do just that. This exercise will assist you in clarifying your responsibility boundaries. It will support you to further comprehend what each person in a situation is responsible for.

A major benefit to this exercise is that it can serve as a guide to those people who tend to over-perform or under-perform. Once you have a clear understanding of each person's role, it will make you more aware of what you may be tempted to do for others that you shouldn't do, or what you may want to push onto others and shouldn't.

Questions To Ask As You Make Boundary Decisions

The following are questions you can ask yourself as you fill in the following chart. The answers to these questions bring clarity, truth, wisdom and guidance.

- What do I think should happen in this situation?
- Who is the most appropriate person to do each of these things?
- What responsibilities would God want me to have? If you're not sure, ask Him.
- What do I believe the other person needs to take responsibility for, in part so that he/she can learn and grow from this experience or situation?
- Considering my own personal situation, the amount of energy, free time and other responsibilities I have, what would be healthy boundaries for me? What should I not take on?
- What are realistic limitations for me right now, considering what I am personally capable of and where I am gifted or not? (Example: It is impossible for me to be available to this person every time they need me.)
- What don't I have the power to change or fix? (Example: I can't take away this person's pain or force them to learn.)
- What are the realistic limitations of the other person or people involved? These are the things that are beyond their control or ability to change.
- What expectations do I have for this person that he/she may not be capable of meeting? Any expectation that is unreasonable needs to be adjusted to better suit the person(s) involved.

Give a brief description of the task or work that needs to be done:

_____

_____

_____

	This Person's Proper Responsibility	This Person's Healthy Boundaries	What's Out of his/her control
My Name: _____			
Name(s) of Other Person(s) Involved: _____ _____ _____			

To Tell or Not To Tell

You may or may not tell others what you believe to be their responsibilities and limits. It depends upon the nature of your relationship with that person. Are you his/her leader, mentor, parent or supervisor? Are you supposed to be their helper in some way? If not, let him/her take care of things by himself/herself. Everyone should be relying on who it is God has put in their life for support. If you feel led, you may opt to talk to the person's leader and then leave it between them.

Pausing part way through the handout, Mike said, "This makes a lot of sense."

"What's that?"

"Talking with my pastor and reading this handout has shown me how much I've been enabling Travis. My efforts to help him have been a disservice to him in the long run. Not to mention the fact that working late has caused a bunch of problems between my wife and me. I also see that I've been taking responsibility that belongs to Travis' supervisor. I need to get out of the loop."

"I think you're right on target," said Jim.

"Another thing I'm wondering," said Mike "is if I have realistic expectations for Travis. Is he capable of getting his work done on time? Maybe this job isn't the best fit for him. Once our supervisor realizes what's going on, will he need to transfer Travis to a different position?"

Jim replied, "Those are great questions for your boss to figure out."

Mike nodded. "Something else that stood out to me on the handout is the issue of whether it's realistic to be available to people every time they need you. I got thinking about what would happen if I were on vacation for a couple of weeks. What would Travis do then?"

"Those are great questions. You're absorbing this material quickly," Jim said, knowing that Mike had reached the root of the issues.

"It makes me mad that I've let this go on for so long. I'm ready to do something about it."

"That's right where we left off on the handout. Tell me what you think of this," Jim said. They both pulled out the sheet of paper again.

STEPS TO IMPLEMENT A BOUNDARY

Think of a situation in your life in which you think you need to set a limit. Choose a situation that seems like it won't spiral out of control and won't surpass your current confidence level or skills. If you're feeling unsure of yourself, narrow your focus or select a smaller limit to assert.

Describe the situation: _____

_____

_____

STEP ONE: Identify a person involved in the situation who is basically respectful and kind. If there is no one in the situation that fits this description and you are new at setting boundaries, choose a different situation with other people. It's best to start setting boundaries with gentle and respectful people first. Avoid starting with those people who are the biggest manipulators and bullies you know. Practice your skills and gain more confidence before you attempt to set limits with rude or irresponsible people.

My 1st Step: The person in this situation that I'd like to talk with is _____

_____

_____

STEP TWO: What do you want to be different in the situation? What would need to change in order for this to occur? Are there certain things you want to take responsibility for and other things for which you want the other person to be responsible?

My 2nd Step: The things in this situation that I want to be different are_____

_____

_____

STEP THREE: Practice what you will say to this person. Focus on being calm, direct and respectful. A basic outline is to state:
a)   how you see things.
b)   what is happening that you don't like.
c)   how it affects you negatively.
d)   what you want to happen in the future instead.
You could practice this out loud or in writing. If it's a sensitive issue, consult a wise and supportive person in your life. Let him/her know your plans, get feedback and explain how he/she can support you.

My 3rd Step: An outline of what I'd like to say is_____

_____

_____

STEP FOUR: Find a good time to talk to the person with whom you want to set a limit. It shouldn't be a rushed or hectic time. It should be in a private setting, as long as you'll be safe. Make sure you've had adequate sleep and food so that your thoughts are clear and your mood is stable.

My 4th Step: The setting and time period in which I will attempt to speak to this person is_____

_____

_____

STEP FIVE: Expect to feel unsure of yourself right before and after you set the boundary. You may doubt whether it is worth it or whether it will do any good. Remember that there is a healthy balance between considering both your needs and others' needs. Healthy limits are protective of both parties' needs and interests.

Stand Your Ground

Be prepared to stand your ground. Some people will challenge your decision and try to deter you from enforcing your boundary. In an effort to get you to recant, people may try to:

- pressure you to change your mind.
- gain more sympathy from you to so that you will do more for them.
- try to make you feel guilty.
- be pushy and demanding.
- be verbally, physically or emotionally abusive.
- disregard your boundary or violate your limits and see how you react.

You shouldn't have to justify your decision or make excuses. If you get resistance, calmly restate your boundary and end the conversation. In order to be successful at maximizing your life through setting limits, you will need to be assertive and persistent at maintaining your boundaries.

My 5th Step: What will help me to stick to my decision and maintain my boundary is_____

_____

_____

Benefits of Clear Boundaries

- Protects the well-being of you and others
- Keeps you from being too busy and overwhelmed with responsibilities
- Frees you from needless pressure and obligation
- Improves mental health
- Ensures time for rest and relaxation
- Allows you to be healthy enough to effectively minister to others
- Prevents you from being taken advantage of or manipulated by others
- Releases you from anger, bitterness and resentment that comes from having poor boundaries
- Prevents burnout
- Provides clear understanding in your relationships of where you each stand, what you both expect and want. This leads to greater satisfaction in relationships.

Jim asked, "How do you think this applies to your situation?"

"The steps seem straightforward and useful. My friend Isaiah would be a good person to bounce my ideas off of. He likes this sort of thing. These benefits sure are attractive," Mike said.

"One thing that comes as a surprise to many people," Jim said, "is that boundaries are not only good for us, but they actually increase our ability to care for others."

"How so?" Mike asked.

"Take the example of lifeguards. When someone is having a hard time swimming to safety, lifeguards do not just jump in the water and go grab the flailing person. They are trained to first call instructions to them. 'Swim in this direction.' If that's not enough, they throw out a life preserver and tell the swimmer, 'Grab this flotation device.' In effect, they are reminding people or teaching them how to take care of themselves. They try to get people to use the equipment that they need for themselves."

Mike was seeing the connections to his own life and how he could change his approach.

Jim continued, "Only if all of these methods fail will lifeguards go in and risk their own safety. At this point, lifeguards perform the tasks for the struggling person. The biggest danger to lifeguards is getting caught in the grasp of fearful swimmers and pulled down into the water. Then both people may drown. It is for this reason that lifeguards have a system for helping the person help himself or herself. If they don't follow this system, they won't last very long. They'll get exhausted or harmed in the process."

"That's good to think about," Mike said. "I can see how this is a good analogy for my situation. If I want to be a helpful person, I need to pace myself, equip others to help themselves and protect my own health and safety."

"You've come to a lot of conclusions in one session. I think we're done for today," Jim said.

Mike nodded. "Yes, I'll see you next week."

"I can't wait to see what happens," Jim said.

That night, Mike's sense of encouragement was bolstered as he read over the handout again and thought over what he might say to Travis. He reviewed a few of the tips and refined his plan. Mike had growing confidence that he could address the problems at work, despite his trepidation for the upcoming conflict.

Questions for Group Discussion or Individual Reflection

1) In which of the Core Categories of Boundaries do you find it easy to set limits, (e.g. time, money, or work)? In which core areas is it hard for you to set limits?

2) What prevents you from setting limits with people in your life (e.g. a fear of conflict, being a people pleaser, wanting to be sure you're viewed as a giving person, etc.)?

3) Are there unpleasant emotions in your life, such as anger, resentment or stress, which are showing you that you need to increase your boundaries? Can you think of a certain boundary or limit that you could set that would rectify things?

4) Use the Steps To Implement a Boundary worksheet in Appendix E to help you prepare to set a limit. The appendix also includes a completed sample Boundary worksheet, which may help you get started.

## CHAPTER NINE

Maximizing Life by Setting Limits

Isaiah, you're not going to believe this, but I'm about to shake things up at the office," said Mike. "You may also find it hard to believe that I'm getting into this counseling stuff."

"You're right. I hardly believe anything you tell me," Isaiah retorted.

Ignoring his remark, Mike recounted his meeting with the pastor and counselor.

"It's important to you to get along with other people. So, I am not surprised you've got yourself into this situation," Isaiah said as steam rose over the foaming milk.

"I guess that it is time to not get along so well," Mike said.

"Perhaps that shouldn't be the only goal," Isaiah joked. "But it may be one of the results of what you're going to do."

"Yeah, probably. Things may not be as diplomatic around the office, but at least the problems will be dealt with appropriately. You know, I don't think it's going to be as hard as I thought it would be. All I needed was some training and assistance."

Isaiah piped in. "Let me tell ya, I'm no stranger to the difficulty of saying no to people. I've had plenty of experiences where I failed to set healthy boundaries. Unfortunately, I did not have the luxury of your counselor or pastor to guide me through the process. I had to wade through it on my own."

"How did you learn to do things differently?" Mike asked.

"Trial and error, my boy! I've gone from not setting limits to the mistake of setting them in very harsh ways. I can't say that I was the most tactful or the best role model, but over time I did improve," Isaiah explained.

"What happened?" probed his attentive customer.

"Well, Mike, the story goes like this. It was a soggy, early spring day. Rainwater was dripping off my nose in an irritating kind of way. Six yards of bark needed to be spread over the yard to keep the weeds down. I had made a commitment to my neighbor to get the project done, and I was a man of my word. Honorable, isn't it? So piously noble that it was ridiculous.

"Most people would have considered me to be a genuinely nice guy. Well, they were wrong. I must admit, it was a hero complex that I had. My wife knew it long before I did. She saw the signs. I would readily agree to take on projects for anyone in need, but I was never particularly motivated to do the tasks that my wife asked me to do. I'm not really sure why it was like this. Perhaps it was because I didn't feel a need to impress her anymore. My pride was more affected by what others outside of the family thought of me. The result was that I would remedy a crisis for others, while creating a crisis in my own home. I was a saint to those who were just acquaintances. It was more prideful than altruistic.

"This job of spreading the bark was no different than all of the rest. Annabelle, my sixty-eight-year-old neighbor, was so grateful. She even invited my wife and me over for dinner afterwards. It was a pleasant evening, but I should have left early to plan for a meeting at work the next day. This was all before I retired from the military. Well, I didn't want to offend Annabelle, so we stayed late, talking well into the evening. Little did I know that I would not be giving that presentation the next day, because I ended up getting a fever from a bad stomach flu. It kept me in bed for the next thirty-six hours. It was good catching up on *M.A.S.H.* reruns, though. You can never see enough of those."

"You ran yourself into the ground," Mike said.

"You got it. Too many projects. You can't say yes to everything. I remember looking at the digital clock showing 3:27 A.M. Sitting up in bed with a garbage basket in hand, I started to rethink my protocol. Seeing the ham and green beans for the second time that night made me think it wasn't worth it. I came to the conclusion that the ethical principle of 'Do no harm' should apply to yourself as well as others. That's when I started to make some changes.

"It was indirect at first. I started making excuses for why I couldn't help as I had before. Sometimes I was even truthful. Then I started to get annoyed and angry, because I felt that people were using me just for my skills. One time I responded to Old Bob's request to put up his fence with a quick comeback that was true but rude. I said, 'Why don't you get your no-good hung-over son off the couch to help, instead of always asking me?'"

"That's terrible." Mike reacted strongly. He then realized that he was doing the exact thing that he despised. When he shared one of his problems with another person, he didn't want them to react in a way that made him seem like a bad person or an idiot. "I'm sorry. I didn't mean to sound judgmental. It was just that I was surprised to find out that you said something like that."

"No worries. I have my faults, just like everyone else. I'm sure I could have picked a few nicer words, or a gentler way of saying it. The fact was that I was angry that I had been the only one helping out. But that was no excuse for my careless reply. Later, I did apologize, but it took a while before Old Bob would speak to me again."

"I hope I never get to the point of lashing out like that," Mike said.

"You may be surprised. Most people who lack boundaries tend to stuff down a problem repeatedly. Then it comes out too forcefully at inopportune times," Isaiah replied.

"I agree with you there. My question, then, is how can you set firm boundaries without being offensive?" Mike asked.

"I started to decide what I thought was reasonable, and what I was able to do for other people without driving myself into the ground. I was a busy person, but deep down I did like helping other people. There just needed to be a healthy balance.

"Finally, I decided that I could only help people with one project at a time and no more than one or two a month. If I had reached my maximum, I would tell them that I wanted to help them but the timing wasn't good for me. I would need to find a later time in my schedule.

"Once I set up this system, I didn't feel nearly as angry or used up. This made me more relaxed, and I didn't tell anyone else off for asking me to help. Instead of hoping people wouldn't ask me for too many favors, I decided ahead of time what was and was not feasible. This made a big difference. I no longer felt like I had to make up reasons for why I couldn't help. Plus, I didn't feel like I was forced into helping. It became my free choice. Funny how that one change made helping people a joy and a passion, rather than duty and drudgery. Somewhere in that timeline I started learning about prioritizing my wife in the process. She became a higher priority than my projects. It probably saved my marriage."

Mike was very interested in this topic, and he was glad Isaiah was the one who had brought it up. "How did it save your marriage?"

"You're cheating now. You want me to give you all the answers."

"I've been thinking a lot about what you said one day, that you looked forward to me 'fighting for my wife.' I can't get that out of my head. There are at least a couple ways of interpreting that."

Isaiah stopped wiping the counter and turned to face Mike. "What are those?"

"The first could mean that I fight to protect her from harm. I would be the chivalrous knight that would fend off attackers or those who would take her away. The second is fighting for a healthy relationship with my wife."

Isaiah listened intently.

Mike went on, "I'm starting to see how setting limits at work will start that process. I'm fighting the adversary, a time-thief of sorts that keeps me away from Sara. By dealing with things that eat up my time, I'm making sure I give our marriage the time and energy it needs to be truly satisfying."

"Loving your spouse well takes hard work sometimes, doesn't it?" Isaiah asked.

Mike nodded. "I never thought my wedding vows to honor and cherish Sara would involve decisions that I made at the office. I hadn't made that link."

"What are you going to do about it now, Mike?"

"Can you tell that I've been stalling?"

Isaiah looked at his watch. "Yeah. Normally you'd have left for work by now."

"My plan is to face a personal conflict at work head-on. I've never dealt with things so directly in the office before. I usually hint at the problem through jokes and hope that the other person catches on. I'm getting nervous."

"Go for it! I have confidence in you, Mike. I believe direct communication will serve you much better than hinting around the subject. I applaud your willingness." Isaiah grabbed the laptop, handed it to Mike and began to usher him out the door.

Mike reluctantly said his goodbye to Isaiah and headed off to work.

THE SHOWDOWN

You're going to make everyone angry with you. You shouldn't rock the boat. The boss is going to think you're dragging down the team. Mike's doubts attempted to talk him out of the task. He was already starting to second-guess himself.

Fortunately, he was pretty good at identifying his faulty thinking patterns by now. He identified that he was Mind Reading, Imagining a Disaster and Being Ruled By Shoulds. He replaced his thoughts with his new knowledge, what he'd been learning from his pastor, counselor and friend. Taking a stand was in his own best interest, as well as being best for Travis and the whole team. Cold feet or not, he was going through with it. *I just want to get it over with, without analyzing it any longer.*

Mike remembered an essential aspect of setting limits: prayer. He asked God to assist him in the process, to help his boss and co-worker to understand the situation, and for a positive change in the workplace. He noticed as he prayed that he had more confidence and assurance that he was doing the right thing. To his surprise, he realized he was not able to continue his faulty thinking patterns at the same time that he was praying. *He laughed. Prayer is my faulty thought blocker! It makes me want to pray more often*, he thought.

Mike entered the front doors and walked up to his desk. He began planning his duties and schedule for the day. What was different was that he deliberately omitted his regular time-allowance for Travis.

The team was ramped up for tomorrow's deadline for their current project. It was mid-morning when Travis sauntered over to Mike's desk. Giving Mike a little playful punch on the arm, Travis sat down next to him and looked at the computer monitor. "So, when do you want to meet up to review the animated graphics?"

Mike couldn't help but notice that Travis was acting as if he had already agreed to help him. How irritating.

Travis leaned over and tapped a few keys on the keyboard, bringing up his part of the project on the screen.

Understanding things more clearly than ever before, Mike saw how Travis was including him in a responsibility that was for Travis alone. By getting Mike to assist in this task, Travis was beginning the process of roping him in to complete his other tasks as well. It was time for Mike to hold his ground. He noticed that his heart was pounding, a symptom of his elevated stress level.

Jim said that we experience discomfort for a reason, so I'm going to use it to my advantage to motivate me to finish the task. We'll see if it goes away afterwards, like Jim predicted, Mike thought.

Here it goes, Mike said to himself. "Travis, I appreciate that you want this aspect of the project to be in good shape, but I need to finish my work on something else. Have you considered asking our project manager for help?"

"I thought about it, but I came to the conclusion that you'd be the best person to help me out. You've always come through before. You have the gift!" Travis said enthusiastically.

Now more educated about how people disrespect boundaries out of selfishness, Mike became annoyed with Travis disregarding his newly set limit. Mike imagined saying, "Yeah right, you want to sit around and have me to do your work for you. Flattery will get you nowhere, pal." However, he didn't seriously want to go in that direction. As he had learned from his conversation with Isaiah, he needed to be careful how he set his limit. Firm, yet respectful.

Allowing his emotion to fuel him, Mike replied by saying, "It's nice to be appreciated, Travis, but I have my own deadlines. I can't help you out today. I have enough of my own responsibilities to keep me busy." Mike felt gratified. He had finally got out the words he had been wanting to say for months. What relief.

Travis changed his tune. The smile on his face suddenly vanished, and he put on a look of concern. "I can't believe you won't help me. Aren't you worried that we won't finish on schedule?"

Now he is trying to pressure me and make me feel guilty. He's trying to pass the problem on to me. What a fool I have been for feeling sorry for him all this time. Is Travis intentionally trying to manipulate me? It feels like it. He should be more professional than that at this point in his career.

Mike had to plan his response carefully. He wanted to be considerate, yet not give in to Travis' demands. "Of course I care about finishing by our deadline, but it won't do any good if I help you with your work and don't get mine done on time. Each one of us needs to make sure that we get our part of the work done." Mike felt satisfied with himself. Things were going well.

"Oh great," Travis moaned. "Now I'm going to be holding everybody up. The project is going to fail, and it's going to be my fault."

Even with all of his preparation, this was still Mike's weakest area. The pathetic plea for help made him feel coldhearted for resisting. He knew that if he helped Travis at this point, he'd be reinforcing the senseless pattern he'd gotten himself into.

He didn't back down. "I can understand you feeling stressed out. I'm feeling some time-pressure too. Why don't you see if our boss can help you out?"

"Don't do this to me. Can't you give me a little bit of your time, just this once?" Travis pleaded.

What are you talking about, just this once? This is a weekly ordeal! As Mike's anger increased, he grew stronger in his resolve to stand his ground. Even though not helping went against all of his past instincts to help out someone in need, he was not going to give in to these appeals. He was sick of the old ways of handling things. His former thinking and ways of relating had been modified. Plus, he knew that Isaiah and his counselor would be asking him how things went today. His built-in accountability made this easier; it gave him additional incentive.

"Sorry, I have plans with my wife for tonight. I promised her that we'd go out together. I need to be sure to get my work done on time so that I can fulfill my promise to her." Mike and Sara were going to play volleyball that night. In the past,

Mike would have tried to wiggle out of the plans and arrange to play a different time. But he was quite happy to keep their plans for tonight.

"Fine. I would have thought you'd be more of a team player, but I can see you're not."

This was a direct attack. Mike no longer felt sorry for Travis—just mad. "Bye Travis."

Travis got up and left. Mike exhaled audibly to the point where he felt he had nothing left in his lungs. *Well, that didn't go as smoothly as I would have liked, but I did it! I'm surprised how much Travis fought me. It makes me think he might be aware of how manipulative he is. In that case, it'll be easier to say no to him in the future.*

Being accused of not being a team player was hard for Mike to shake off. It made him feel like a victor and a traitor at the same time. Fortunately, Jim had prepared him for this. His counselor had mentioned that he might feel this way after setting a limit, especially if the other person laid a guilt trip. This brief encounter with Travis made way for a significant shift. Mike was proud of his accomplishment. *I made a decision based on my values instead of letting circumstances dictate my choices. And I want to keep it that way. I did not attack; I fortified. I built up my defensive walls to protect from onslaughts threatening to consume my time and energy.*

This echoed the conversation Mike had had with his pastor. Mike knew that this was a pivotal point in his life. It was a choice that would make a difference. He felt a sensation that he had had while skydiving. After launching out of the Cessna, there had been freedom from the regular constraints of life. Jumping out of the plane had been exhilarating.

Taking a risk and going for it was Mike's new M.O. It was his strategy of choice and much preferred to the old unwritten rule of politely taking the path of least resistance.

LIKE THE OLD DAYS

Because of Mike's success at work, he got home on time that evening. Sara was stunned that he was home early enough for them to play volleyball together. Mike wanted to tell her about the events of the day, but he was concerned that it may be hard to have that conversation and not reveal the fact that he had started going to counseling. Someday he would have to tell her that he had met with a counselor and their pastor, but right now he felt too uncomfortable.

Heading out to the gym, Sara kissed him on the cheek and gave him a big smile. Mike sensed her tenderness and looked forward to their night together. Warming up on the court, he noticed Sara's athletic legs and saw afresh how attractive his wife was. They started playing and laughing like in the old days. Their strong team-work came together again. Sara would set the ball up high, and Mike would spike it down forcefully on the opponents' side. Once, after Mike scored a point, Sara glanced at him, smiled and said "nice shot." It was followed by a second look of admiration at the person she had married.

It was the best time that they had had for a long while. Mike thought to himself, *I feel like I am fighting for my wife.*

Questions for Group Discussion or Individual Reflection

1) How have people tried to resist you setting limits with them? Describe one of these situations and explain what happened next. Did you back down? Did you try again later? Did the other person concede?

2) Have you ever had to modify a relationship or have time apart because another person would not respect you or your limits? If you want to, talk about this experience with a friend or your small group.

3) What obstacles are you facing right now that are preventing you from setting a limit that would improve your quality of life or your health? It may be a limit at home, at work, at church, or in a relationship. What would motivate you or otherwise help you to overcome these obstacles?

4) What benefits have you experienced after you set a limit and enforced it?

SKILL #4

CARING FOR YOUR BODY

CHAPTER TEN

The Results Are In

"A re you kidding me?" the boss ranted. The whole team squirmed under his rebuke. "Why is the project not finished? How come I didn't know about this ahead of time? Do you realize what this could mean for our contract and the company's reputation?"

The boss got the low down from the person over each division. Mike's portion was completed accurately and efficiently. Each part was finished, except for the section done by Travis. Put on the spot, Travis explained, "This was the hardest part, and when I asked for help, Mike didn't give it to me. Instead, he went home and left me to do it myself. How is that for teamwork?"

Steaming over how Travis was shifting the blame, Mike could feel his blood pressure rising. He cringed under the discomfort of the situation. He wasn't used to having to give an explanation for failure. *Travis is trying to make me look bad in this meeting. This is just one temporary ramification of me not helping him. It's not going to make me change my decision, even though that's exactly what Travis would want. The truth needs to come out. I'm not going to apologize. He needs to take responsibility.*

Yearning for justice, he said, "We've all been extremely busy with this timeline. Each of us was given a specific task and ample time to ask for assistance. Travis just came to me yesterday, and I told him I needed the time to complete my own task. I informed him that he should seek assistance from you early on in the day, so that his part would be completed on time."

Mike's supervisor and the rest of the team seemed satisfied with this answer, and the ball was back in Travis' court. But Travis had nothing left to say. His cover had been blown. He had no more tactical maneuvers. Admitting that he needed help from his boss yesterday would have prevented this mess, but he had been loath to do so. Now, it was apparent to the group where the deficiency lay. The burden that Mike had shouldered for so long was now clearly exposed for what it was. Mike was embarrassed to admit to himself that he had played a part in this game for so long.

It was a defining moment. Mike had managed to correct a situation by setting a boundary in place for proper responsibility. He had set things in proper order and put an end to the inadvertent enabling. *What freedom! I could get used to this.*

As hard as it was to set limits, Mike saw how vitally important it was. He would no longer play the role of the Enabler or the Grand Hero. The strides he had made with his thinking patterns previously had all been internal, yet paved the way for his outward victory at work. *Facing conflict head-on and setting a limit with Travis made such an impact. And it was such a short conversation. I could do it again. Next time, it won't be so hard.*

The Master

The blood tests results were back, and Mike's appointment was scheduled. This time he was inclined to be more forthright with the doctor. He didn't want to mess around. Grateful that he wouldn't have to have blood drawn again, Mike sat upright on the exam table. The disposable paper lining crinkled underneath him as he inhaled the scent of the countertop cleanser. *I wonder what kind of disgusting bacteria are growing all around me right now*, he thought. He conjured up images of a giant abscess being drained by the doctor with a prick of her scalpel blade. Pressurized hollandaise sauce splattered and covered the walls with the dripping ooze. *I hope that Dr. Chang was wearing glasses and a face mask. What a time to be caught with your mouth open.* He was now glad for the scent of cleanser and assured himself that the room was regularly disinfected.

Mike laughed at his vivid imagination. It was this same imagination that had given him chest pain at his last doctor's visit, as he envisioned giving himself insulin injections for the rest of his life. Today, he was in a whole different place. Much better at thwarting off the insidious attacks of the mind, he was less at risk for anxiety attacks. He could more readily identify how unrealistic his thoughts were and assure himself that this room was probably not going to infect him with the swine flu or SARS.

A knock on the door and a second later, Dr. Chang's pleasant face appeared, her stethoscope swinging gently as it hung from her neck.

"Hi, Mike. How are you?" she asked.

"Much better, thank you," Mike replied. "Things have improved since I saw you last time."

"That's great to hear. What's been going on?"

"I took your advice. I saw the counselor that you recommended, and we're making good progress."

"Fantastic!"

"Yeah, and I took care of my problem at work, too. Now I can focus on my health some more."

"Wonderful. Your life is a perfect example of the Pentagon of Change that I showed you. You've made improvement in one area, and the benefits are trickling into other areas.

"Take a look at this: your blood pressure is down today. Also, your lab results show that your blood count, liver and kidney tests are normal. Your cholesterol is mildly elevated, though, and your blood sugar's 114. That's not quite normal, but it's not in the diabetic range. At least not yet."

"What do you mean, 'not yet'?" Mike asked.

"Your level is considered to be 'impaired fasting glucose.' It's a little higher than normal, and it puts you at risk for developing diabetes. Plus, you have an aunt with diabetes, which also increases your risk. We'll need to keep a close eye on your blood sugar to make sure that it doesn't keep going up. What this means, Mike, is that we need to talk about what you eat, your weight and how you exercise.

Dr. Chang observed Mike taking a big breath. "Okay, before I get into this too much, let me ask you a few questions first. I remember that last visit you were quite stressed out. How is your stress level now?"

"Better now that I'm putting in less time at work. I still have some other things going on, though."

"Let me guess: finances or relationships?"

"Relationships," Mike answered.

"Let's see, your chart says that your wife's name is Sara."

"Yep, that's right. We've been spending more time together, and that's helped. But we still need to work through some things."

"Okay, how's your sleep?" Dr. Chang asked.

"I still don't do enough of that."

"Do you exercise?"

"I recently started playing volleyball again, but otherwise I've been a couch potato for the past few years."

"How much do you eat healthy food versus junk food?

"Junk food. Now you're onto something. I've got experience with that."

Dr. Chang smiled.

Behind Mike's own smile, his inward thoughts were not as confident. *Whoa, she just targeted several areas I need to work on. Am I going to be able to pull this off? Maybe I should put my effort in other areas where I'm more guaranteed of success.*

Mike liked having a sense of mastery. He had grown used to being on top of his game in his career and in social situations. In these environments, he was able to rely on his humor, wit and intelligence. If he couldn't be assured of success in some area, he had an unconscious rule in his mind that he shouldn't try at all. The fear of potentially not being able to master something had at times paralyzed him and prevented him from trying.

It was similar to his faulty thinking pattern of Needing to be Right. Unfortunately, this faulty thinking pattern had negative consequences for maintaining his health. He had put on some extra weight and was unsure if he would be able to shed those extra pounds. In the past, the fear of failure kept him from trying, which made it certain that the weight would not come off.

This time it's going to be different. I'm going for it. If I fail, at least I will have given it a good shot. But I don't think I am going to fail.

"Success happens one step at a time," said Dr. Chang. "Many patients feel overwhelmed at a time like this. For that reason, I put together this questionnaire, which helps people to identify specific areas for improvement. Then they can decide where to start and formulate a plan. Please fill this out while I go see another patient. My nurse will make a copy of it for you to take home with you. I'll be back in a few minutes."

Physical Health Self-Assessment

1. What percentage of the time do I feel stressed out?
   a. Occasionally
   b. Sometimes
   c. Often
   d. Most of the time

2. Do I have any recreational activities that involve exercise (i.e. soccer, skiing)?
   a. Yes
   b. No

3. How many days a week do I get sufficient sleep so I feel rested when I wake up?
   a. 6-7
   b. 3-5
   c. 0-2

4. How often do I eat fast food a week?
   a. 0-1
   b. 2
   c. 3+

5. How many soft drinks (non-diet) do I drink per week?
   a 0-2
   b. 3-4
   c. 5+

6. How many days a week do I exercise for 20 minutes or more?
   a. 4+
   b. 2-3
   c. 0-1

7. How many drinks of alcohol do I have per week?
   a. 0-7
   b. 7-14
   c. 15+

8. Do I use recreational/street drugs?
   a. No
   b. Yes

9. Do I regularly reward or comfort myself with food?
   a. Rarely
   b. Sometimes
   c. Often

10. How many caffeinated drinks do I have a day?
   a. 0-1
   b. 2-3
   c. 4+

11. Do I smoke?
    a. No
    b. Yes, less than half a pack a day
    c. Yes, half a pack a day or more

12. How many servings of fruits and vegetables do I eat every day? (an example of a serving is a medium sized apple or a half a cup of chopped vegetables)
    a. 5+
    b. 3-4
    c. 0-2

Mike completed the last question, and Dr. Chang came back into the room: "I see you've finished filling it out. Remember that this is a tool to identify areas that you first want to work on. Let's see where things are currently. As you probably figured out, the answer 'a' was the healthiest option for each question."

Mike said, "I answered 'a' six times, 'b' three times and 'c' three times."

Dr. Chang chimed in, "Not too bad. But there is room for improvement. Fortunately, nowadays most people know a significant amount about health. The media pumps out many articles and news stories each week on issues of health. As a result, the general public is getting better educated about health and wellness. Even so, it's the rare person that comes to me saying that he/she is doing all of the right things. That's because the problem with the vast majority of people isn't a lack of knowledge. It's the implementation that is the hang-up. Just like we talked about during your first visit.

"With the amount of responsibilities most people have, it's hardly realistic to work on all areas of their health at the same time. You need to pick and choose what to focus on at a time. It's very important to start slowly with just a couple areas of change. This way, you'll have a much better chance of following through with it. By the end of today's visit, I'd like you to select a couple of things to work on. You can use the self-assessment handout to help you choose.

"Before we get to that, I think it's helpful to look at obstacles that get in the way of change. Once you've identified the barriers, you can find ways to overcome them. Then, you're off and running to accomplish your specific goals. Take a look at this sheet. These are some of the reasons people give for why they have poor health. You may relate to some of them. For each barrier listed, a possible solution is offered."

Barriers to Health Improvements and Their Solutions

BARRIERS TO IMPROVING YOUR HEALTH	SOLUTIONS TO THESE BARRIERS
I don't know where to begin. I'm overwhelmed because I'm so out of shape.	Many gyms offer a twelve-week introductory class tailored for beginners Start low and go slow. Aim for a goal of eventually exercising thirty minutes, several times a week.
I'm too tired. I don't have the energy.	Exercising gives you more energy. You'll be feeling more energetic after a couple of weeks. Exercise helps you sleep better, too, which in turn gives you more energy.
I don't feel motivated.	Foster healthy thinking patterns and an attitude for looking to learn new things and have new experiences. Set your eyes on your goals. Think about what it will be like to have achieved them— how good you will feel with the outcome.
Healthy food is more expensive, and it takes too long to cook.	Cook in bulk and eat leftovers. Freeze portions. Cook with friends. Use one of the many low-budget cookbooks.
I'd rather spend time with my friends and family.	Socialize and exercise at the same time. Start a new sport together.
I don't have support or accountability.	Find a partner, join a class, start a team sport.
I don't have the time.	Being healthy energizes people, and as a result they become more efficient and effective. The consequence of poor health is more time wasted on caring for the illnesses.

Cost of Gym Membership	Many gym memberships cost less than the cable bill. Some churches organize gym activities and they're free. Buy a few exercise videos you can work out to in your home. Walking and stretching are great for you, and they're free.
I'm in too much pain. I have bad joints.	Swimming and water aerobics are good for those with bad joints and fibromyalgia. Keeping active is one of the best ways to decrease pain for most people.
Fatty foods taste better.	Learn new things to cook. Add spices instead of oil and fat. Explore new options like certain ethnic foods that are lower in fat.
I can't give up my comfort foods.	Learn to manage your mood in other ways. Call a friend, journal, get out of the house, prepare healthy snacks to have on hand.
Sleeping takes up too much of my time from doing things I need to get done.	If you get sufficient rest, you'll have more energy to work. You'll work faster and smarter. You'll be sick less often, so you won't lose work time due to illness.
I'm too busy taking care of my young kids.	Walk with strollers at parks or malls. Many gyms have inexpensive daycare.
I'm never going to have perfect health or look like a model or bodybuilder.	Recognize that this is a faulty thinking pattern of Thinking in Extremes. Identify when your thinking is becoming polarized. This type of extremist and pessimistic thinking is common and undercuts motivation before you can even get started.

"I can relate to some of those," Mike said.

"I thought you might," said Dr. Chang.

"Being too tired and busy is the story of my life lately. I've been working on setting limits on the things that perpetuate this problem. Like I said earlier, I now have more time and energy to focus on my health. It's good to see that I have already eliminated a barrier!"

"That's great!" Dr. Chang was happy for Mike. "It's good to celebrate your accomplishments along the way. By the way, has Jim talked to you about how emotions can affect your health, such as anger, jealousy and bitterness?"

"He briefly mentioned that anger is a helpful tool that indicates that I need to make a necessary change in my life," Mike replied.

"That's true. Emotional Intelligence training is one of his specialties," Dr. Chang replied. "And emotion has a powerful influence on what we eat and how much we exercise. People often eat according to their mood or stress level, which is where we get the term 'comfort food.' It isn't surprising that food is what many people turn to for comfort when they go through hard times, because food is frequently associated with celebrations and rewards."

"That is not so much the case for me," Mike said. "I don't eat according to my mood; I eat whatever is the fastest and most convenient. When it comes down to it, I need to make some decisions and stick with them. I want to feel better, so I want to be committed."

"Yeah, and if you stick to your new plan for ninety days it will become a habit, a new way of life," she added.

Mike was eager for this. He knew that once something was a habit, it took much less energy to maintain it.

"One last potential barrier to consider is a religious one. I don't know too much about your faith background," said Dr. Chang, "but I have found that some faith groups adhere to the idea that only spiritual things matter so they forget about the physical realm. They rationalize that they are going to die no matter what, so why worry about caring for their bodies in the meantime?

"It's true," Dr. Chang continued, "In the grand scheme of things, we're not going to be around here very long anyway. From an eternal, spiritual perspective, the Bible says we'll get new, completely restored bodies in heaven. My thought, though, is that we honor God by taking care of the bodies He's given us. It's a way we can be good stewards. Plus, if we take care of the body we have now, we'll enjoy day-to-day life even more. We'll be freer from illnesses, disease and disability. It also helps with ministry, since with good health we are better able to serve others.

Our mood will be more stable and upbeat. We sleep better...."

Mike interrupted her, "Yeah, I've noticed that when I actually do exercise regularly, I sleep a lot better. Plus, I have more energy, and fewer aches and pains."

"Ah, you've experienced the benefits of taking care of your body," Dr. Chang said. "That goes a long way for staying motivated. Now, I do want to mention something about the opposite extreme. While some people only want to take care of their spiritual health and neglect their bodies, other people focus only on their bodies and neglect their spiritual well-being. I'm emphasizing that both are important. And as your doctor, I want to support you towards physical and spiritual health."

Mike appreciated her prioritization of both physical and spiritual health. "Wow, a doctor who is encouraging me in both my spiritual and physical well-being. I've never had that before. Thanks. I just got thinking, there's another benefit to being in good shape. I'm better looking," Mike said smiling.

Dr. Chang laughed. "Mike, you just reminded me of another patient I saw in the past. She was a hard-working young student who was feeling depressed, cooped up studying in her dorm room most of the time. She started having a difficult time getting things done, because she was dragging so much. At one point, she decided to start exercising regularly. She enjoyed swimming and began to get back into it gradually. At first, she would go for just twenty minutes once or twice a week. Over a few weeks she increased this to forty-five minutes three times a week.

"When she came back in to see me, she told me that she felt like a new person. She wasn't depressed anymore and as a result found it much easier to be productive. Her story is another example of how change in one area of our lives can have a major impact in another area. To her surprise, she didn't think that as a student she would have time to exercise so frequently. Yet, because she felt more energetic and full of life, she found she accomplished more in the remaining time that she had."

"I like the sound of that. The notion of having more energy and working faster so that I can spend less time at work is definitely appealing to me," Mike said.

"I'm sure. Many benefits come from caring for your body, including the coveted increase in efficiency and productivity."

I'm all over that. And she's right—I am like that student. I can have that same kind of success.

"We've talked about several topics of health today, Mike. It's good to pick somewhere to start and build momentum from there. What would you like to focus on first?" the doctor inquired.

"My biggest concern is fighting off diabetes. I would hate to have to constantly monitor my blood sugar levels and take insulin shots. Obviously, some weight has got to come off, which I think would also lower my blood pressure and cholesterol. I'm thinking that I want to drop twenty pounds. How does that sound?"

"I like it. I find that people tend to do the best when they add in activities and foods that they like which are also good for them, rather than only concentrating on avoiding what's bad for them. What have you enjoyed in the past?"

"That's easy. I like to play sports and watch sports, especially basketball." Mike thought for a second about what good things he wanted to add in to his lifestyle. "I want to focus on playing sports to get some more physical activity. My wife and I are members at the YMCA, but haven't gone very much. It would be fun to start playing pick-up basketball with the guys again regularly, and play volleyball with my wife.

"Maybe I could combine watching sports with getting in shape myself. Instead of sitting on my couch watching games, I could head to the gym a couple times a week and ride the stationary bicycle while watching the games. I love the NCAA basketball season, because there are always games on."

"You're filled with good ideas. It looks like you have a prime opportunity to change your level of activity. Start out slow and gradually increase your activity towards a goal of about two and a half hours a week. This much physical activity is shown to decrease your risk of diabetes and hypertension as well as heart attack and stroke. Do it for ninety days, Mike, and it'll be your new lifestyle."

"I'll work on that. I'd like to start with some simple changes in my diet, also. Now that I'm doing less overtime at work, I'm going to limit my fast food to a max of once a week and cut out soda. I've heard you can lose significant weight just by doing that. I'm looking forward to eating more of the healthy foods that I like but rarely eat. Maybe down the road Sara and I could work on that together? She's told me she wants to spend more time together, and I'm sure she'd like more help with the cooking.

"You have picked several things to start off with already. That's plenty. Why don't you start with those. We'll check in again once that's been in place for a while. It'd be good if you included someone else in your plan. Having the support of a spouse or exercise partner makes many people more successful, partly because it's often more fun if it's social. Plus, you then have the accountability to keep you on track."

As Mike left the office, he felt good about his decisions and appreciated the advice of the doctor to keep a narrow focus. He did work better this way. It also met his desire to be able to feel competent. He knew he'd have a greater chance of success if he stuck to a clear simple plan.

QUESTIONS FOR GROUP DISCUSSION OR
INDIVIDUAL REFLECTION

1) Complete the self-assessment if you haven't already. What areas of your physical health could use some work?

2) Where do you want to start? To start, pick only two behaviors or goals to work on.

3) What motivates you to improve your health? Think about any success you've had in the past in taking care of your health. Are there any ways you could build on your past successes and the lessons you learned in order to achieve your current goals from question two?

4) Implementation comes through breaking a goal down into steps and starting at the beginning. Select one of your goals from question two and break it down into simple steps. (Example: My goal is that I want to get more sleep. Steps: I need eight hours, so that means I need to start getting to bed by 10 p.m. instead of my usual 11 p.m. I'll have to record my favorite TV show that comes on at 10 p.m. and watch it at a different time. I need to commit to this and focus on how much better I'll feel with more rest.)

5) See Appendix F for more Quick Health Tips.

## CHAPTER ELEVEN

Life Style

I haven't seen you in awhile. So, what'll it be? The usual?" asked the friendly barista.

"Decaf this time."

"You gotta be kidding me." Isaiah staggered as if he was about to fall over. "Is there no stability in the universe? How can I continue on in this profession not knowing what to expect from one moment to the next. You look a little different, too. Maybe it's caffeine withdrawal."

"What? Can't a guy make a change in his life once in awhile? Plus, it's the afternoon. I've cut back on my caffeine intake, but I'm not sure if I can cut out my pick-me-up in the morning. Do you want to hear what else has been going on?"

"I work here. You have a captive audience."

"Well, I started to exercise again." Mike said this with pleasure in his tone, happy with this particular change.

"Really?"

"Yeah. Sara and I started playing volleyball Friday nights. It's good for both of us to get some exercise, and we've been having more fun together than usual. Another thing that I've been trying to do is work out on the cardio machines when I watch basketball games. When I've done that, I've gotten so into the games that I hardly noticed I was exercising."

"Nicely done."

"Almost. It was working for the first couple of weeks," admitted Mike. His face began to look despondent. He wondered if he was going to be able to pull off the goals that he came up with his doctor. "But as time went on, it was hard to be motivated to get my butt over to the gym. I ended up watching the games at home."

"Maybe the personal trainer from the *The Biggest Loser* reality show will be available when the season is over."

"Nah, that's not my style." What Mike was really wondering was if Isaiah would be his workout partner. But he was hesitant to ask. He knew Isaiah in a casual way, and it would be asking for the friendship to take on a new dimension. He didn't know if Isaiah would be interested in that. *What if he said no? That could make things awkward in our friendship*. However, Mike wasn't sure whom else he could ask, so he took the risk. "What I really need is someone to join me. What do you think? Do you want to watch some Duke hoops at the gym while exercising?"

"Sure, what else do I have to do in life? It would be good for me to get these old bones moving again. The only thing is that I'm much older than you are. I'll have a hard time keeping up."

"That's fine. No problem. You can go as hardcore as you want. The good thing about the YMCA that I go to is that there are people with all body shapes and sizes who exercise there—even people who are your age," Mike said teasingly.

"I must warn you: I'm a UNC Tar Heel fan."

"Hmm. I may have to re-think my invitation. Well okay, I'll just pretend not to know you during rivalry week."

"That works for me," chimed in Isaiah. "Maybe we could do a little wager on the game, and when Duke loses you can buy me lunch."

"You're on. I'd be happy for you to buy me lunch," Mike said. "You know, one of the good things I've found from working out is that I'm already feeling more energetic."

"I'll probably be ready to run a marathon after March Madness," responded Isaiah. "Nothing like basketball all day long to keep you on the treadmill. Can we bring pretzels and pizza to the gym?"

"Oh yeah, we can sneak it in. If that doesn't work, we'll bribe the staff with a piece." Mike wasn't sure how things were going to pan out with Isaiah as his exercise partner, but he knew that he needed some help getting going. Leaving the café, he was somewhat afraid of the commitment in case he might change his mind. Now he had built-in accountability with Isaiah. In a way, it had been nice to have anonymity at the gym and in his plan. However, if he kept trying to do it on his own, he'd likely stay right where he was—not going to the gym. Taking a step to live in community with others was both a step into the unknown and a step towards health.

Over the next couple of weeks, these two basketball fans hit the gym twice a week. Their favorite teams hadn't played each other, so their friendship remained intact. Mike was happy that he had asked Isaiah to join him. Meeting up with him made it so much easier to make it to the gym, and they had become better friends through it. At home one night while Mike was getting changed for bed, he viewed himself in the mirror and noticed that he was looking slimmer. *Hmm, it may have something to do with the fact that I'm sucking in my gut.* Undeniably, his pants hung a little lower on his hips, and without a belt his pants would drag on the floor. *Who says that I'm not in with today's youth?*

He was relieved to know that he was making progress. *Exercising like this, I'm burning up calories faster than the government can burn up my future social security savings,* he thought to himself with a smile. Weighing himself on a scale wasn't appealing to Mike. It put too much pressure on him and reminded him of family members that stressed about their weight but did little about it. They were always depressed with the results of what they saw on the scale, and it paralyzed them instead of motivating them. Mike wanted to avoid this. He chose to go by the way he looked and felt rather than a number on a scale.

Grateful that he had more time to exercise, Mike celebrated the payoff from setting better boundaries at work. This freed him up to do the things he enjoyed and knew were important for his health—things he been longing to do but had been having difficulty putting into practice. Not surprisingly, the biggest obstacles for Mike had been a lack of time, motivation and accountability. Now that he had overcome these barriers, he was reaping the benefits that come through regular exercise.

The first thing that Mike noticed was that he was sleeping better. Normally he had difficulty falling asleep and staying asleep. Ever since he had cut down on caffeine and started exercising regularly, though, he had been sleeping soundly.

Mike's sleep affected how he reacted to Sara. In the past, he would have quickly become irritable with Sara's demands on him. Now that he was getting better sleep and had less stress at work, he was less easily irritated. Thinking back, he realized he hadn't had any anxiety attacks for a few weeks. Whether this was due to his exercise or having less pressure at work, he wasn't sure.

GAME ON

"Twenty seconds to go. UNC is up by one," Isaiah pointed out.

"I know. It's nerve-racking." Clutching the support handles on the treadmill, Mike's knuckles turned white as he listened to the commentator's remarks: "Duke has the ball and is spreading the floor to take the final shot. Ten, nine, eight…driving up the paint, UNC cut off the lane, Duke kicks it to the three-point arc. He puts it up just as the clock expires. Unbelievable! Nothing but net, baby! What a finish! Duke upsets number one UNC by two here at home at Cameron Indoor Stadium."

"I don't believe it," said Isaiah.

"Get used to it!" Mike said glowing.

"I feel sick," commented Isaiah.

"You're just trying to get out of buying me lunch. It's not going to work."

As Mike got down from the treadmill, he noticed that his left knee didn't hurt. He had forgotten to mention it to Dr. Chang that it had been bothering him. He knew that nothing was broken, but over the past year every time he moved it in certain ways, he'd feel a painful twinge.

"Ever since we've been working out here, my knee is doing better."

"That's right. Stronger muscles are better able to protect your knee. Plus, your endorphins kick in with exercise and they act as a natural painkiller. I think you're addicted."

"You know me. So, what's for lunch? I feel like a turkey sandwich," Mike said.

"Look's like your eating habits are changing too," Isaiah observed.

"It seems like ever since I've been exercising, I crave healthier foods. Dr. Chang told me to start off small, so I cut down on fast food and soda. Did you know that a can of Coke has 150 calories?"

"No, I did not. I'm not sure I want to know how many calories are in the drinks I make," Isaiah said.

"One can of soda has 150 calories. I read that taking in an extra 3,500 calories makes you gain one pound. With a little math, an extra 150 calories per day ends up being just over fifteen pounds for the year. It makes me want to give up this lousy drink for good. Do I really like it that much? Not really. I just drank it because it's available and customary. So I've switched over to water."

"That's a small concession for a sizable benefit—a good return on your investment."

"So far, I've been able to handle a few small changes. Those alone paid good dividends. I'm looking forward to getting my blood pressure, blood sugar and cholesterol checked again, because they're going to be better this time."

Life was looking up. Who knew exactly what size or shape Mike would end up? That was not his goal, exactly. His goal was to have better health. However, his concept of health was broader than it had once been. Before, the most valued sign of health for him was to look athletic. Undoubtedly, this was an important part of the repertoire, but it was only a piece of it. In fact, the outward appearance of his health could be compared to the mere ten percent of an iceberg that was visible for others to see. He cared about looking good, but he also cared about a healthy state of mind, strong relationships, and a body that would be well enough to live a full life.

It was surprising to Mike that the catalyst for his outward transformation had been the internal modifications to his thoughts and decision-making process. Sometimes, it felt tedious to work on his thinking patterns, but it seemed to make a big difference. It was the inward changes that had made the outward changes feasible.

Questions for Group Discussion or
Individual Reflection

1) Have you ever had an experience where an inward change helped you to make a change on the outside? If so, describe it.

2) What would be a fun way for you to get exercise? Is there a certain hobby or sport you used to play that you could pick up again?

3) What many people describe as the signs of your body aging can be explained as symptoms of disuse. How does your body feel different when you exercise regularly? (Do you ever notice that you feel younger? Are your joints and back less stiff and achy? Do you have more energy or sleep better at night?)

4) Are you a person who benefits from having an exercise partner or not? If so and you don't have one at this time, whom would you like to ask to be your exercise partner?

5) What are just a few changes you would like to consider making to improve your diet? Remember that it's good to add in healthy, tasty foods and not just take away unhealthy foods.

RAISING YOUR EMOTIONAL IQ

CHAPTER TWELVE

The Pastor's Perspective

H ave you lost weight, Mike?" Sara saw his discipline in exercise. She took notice of the improvements in his fitness and appearance.

"Yeah, what do you think?" Mike replied.

To her it seemed like he was instantly transformed by his own sheer willpower. It didn't help that Mike hadn't shared with her all of the inward changes that had taken place. This had some unexpected effects on her.

"You definitely look better than you used to," Sara said.

"Hmmm, thanks, I think," Mike said.

Seeing improvement in others can bring out the best and the worst in an individual. One person may celebrate a friend's newfound successes; a different person may secretly (or openly) react with jealousy. Sara was capable of both. With her husband, she tended to be jealous. What she had long desired had come to pass, but when it did, there was bittersweet joy. She was happy that her husband had finally listened to her and was making a change in his physical fitness. Yet, she was threatened by his discipline exceeding hers. She didn't like him reaching the point where he was no longer the object that needed to be fixed. Until now, her issues had been able to go under the radar. Now, her own weaknesses had become more apparent, and she dwelt on it. She felt insecure and inadequate in contrast to the growing strength she saw in her husband.

Fueled by the comparison, Sara's engines were gearing up to propel her towards her own change. In the past, though, she tended to slip back into the same old patterns when she made an effort. She always failed to make a lasting external change, because internally she was still the same.

Sara felt a bit guilty and began backpedaling. "Don't get me wrong. It's not like you were huge. I think you look more fit now, and that's attractive."

"I'm glad you think so," said Mike, still feeling somewhat insulted.

At this point, Sara's areas of faulty thinking were unknown to her. She did not recognize her habit of Thinking in Extremes, which led her to alternate between thinking that a stringent diet of eating very little was the answer, to binging because she was so hungry and thought she deserved some extra. This experience of not seeing change in her outward appearance quickly enough sent her into a spiral of despair. It was all or nothing. She needed fast perfection or she felt like a complete failure. Unconsciously, she translated her feelings into labels for herself: "quitter" and "useless." She was caught in the trap of Assuming Emotion is Truth. Plus, this lone struggler had no support or accountability. When she was tired and didn't feel like working out, she could easily stop and no one would pay attention.

Unlike her husband, Sara did not have difficulty setting limits, nor did she avoid conflict. Rather, boundaries were her forte. If only her assertiveness were combined with an understanding of how to use her emotions productively.

SECRECY LURKS

Meanwhile, Mike was debating with himself in his head. *Should I tell Sara or not? How would she react if I told her I spent time with our pastor, or that I've been going to counseling? She doesn't know about the changes I've made at work, because explaining that may lead to revealing what I've been learning in counseling. I know I should tell her what's been going on with me, but her outbursts make me feel too vulnerable.*

What Sara did know was that Mike was coming home from the office earlier. Mistakenly, she assumed that it was because there was less work to do, not knowing the truth that Mike had taken the initiative and set limits. Since Mike wasn't being open with her, she wasn't able to give him credit for his achievements. Another consequence to Mike's secrecy was that Sara continued to feel less prioritized than his work.

Having difficulty verbalizing what she was feeling, she approached her husband with displaced frustration. "Mike, why are you taking off and going to the gym without me? It seems like you're always going with Isaiah. I feel like I'm stuck doing all the chores around the house, and I can't do the things that I want to do."

Immediately, Mike's defenses went up. He was under attack. Frequently, when she was feeling miserable, Sara had difficulty identifying what exactly it was that was making her miserable. As a result, she often attributed her despair to the wrong thing. Neither of them realized that this time there were several reasons for her anger: she felt jealous of Mike's success, like a failure herself, and believed she came in second after Mike's job. As had happened many times before, in the midst of Sara's confusion, Mike became the target.

Uncomfortable with her dissatisfaction aimed at him, Mike did what came most naturally—minimization and deflection. "I don't know what you're talking about. It's not that big of a deal. We only go a couple times a week. You're welcome to come anytime. Just let me know when you want to go."

He was sincere in his invitation, but he neglected to share his own difficulty with self-discipline before he got a workout partner. He also failed to notice that he used a tone that Sara interpreted to be mildly condescending. This made her feel even worse about her failed attempts. In reality, Mike didn't bring up his own struggles because it was such an unpleasant topic for him. Mike's intention was to cut off the conversation in order to avoid further emotional confrontation with his wife. His plan backfired.

Sara replied angrily, "You do this every time, Mike. You make it seem like I'm not trying very hard. Don't you care about how I feel? How can you be so insensitive and unsupportive?"

Flabbergasted, Mike exclaimed, "What are you saying? I was inviting you to come and work out with us. Why are you reacting so harshly?"

"You know that was a half-hearted invitation. Don't you understand that how you say something contributes to the meaning? You make it seem like everything is easy for you and it's incomprehensible that someone would have any problem with trying to get in shape."

Sara's highly charged emotions sapped Mike's energy. It was more than he could handle. "I can't deal with this right now, Sara. Why don't we talk about this when we've cooled down?"

Still riled, Sara pushed him even further, "Oh great, I bet you're off to work again. I still think you care more for your work than you do about me."

Mike was incensed. He had been making giant gains in that area and felt that he had made meaningful strides in prioritizing her over his job. *Can't she see how much I have done for her already?*

The hurt from Sara's comment quickly cascaded into rage from the injustice. Mike knew that if he wasn't careful he could say words that would leave an indelible mark on their relationship. *I hate this. Give me a root canal, but don't make me endure any more of this.* Mike grabbed his jacket and turned away. He could no longer look at Sara. He questioned, *Should I explain what I've done for her?* He quickly changed his mind. Proud of his accomplishments, he wanted to keep them protected from her criticism. Coolly picking up his keys to go for a drive, Mike coped by engaging his automatic defensive stoicism. Placidly, he said, "You're wrong, but I'm not going to argue about it. I'll see you later." He hated this heated emotion, and he would never have guessed that one day he'd come to appreciate it.

Surprised by the Pastor

Mike was not the type to let his anger go uncontrolled through verbal lashings or rash actions. Rather, his type was the opposite unhealthy extreme. He capped the emotion deep inside him and gave it no outlet. It stewed, boiled and fermented. It took enormous effort to contain it. Eventually the gangrenous mash gnawed and eroded other parts within him. As the emotion finally began to subside, the sticky ooze still clung to the central part of his being and left him irritated and depleted.

While he was driving, Mike thought about his anger. *How can I be a Christian when I have this rage that comes up so easily? Why does our marriage bring this out in me? This can't be normal. Christians aren't supposed to be like this. Isn't anger a sin? Does this mean that I'm evil?*

What had previously been anger at his wife was now becoming self-disgust. Despite his counselor's training in thinking patterns, Mike was blinded by the power of the events at hand, so he didn't see his own Negative Filtering taking place.

Fortunately, he was now accustomed to sharing his problems with other people instead of keeping them in his own private world. *Who could help me right now? Doctors and counselors are such a pain to get a hold of in the moment. Maybe I could talk to Isaiah or my pastor.* Mike was near his church, so he stopped by to see if Pastor Tony was available.

Upon entering the church, Mike spoke with the receptionist. She said that Pastor Tony was busy right then, but he would be available to talk for a few moments after his meeting. Sitting down, Mike smelled the scent of fresh lavender, which began to have a therapeutic, calming affect on him.

Pastor Tony rounded the corner, "Hello, Mike! Good to see you."

Mike managed a weak smile. "Hello. I was wondering if you had a few minutes to talk."

"Sure. Come on into my office." The pastor listened intently to the scenario that had transpired between Mike and his wife. He quickly saw that Mike felt he needed to run from the confrontation with his wife. It seemed like Mike considered himself unworthy to be a Christian because of his repeated anger at his wife.

The pastor quietly said, "I'm sorry you and your wife are going through tough times. It seems that the emotions that you're experiencing are particularly troubling to you. I'd like to talk with you about that, if that's okay."

"Sure, what have I got to lose?" agreed Mike.

"I believe that many people have incorrect beliefs about emotion, and it leads them to many problems. Their mistaken ideas also prevent them from making good use of their emotions.

"The way I see it, every person has certain emotions that they like to feel and ones that they don't like to feel. For instance, most people appreciate and even strive to feel love, joy and excitement. Some make great efforts to attain these emotional states, some legal and some illegal, if you get my drift. On the other hand, most people also strive to avoid certain emotions like sadness, grief, anger and disappointment. Overall, they believe it's okay to have certain emotions but not others—that some are bad or unacceptable. Mike, it seems like you are one of those people."

Mike nodded in agreement. "It's not as if I don't feel any emotion, it's just that emotions like anger tend to completely drain me. They don't seem to have any purpose, and they're exhausting. If anything, they seem to get people into trouble."

Pastor Tony leaned on his desk and rested his chin on his fist. "I would agree that emotions can take effort and they can cause trouble if they are not appropriately handled. The problem that I see frequently is that people avoid them or pretend that they don't experience unpleasant emotions. I have even met people that say they never feel sad, angry or disappointed. They grow calloused so that they can no longer feel or identify their own emotional states. In a way, these people have become experts at shutting out these emotions, at least on the surface. Others try to block out the emotions by using drugs, or ease the discomfort with alcohol. The problem with these coping strategies is that the cure is very temporary and what may start out as a harmless habit sometimes ends up as an addiction."

"That is definitely not me," Mike was quick to add, to make sure that his pastor had the right idea about him.

"Oh, I was not meaning to insinuate that at all. The point that I was getting at was that some people I've met try to avoid any and all unpleasant emotions. However, I think that God gave us our ability to experience emotion for a purpose—that each feeling can be productive and useful. Emotions are not meant to be a hindering force, or a mere annoyance. They are put in place to inform us of our core needs and to tell us when they are being met or not. They are also there to provide the drive to get our needs met.

"Altogether, they are means to help us to experience life in a full and exciting way. Without emotion, how would we know if we were enjoying life, or if we were satisfied with various aspects of it? What would happen to passion? Life would be so boring without emotion.

"Let me show you what I mean. A gentleman in our congregation is a counselor, and we've had some discussions about the purpose of emotion. After we talked, he put together this handout summarizing our conversations." The pastor laid a sheet of paper on the desk between them.

The Two Categories of Emotion

The Bible says we are created in the likeness of God (Genesis 1:26). One aspect of this is that we are able to feel emotion. Like God, we have a wide range of feelings through which we experience the world and its events. There is intentionality to this. God gave us the ability to feel emotion for a purpose.

PLEASANT, COMFORTABLE EMOTIONS	UNPLEASANT, UNCOMFORTABLE EMOTIONS
These emotions are called Reinforcers. They tell us something is happening that is good for us, that a need is being met, or what to keep up in our lives.	These emotions are called Change Indicators. They tell us something is happening that is not good for us, that a need is not being met, or that we need to make a change.
EXAMPLES:	EXAMPLES:
Happiness	Sadness
Joy	Fear
Peace	Jealousy
Love	Disappointment
Contentment	Anger
Confidence	Loneliness
Excitement	Grief
Our society typically calls these our "positive" feelings.	Our society typically calls these our "negative" feelings.

Are There Good and Bad Feelings?

- Oftentimes emotions that are unpleasant or uncomfortable to experience are inappropriately labeled as "bad" feelings.
- Similarly, emotions that are pleasant or comfortable are labeled as "good" feelings.
- However, emotions are not "good" or "bad." Nor are they "positive" or "negative." Every emotion has been designed to have a good purpose. As long as they are managed well, every emotion can have a good effect, too.
- God intentionally made certain feelings uncomfortable to help us be motivated to make positive changes in our lives. He knows that we sometimes need some urging or assistance to do what's right and good. For instance, feeling convicted makes us think about changing our behavior. It is a feeling that indicates a need for change.
- Emotions are automatic, just like pain is automatic when you hit your thumb with a hammer. Anger, like pain, is not the root issue. The problem is whatever caused the pain or anger. Unpleasant emotions help us to identify that there is a problem that needs to be addressed.
- Similarly, God deliberately made certain emotions pleasant to feel. This way, we are motivated to repeat the actions or choices that brought about that feeling state. Take for example the feeling of joy. When we find friends that bring us laughter and joy, we are strongly motivated to develop these relationships and create strong friendships. These enjoyable feelings reinforce keeping healthy, beneficial things in our lives. They can also lead us to attain things for the first time in order to get certain needs met.
- It takes retraining of our minds to get in the new habit of referring to emotions as pleasant or unpleasant, comfortable or uncomfortable, instead of calling them good or bad. Using these new labels is advantageous, though, since they can improve our attitude toward emotion and pave the way for responding to emotion productively.

Mike didn't know what to say. He had been to church before, but he never thought much about how God created humans to be like Him in some ways. To Mike, emotion seemed like too petty of a thing for God to care about or experience. But his understanding of God was beginning to change.

The pastor began speaking and re-focused his attention. "Mike, let's apply this information to the anger you're feeling in your marriage. Anger was classified in the chart as an unpleasant emotion. I bet you don't have any argument there?"

"That's for sure," agreed Mike.

"The suggestion was that it's uncomfortable for a reason; it indicates change is needed. Take the example of child abuse. When you or I hear a story of abuse, our natural reaction is to be mad about it. Our anger compels us to recognize injustice and to be energized to correct that injustice. Imagine this: What would the world be like if we weren't able to feel anger? What would happen in all those situations where children are getting abused?"

"Well, if no one got angry about it, then no one would ever do anything about it. The abuse could go on forever." Mike was slowly absorbing what the pastor had to say. This was not his usual understanding of anger. He was intrigued but as of yet still unconvinced. "I can see how anger is important in that situation, but what about in my life? What place does anger have in my marriage?"

Pastor Tony noticed Mike's furrowed his brow and decided to explain what he meant in further detail. "A general way of looking at this is that because there is sin in this world, people are bound to hurt each other. Anger is designed to help people identify those situations and motivate them to correct those problems. As long as people are getting hurt or mistreated, people need to be able to react with anger. Anger energizes people to seek justice; it fuels them to right a wrong. Married people are bound to hurt each other every now and again. Anger is what leads them to do something about it so that healing and reconciliation can occur."

Mike mulled over what the pastor had to say. "Okay, I think I'm following you. I've hurt Sara in the past by prioritizing my work over her. She has a right to be mad. Her anger could serve the useful purpose of trying to correct that situation.

"On the other hand, she's hurt me by lashing out at me. Her harsh words are disrespectful, and it's appropriate for me to be angry at how she treats me. I think I see the problem more clearly now. Our emotions suit the situation and can be beneficial. Sara and I are starting off with the proper reactions, but we don't know what to do next. So we never get to the healing and reconciliation part."

"There you go. That's one of the most common problems. A lot of people can recognize what they're feeling and why, but they don't know what to do about it— they don't know how to use their emotion to respond effectively. As a result, feelings get bottled up inside. This pent up emotion can have many side effects. When people try to keep emotion trapped inside, it tends to still come out some way or cause other problems. Sometimes people bottle up anger and then explode. Others store up their feelings and become depressed or anxious. You wouldn't believe how many health issues have a strong connection to people not dealing appropriately with emotion. Things such as insomnia, irritable bowel syndrome, eating disorders, headaches and other chronic pain, can all be tied to emotion that has been squelched. As you see, this short-term coping mechanism of denying emotion is not very effective, nor is it healthy."

As he thought about his own anxious tendencies, Mike could now link to his own life what the pastor was saying. "You could say that I fit in with some of that description. I don't think that I've ever thought about emotion this way before. I guess I've always tried to avoid feeling certain ways. Probably the ones I avoid the most are ones that feel the most uncomfortable to me, like anger, sadness and disappointment. I often try to pretend they don't exist and hope they go away. This may explain some of the health symptoms that I've had in the past. No wonder I ended up in the ER."

"Mike, you're not the only one. Physical symptoms are definitely tied to our emotional well-being. How much we're going to deal with the root emotional issue depends upon our attitudes toward emotion. There are common negative attitudes toward emotion that make people not want to deal with how they're feeling. A lot of people view emotions as irrational, weak, draining and too time-consuming. How we think about emotions affects whether we'll use them to our benefit or squelch them."

"If I was completely honest, I'd have to admit that I agree with all of those common negative attitudes toward emotion." Mike said. "It seems like what I do is pick and choose which emotions I like and which ones I don't like. I mean, some emotions are such a pain. Plus, I can't imagine that God would want me to be angry all the time."

"I appreciate your honesty," said Tony. "That is very helpful for you to know, because the direction you were headed with those negative attitudes toward emotion would lead you to be perpetually stifled and limited emotionally. It's important to recognize your negative beliefs about emotion and interrupt them. As long as you think something is useless, such as emotion in this case, you won't be motivated to make any improvements in that area. With your beliefs the way they've been, you've been hindered from using your emotion effectively. Whereas, if you modify your beliefs and attitudes toward emotion to acknowledge the ways emotion can be productive and beneficial, you stand to greatly enhance your relationships, work performance, decision-making and general state of mind.

"I agree with you that God doesn't want you to be angry all the time. I think His plan is for us to deal with our feelings when they come up and then move on.

Can we come back to that later, because I'd like to talk about something else first?"

"Sure," Mike said.

"I think it's interesting to consider how God is an emotional being and to take a look at what the Bible has to say about handling emotions. Some people don't realize this, but it is clear in the Bible that God has a wide range of emotions Himself, and He responds to situations according to how He is feeling."

Pastor Tony is spending a bunch of time with me talking about this stuff, Mike thought. *It's really nice of him. Never once have I thought about God as an emotional being. It makes Him seem so much more real and personal.*

"Throughout Scripture," explained Pastor Tony, "We read that God has strong feelings. They arise out of His relationships and interaction with people. Doesn't that sound familiar? Most of the time, it is in our most intimate relationships that we usually experience the strongest emotions."

"That's certainly been my experience. Sara, the person that I love the most, can be the most irritating."

"Irritating? That's it? You left your wife in the middle of an argument. You drove off and came here to talk to me about it. That sounds to me like you were more than just irritated," the pastor said.

"What are you getting at?" asked Mike.

"I think you're understating how you feel. Be honest. Say it like it is!"

"Okay, you're right. I was really mad," Mike said.

"That's better. You may even have been furious. Whatever the case, I think it's important to call it what it is. A lot of people minimize how they're feeling. They may feel devastated but say they are just a bit disappointed. They may feel deeply depressed but only admit to feeling a little down. It seems they're embarrassed or uncomfortable admitting the strength of their emotion, as if there's something wrong with them. Actually, I think that strong emotion is really valuable: the stronger the emotion, the greater the potential change that can be generated.

"Take for instance the biblical example of when Jesus felt much grief over the death of his friend Lazarus. In the book of John, it says Jesus wept over his death. He sensed the anguish of Mary and Martha, too, and remembered their request for Him to help. All this led Jesus to bring Lazarus back to life. He took action in response to how He and others were feeling.

"Another aspect of God responding to His emotion is in the Book of Psalms where it says God 'will have compassion on the poor and needy, and the lives of the needy he will save' (Psalm 72:13, NASB). It's His compassion that compels Him to act.

"God's love is also a powerful force that impacts His decisions," Pastor Tony continued. "Talk about strong emotion: God loves more deeply than any human can imagine. It was His immense love that led Him to send Jesus to earth as our Redeemer. That same love directed Him to develop covenants with the Israelites, to establish promises for the relationship between Him and His people.

"I am very thankful for these promises and for God's love for me," said Pastor Tony. "Without it, my life would be a mess. I have been comforted and strengthened knowing the unyielding, steadfast nature of God's love for me. It's God's expression to me that He is on my side and wants good things for me. That's where I get my strength to continue on in ministry."

"I've wondered about that," said Mike. "It's amazing to me how you can continue to take care of hurting people all of the time without burning out."

The pastor was quick to respond. "Oh, it's definitely not by my own strength or abilities. If it were, I would have quit long ago. Experiencing God's love for me energizes me every day. I'm grateful that He's an emotional God."

"I'm beginning to appreciate that, too," Mike said. Sensing his pastor's closeness to God, Mike felt drawn to have a similar type of relationship with God.

Pastor Tony shifted in his chair. "One of the things that's different between how God reacts to His emotion versus how humans do is that God always does so perfectly and naturally. Humans usually need to think it over a while, maybe pray, and come up with a plan before they respond well to a situation."

"Yes, I could see that," said Mike, "Especially with where I'm at right now. It wouldn't be good for me to react without thinking during times like this with Sara. My first response to her often isn't the one to go with."

"My first response often isn't the one I should go with either," said the pastor. "Those who hastily act on every emotion are bound to get themselves in trouble. Uncontrolled emotion can cause havoc in a hurry, and the cleanup can take a long time. It's no wonder that a lot of people think that some emotions are wrong or sinful. The problem is not the existence of the emotion; instead the problem is the fact that the emotion is managed inappropriately."

"Do you mean that it's okay to feel jealousy or anger?" asked Mike.

"Here's the thing. Any emotion that the Bible says God has felt must mean that it's okay, right?"

"Yeah, I guess so," replied Mike.

"Well, the Bible gives accounts of times when God felt jealousy and anger. In the Old Testament, God was jealous on several occasions when the people were worshipping false gods and idols, like the golden calf. In the Book of Exodus, God even says about himself, 'I, the Lord your God, am a jealous God'" (Exodus 20:5, NASB).

"That's pretty clear. Hard to argue with that," Mike said.

"Similarly, many people mistakenly believe that being angry is wrong. That's such a problematic belief. First of all, God experiences anger many times in the Bible. Since God is perfect and holy, and He is sometimes angry, how can anger be a sin? It just doesn't compute. Teaching that anger is a sin causes many people to avoid their emotion of anger. It's what you do with your anger that matters. The Bible is clear that when we are angry we are not to sin (Ephesians 4:26). It is important to separate the emotion from the actions that take place as a result of the emotion."

Mike felt stunned. He had believed this false notion for so long that he assumed it was the truth. He was getting it now. As they were talking, an example of what the pastor was talking about came to mind. "I remember that God was angry with the Israelites on multiple occasions in the Old Testament."

"That's right. God became angry because of the injustices and the broken promises to Him. God was appropriately angry just as either one of us would become angry in an instance of injustice or a broken promise. The good news is that God is patient with us; He's slow to anger. When He does decide it's time to respond, His emotion gets translated into corrective action."

After a pause Mike asked, "How did God correct things through His anger?"

"Well, He gave them lots of warnings first. They persistently refused to respect Him, so He sent them into exile. The Bible says God was hurt so He hid his face from them. You might say He set a boundary with them, because they had been treating him badly. After a while, God reunited the nation and put faithful people in leadership to re-establish it."

"That seems like a good plan. If only I had the power to exile certain team members from my workplace and put new leaders in place," said Mike, already smiling.

"Wouldn't that be nice?" Tony asked playing along. "Yeah, I think that's what some new CEOs do when they are hired to come in and fix up a failing company. Sometimes a system is so messed up that it does need to be rebuilt from the ground up."

Mike thought these things over and considered how he might apply them to his life. It was a completely new way of thinking about emotion. *So I am not an evil person because I get angry at my wife. Feeling angry is a God-given response to being mistreated. Has all of my self-condemnation been unnecessary? My response of shutting her out was probably not the best response. I wonder what I could do instead? What would God do? He's had a few more years of practice than me. From what Pastor Tony has been saying, God probably would have addressed the issue instead of running from it. I really don't feel like doing that. It would be awkward and painful. But it must have been just as painful for God to address His anger with the Israelites.*

Waiting for Mike's glazed eyes to re-focus, Tony asked him, "Can I give you a suggestion?"

Mike took a breath and said, "Sure. Go ahead."

"Staying angry or experiencing any of the unpleasant emotions for any length of time can be exhausting. I recommend you respond as best you can in your relationships and learn as you go. Think things over a bit before you act or speak up, but laboring over it for a long time will wear you down."

"You're not joking. Trying to analyze problems or relationship issues is draining. It's kind of like going shopping all day. I think one of the reasons I've been avoiding certain feelings is because I get so tired trying to deal with them."

"I know what you mean," said Tony. "Chronically experiencing unpleasant emotion can take a lot of energy. Then again, the better you get at recognizing and using your emotion for a beneficial use, the less draining it becomes. If someone does something that makes you mad, go talk to them about it, problem-solve the situation and move on. If you don't—if you avoid your emotion—it won't go away.

"God doesn't want us stuck in an emotional quagmire all of our days. There are certain emotions that God urges us to learn from and to respond to quickly. He doesn't want us to dwell on or get stuck feeling uncomfortable emotions like fear, worry or resentment. He knows that if we go on feeling these certain emotions for an extended time period, it's not healthy for us spiritually, physically or psychologically. Instead, God wants us to quickly respond to our unpleasant emotions and let them propel us to do what's necessary for things to be resolved."

Pastor Tony folded his hands and placed them on his desk.

Mike reached up and placed his hands on his head. "Well, when I came here I wasn't expecting so much information on this topic. I need to think this over some more. I can tell that I already think about emotions much differently than I did before our conversation. It's going to take some time to sink in, though, and to begin to influence my actions."

"That's expected. You're better off than some people. I've met people who dislike emotions so much that they refuse to listen and learn from their emotion at all. I think other people are unaware that deep down they have negative attitudes toward emotion, and because of that they are blocked from living life to a full measure, with passion and emotion. Over time, as we grow in our understanding and productive use of our emotions, we can become more aware of these covert beliefs and re-structure them."

"That's what I want to do," Mike said. Both he and the pastor were standing up to finish the conversation. As they got to the door, Pastor Tony asked, "Would you like me to pray for you and your wife?"

"We could sure use it," Mike said.

Pastor Tony prayed for strength and wisdom for Mike as he began to use his emotions constructively in his relationship with his wife.

Mike was grateful and felt more confident that this might be possible. "Thanks. I'll see you on Sunday."

"Take care, Mike."

Now in full realization of his habitual emotional avoidance, Mike focused his thoughts on what caused him to be angry. He had recently responded to his feelings of resentment toward Travis and refused to do Travis' work. He reflected on how once he had dealt with the issue, he no longer felt angry at work. The emotion only lingered until he responded to it. *Ahh—success.* Using his emotion effectively had already worked in his life. *If I had known about this earlier, I could have used this emotion to identify the problem and take action much more quickly*, he thought.

The issue with his wife seemed to be much more challenging. When it came down to it, they both easily insulted the other and stubbornly left it at that. Wounds did not heal. As a result, it didn't take much to reopen the wounds and make tempers flare. It was not the fault of the emotion. The anger was doing its proper job by pointing to a problem in their communication. How was it possible to resolve the repeated offenses that kept Mike locked in his anger? He was intrigued and fascinated by the new world of emotional intelligence. *If I can even get some of this down, I will definitely have a better marriage.* A mental shift had taken place: he could see the benefits of emotions. *What I could use now is some help putting all this into practice*, Mike thought. He knew where to turn: Jim.

Questions for Group Discussion or
Individual Reflection

1) What is your attitude toward emotion? For instance, do you tend to see your emotion as annoying or useful, motivating or distressing?

2) How is your life enriched because you are an emotional being? What do you like about having the ability to experience various feelings? (Example: As a parent you may value being able to feel love for your child. Example: You're glad you can feel anger in order to stand up for yourself.)

3) This chapter described God as an emotional being who created people to have emotion, too. Did this cause you to see God or yourself in any new way? Can you think of a Bible story in which God acted according to His emotion? How could this model for you how to respond to that emotion in your own life?

4) People tend to get stuck feeling certain emotions that they don't understand well or don't know how to respond to very well yet. What emotions tend to linger within you?

5) If you have ever used your emotion productively before, describe that experience.

## CHAPTER THIRTEEN

The Taming
of the Shrewd

T he light shone through the window and illuminated the area where Mike was seated. Mike looked at the photo of Jim and his family that was sitting on the counselor's desk. *What are conversations like around their dinner table? Does each family member check in about how their day went and discuss how they're feeling?*

Jim sat down across from Mike and asked, "How are ya, Mike? What's your week been like?"

"Not bad. I've made some changes at work, and now I'm not pulling so much overtime. I really like that. Sara and I are still at odds, though. I need your help with that, Jim. I had an appointment with my doctor recently, and she said one of your specialties is Emotional Intelligence. Also, Pastor Tony was explaining some of the theory of it to me and how that related to the unresolved conflict between Sara and me. I could use your help putting things into practice now. What do you think?"

Jim replied, "Sure, I could go for that. But what happened to you? A short while ago, you would've been very reluctant to bring this up."

"I can't say that I love this topic. It's awkward to talk about something as personal as how your marriage is going and what you're mad at each other about. I mean, who talks about this kind of stuff? This is confidential between you and me, isn't it?"

"Of course. Everything is confidential here unless you tell me that you are planning on killing yourself or harming someone else."

"Hmm, let me think…" Mike said facetiously. "Nope, not today. I've got tickets for the Final Four basketball tournament."

Jim smiled. "I didn't think that was an issue for you. How did you get tickets anyway?"

"I won them at a company party."

"Nice. Should be some great games. Have fun," Jim said. "You obviously have certain things you want us to talk about today. That's great, Mike! I'm glad you're taking the lead and deciding how you want to use your time here. You know, if you ever want your wife to join us, she's very welcome."

"Sara come here, too?! Well, aaahhh, she doesn't even know I'm coming to counseling."

"She doesn't?" Jim was surprised. "Why did you decide not to tell her?"

"I wasn't sure how she'd respond. I didn't want her to make a big deal of it."

"Oh okay. I respect your decision, Mike. You know, though, having her be involved could be really advantageous for what you're working on. When you're ready, I'd encourage you tell her you're coming, and maybe even invite her to come."

Mike thought about it for an instant. He agreed that it would be a good idea, but was reluctant because of the can of worms it could open. *Maybe I'll tell her later.*

"After talking to your pastor, what do you think needs to happen?"

"First of all," Mike replied, "I realized that my anger doesn't go away when I pretend it doesn't exist. I'm willing to address it now, and I'm trusting that you have the solution to make it finally go away."

"Oh no—the pressure is on." Jim put on a false grimace and gasped. "Alright, I think I can help you. But how about we look at it a little differently? I see my job as equipping you with some knowledge and tools, and then supporting you as you decide on a solution."

"That sounds reasonable," Mike replied.

Jim explained his perspective, "You're intelligent, successful in your work, you've found a life partner and you own a home of your own. Most people probably look at you and think things are perfect in your life. However, you know by taking a look inside yourself that there are hurts, pain and significant anger hanging around. Most men try to hide areas of pain and hurt because they view it as weakness, or that it may mean they're inadequate somehow. As a result, they ignore these areas, and improvement never comes. It's been a privilege to watch you courageously open up your life for evaluation and potential change. Coming to counseling can be a hard thing to do, but you have what it takes."

Jim went on, "I see how you're currently in that same process when it comes to emotions in your life. It's new territory for you, and you don't feel highly competent at dealing with them. Even so, you're not shying away. This is an opportunity for you to let your strengths work for you in a new area that you're not yet strong in.

"You see, there are many types of intelligence: academic, musical, interpersonal skills, languages, engineering, athletics, emotional awareness and more. You're naturally gifted and professionally trained in several of these areas, but you are a novice in that last category. The good news is that with most types of intelligence, improvement comes with practice. So you can raise your emotional intelligence, or EIQ as it's sometimes called. Your various types of intelligence that are high will aid you in this area of lower intelligence."

Mike replied, "I used to think that was an oxymoron—'Emotional Intelligence.'"

"In some people's lives, it does seem like an oxymoron, since some people do foolish things when they're emotional. The way I look at it, emotions all have a purpose. They cue us to pay attention to certain things going on in our lives. They can be like an oil pressure light going on in your car, telling you there's something's wrong and it needs to be fixed. If you ignore the light indicator, your whole engine may seize. Likewise, the emotion of anger makes us feel 'lit up' and helps us to identify that there's a problem that needs to be repaired. Take for example the situation of someone flirting with your wife. The normal, healthy response is to be angry and jealous. These emotions alert you that your relationship with your wife is being threatened."

"Sure, that would make me angry. I'd have a hard time thinking about anything else if some guy was busy flirting with my wife." Mike could feel himself getting angry thinking about the hypothetical example.

"That's the most fitting reaction," Jim reflected. "Oftentimes in life, we can be pretty busy, and we need a loud signal to get our attention. Anger is usually loud enough to get most people's attention and urge them to prevent further damage or injury. It's highly motivating. The fact that you'd have difficulty thinking about other things if someone was flirting with your wife is a good thing. Anger propels us to focus on the problem at hand, to speak up and take action. It is one of those unpleasant emotions to experience, and that's what makes it highly motivating.

"It's very fortunate that we're designed in such a way that we're propelled by our emotion. The way things are, if we try to ignore them, they keep blaring. I think of it like a dripping faucet. I grew up in an old house, and some nights when I was trying to fall asleep I'd hear the irritating 'plunk plunk plunk' of water drops from a leaky faucet. I'd lie awake trying to ignore the sound and fall asleep, but it rarely worked. I'd have to get up and tighten the faucet.

"To me, this is a good representation of trying to tune out emotion. You end up lying awake at night, thinking about the situation that's upsetting you. You lose sleep over it, whether you're acknowledging the emotional impact the situation is having on you or not. Sometimes you spend more energy avoiding the situation than you would dealing with it. This could be why the Bible says, 'Do not let the sun go down on your anger' (Ephesians 4:26, NASB). In other words, don't go to bed with the faucet leaking. Get up and do something about it so you can sleep well at night."

As Mike was thinking about this, he realized that it kept coming back to the same issue. "I find that when I'm angry, I know what's wrong, but I don't do anything about it. I stop short because I'm worried that if I act on my anger I'll get out of control and hurt people or do something foolish. I don't want to do that, so I don't act on my anger."

Jim waited a moment to allow Mike's revelation to sink in. This was a major breakthrough. "In that case, you can see that the emotion of anger is not the problem; it is your response to it. You're afraid of handling things poorly. That'll be a good thing for us to focus on. Good work, Mike. Your new insight will allow us to narrow in on where growth is most needed and use your strengths to your advantage."

It was apparent to Jim that momentum for change was building. "Being passive when something we care about is being violated tends to cause us to lose our self-respect. Being a pushover also tends to cause others to lose respect for us. Conversely, when we stand up for our values and what is right, and if we honor how we're feeling and respond to it, it boosts our self-respect."

Mike couldn't deny it. He understood and felt a sense of responsibility and remorse for neglecting his God-given capacity for emotion. "Jim, I want to be able to deal with my anger quickly. I have always thought that with anger there were only two options: ignore it or overreact. Now, I see a third option. I can react to it wisely and productively. I just need to figure out how. What do I do, counselor?" Mike raised his eyebrows with his typical tongue-in-cheek question style.

"You're such the eager student. Sit tight. We'll have you cured in no time," said Jim, smiling. "To begin with, let's look at this worksheet together. It's a great tool to help you come up with a plan of action for responding to your emotion."

Mike took the handout and reviewed it.

Allowing Your Emotions To Succeed:
How can they help you? Will you let them?

Frequently, people view their emotion as the main problem. A woman may think, "I'm feeling so sad. I wish this feeling would go away." A man may think that he is a terrible person, because he is full of anger all of the time. A third person may say, "I'm fearful of this situation in my life. I wish I weren't so anxious." They're blaming themselves or their emotion for their suffering.

Many people simply want their uncomfortable feelings to quietly slip away, as quickly as possible. They want to get back to feeling "normal" so that they can get on with their tasks. In this manner, it is the emotion that is mistakenly being seen as the obstacle or hindrance.

This worksheet is a tool for evaluating the good purpose of a certain emotion that you're feeling. You can be guaranteed that emotion is there for a reason. It's not there to make you suffer but to assist you—to teach you and guide you. Emotions are meant to serve a wide variety of purposes in your life. This exercise allows you to consciously and deliberately determine how you can benefit from what you're feeling right now and to develop a plan of action.

Identifying The Emotion and Its Role

1) What emotion have you been feeling lately? (Just pick one.)_____

2) Can you identify which situation, circumstance or person this feeling seems to be related to? _____

_____

3) Based on The Two Categories of Emotion, this emotion belongs in which category?

   ☐ A "Reinforcer" Feeling   ☐ A "Change-Indicator" Feeling

4) The general functions of emotions are listed below. Which general functions do you think this specific emotion typically performs?

   ☐ Focuses our attention   ☐ Guides and instructs us
   ☐ Motivates us   ☐ Helps us to adjust

☐ Supplies us with energy and strength

☐ Gives us new information

☐ Aids us in decision-making

☐ Protects us or what we value

☐ Prepares and equips us

☐ Brings enjoyment to life

What Is Your Emotion Trying to Accomplish?

1) What could this emotion be attempting to get you to understand about your situation, yourself or what's important to you?

Example: I'm feeling lonely. Maybe I need to spend more time with friends.
Example: I'm feeling unsatisfied at work. Perhaps I'm not being challenged enough.

My emotion could be telling me: _____

_____

_____

2) What could this emotion be showing you that you want/need for yourself, for your situation or your future?

Example: I need to go out with my friends more or else I'll be lonely and bored.
Example: I need to find a job that suits my abilities better.

I want/need: _____

_____

_____

3) What might this emotion be guiding you to do? What action might it be urging you to take?

Example: I'm going to make plans ahead of time for the weekend, so that I can count on getting together with friends regularly.
Example: I want to research job openings in my field or see if a transfer to a different department in my company is available.

What I may do is: _____

_____

_____

4) What might it be leading you to say, and to whom?

Example: To the friend I lost touch with, I could say, "I'm sorry I dropped the ball on our friendship. I miss getting together. Do you have any free time this week?"
Example: To the human resources department at work, I want to say, "Are there any new job postings this week? I like my job now, but I'm open to other possibilities, too."

I could say: _____

_____

_____

5) Now that you've put together this plan, you probably have a better idea of some of the good that this emotion is trying to do for you. What do you think you may gain by following through on the plan you just made?

Example: Our relationship will be a lot better, and we'd both likely be happier.
Example: I could get a job that's more fulfilling and satisfying.

What I could gain is: _____

_____

_____

It's Your Choice: Friend or Foe?

You are free to choose to what extent you allow your emotions to serve you in your life. You can choose to make them the enemy or your servant, your friend or foe.

If you ignore how you're feeling, your emotion will not go away. This is because you will be blocking it from bringing the solution and positive changes to your life that are needed. Your feelings will linger until you respond to them.

If you choose to accept your feelings and work with them to accomplish their purpose, you stand to gain great benefit. The good news is that once an uncomfortable emotion has achieved its purpose, it goes away rapidly.

So what will it be? Will you partner with your emotion and let it accomplish its purposes? Will you opt to let your emotions work for you or consider them your opponent?

Setting down the worksheet, Mike said, "Well, to answer the first few questions, you don't have to be a rocket scientist to know that I've felt angry toward Sara, and it's because of how she talks to me. It drives me nuts how she speaks to me harshly and makes disrespectful demands of me. The feeling is definitely a "change indicator," because it's so unpleasant. The other day I had to get away from her, because it was so uncomfortable being around her. As for the general functions of an emotion, I think that my anger performs all of the functions on the list in the worksheet, except for two. I don't really see it helping me to adjust to anything, and it definitely doesn't bring enjoyment to my life."

"Very good, Mike," Jim said. "I think that many people would agree with you that anger is unpleasant to experience, and because of that, it can be one of the most motivating emotions to bring change. Let's move on to the next section. What do you think your emotion is trying to accomplish?"

After briefly scanning the second half of the worksheet again, Mike took a minute to collect his thoughts. "Well, for number one, my emotion could be telling me that Sara and I need to work on our communication skills. For question number two, my anger is informing me that I want, and in fact I think I do need, to be treated respectfully by Sara. Also, I think that it is showing me that I need to fight for a better marriage, which I might be successful at if I can use my anger wisely and productively."

"It can be hard to identify what needs and wants your emotions are representing," the counselor said. "It's also challenging to put together a plan of what to do that is not overreacting or ignoring the emotion. Your responses seem to fit the situation from what I've observed. Question number three asks, 'What do you think you might do in response to your anger?'"

"What I may do is show her that I'm prioritizing her above my work," Mike replied. "She accused me of not doing this in the past, and she was right. I now need to inform her that things are different because I made intentional changes at work. In addition, it would be good for me to spend time with her doing the things she has asked me to.

"As for question four and what I think my emotion might be leading me to say and to whom, I think I need to tell Sara that I felt hurt by how she treated me during our last fight. I know it's not only her problem. Both of us need to learn how to handle conflict better. In order to accomplish that, I think it's important for me to tell to her how I would like to be treated in the midst of an argument. Even if we disagree on something, I would still like her to speak respectfully to me. Plus, to be fair, I think that she would appreciate it if I asked her how she would like to be treated during a fight as well."

Jim was impressed by his client's plan. "I like how you are expressing to her how you feel rather than telling her off, or listing all of the things that she did wrong. Describing how you feel usually gets you off on the right start and makes her less defensive than citing all her wrongdoings. You've come up with great ideas, Mike. Number five asks what you think you could gain by implementing the plan."

"I guess that we could have a better marriage," Mike said, only half believing his own statement.

"You don't sound very convincing, Mike. Let's try to break it down some to see some specifics of what would happen for you, your anger and your relationship if you were able to respond to your emotion successfully."

"Alright. From our earlier conversation, you said emotion tends to go away when we deal with it, right? So going with that premise, eventually I'd be less angry with her once she and I have interrupted our unhealthy patterns of relating and are getting along better. Also, Sara would realize what I've been doing for her and she might appreciate me more."

"Imagine how you would feel about your wife if you didn't feel angry at her and if you felt like she respected you. Would it be worth the effort to implement the plan you just created and achieve those benefits you mentioned?"

"If I weren't angry with her so often, then there'd be more opportunity to feel love and happiness in our relationship. If I went through with this plan, I could easily see how we would have a more loving relationship," Mike said.

"It's up to you, Mike, if you want to go through with it. I personally would like to see you and your wife gain those benefits, but I'm not the one who would have to do the hard work." Jim could tell that Mike was starting to buy in to the idea that it was in his best interest to deal effectively with his anger. The counselor knew that if his client could have a constructive experience responding to his anger and it turned out well, he would have a more positive attitude towards emotion in general. To prepare for this, Jim brought out a second handout that would demonstrate to Mike how other emotions could be very useful as well. "I want to send this sheet home with you today, Mike. This chart is a short summary of the functions of six common emotions. It also explains what happens when people ignore those emotions. I hope the chart serves as a good resource for you in the future, and helps cement what you're learning now. My other clients have found it to be useful, and they've said it's one of their favorites."

The Purpose of Our Emotions

In order to have the most beneficial, productive and meaningful response to our emotions, it is necessary to become familiar with their potential purposes. We need to understand the ways emotions can serve us in life. Otherwise, without understanding this, emotions may merely bother us, annoy us, slow us down, or simply interfere. This chart explains the roles of some of the most common emotions and can help us to assess our own responses to our feelings. It can assist us to determine whether we tend to allow emotions to help us, or if we have not yet learned how to make them work for us. In the last column, circle whether you typically use this emotion or avoid it.

Through this chart, we can see that our emotions help us in many ways. They assist us to deal with life, understand it, progress through it, have energy for it, and take notice when we need to make changes and adjustments to it.

The Emotion	The Role or Function This Emotion Serves	The Effects of Avoiding This Emotion	Do I Use or Avoid This Emotion?
Love	Helps us to bond. Builds intimacy. Propels us to take care of each other. Helps us to commit and stay together.	Isolation, loneliness, neglect of people or relationships, sadness.	Use/Avoid
Fear	Informs us to get prepared, make changes for the future, trust in God more, or avoid danger.	Chronic anxiety, Stress-related health problems, often left unprepared or ill-equipped.	Use/Avoid
Anger	Gives us energy and strength to deal with problems, protects us from being mistreated, and motivates us to make changes, speak up or seek justice.	We're taken advantage of, mistreated, or we allow harm to come to someone or something we care about. We allow injustice to go on. We lose self-respect.	Use/Avoid
Sadness	Lets us know our needs are not being met, that there are more good things for our lives than what we have. Tells us to keep searching.	We settle for less than satisfactory. We don't stop to realize what we are missing. Eventually we can get depressed.	Use/Avoid
Regret	Helps us pay attention to our mistake, so we don't repeat it. It leads us to repentance and teaches us how to do things differently.	We don't learn from our past. We get stuck in bleak cycles. We keep making the same mistakes over and over.	Use/Avoid
Contentment	Informs us we have some things on track and that several of our needs are being met. Instructs us to keep doing the good we are.	We refuse to allow ourselves to be satisfied. It leads to perfectionism, restlessness, impatience and irritability.	Use/Avoid

"Looking at this list of the function of emotions, I can see there are several ways that anger is at work in my life," Mike said. "It definitely motivates and energizes me. In the past I think I ran from anger, because I thought that it would energize me to the point of being out of control. I wanted to keep things in control. I can now see that my anger is helping me to face the fact that there is a problem and that I'm feeling hurt by how my wife treats me. When I'm angry, I have a hard time thinking about anything other than what's bothering me. So I would definitely say that anger makes me focused."

Jim nodded and added, "Anger also protects your marriage from accumulating baggage—it drives you to get under the hood and fix the problem, instead of letting it continue to the point of irreversible damage," Jim said.

"Ironic isn't it?" Mike replied. "This is the opposite of what I would have said earlier. I would have thought that anger is a destructive force instead of protective one."

"When anger gets mismanaged or bottled up, it's then that it can be used destructively," Jim explained. "But when anger is recognized and used properly, it serves to protect and preserve. People who learn to identify, use and control their emotions perform like accomplished lion tamers. They are still in charge of a formidable force, but that force is much less likely to be destructive and violent. It is the shrewd that tame their emotions. No longer are they wild, but they are safe and reliable in relationships and social situations."

Mike took in what Jim was saying. "I can't say that I'm eager to start using my anger to deal with the issues at hand, but I am at the point where I know that I need to step up. Doing this takes more courage than it does to pretend that my anger doesn't exist."

"That's for sure," Jim acknowledged.

"Looking at the functions of other emotions on this chart," Mike said, "I'm surprised that emotions have such a clear purpose. I never thought it could be that straightforward.

"It's also surprising," Mike continued, "that there is a clear deficit in your life for each emotion that you avoid. It makes me think about what my friend Isaiah said to me a while back. He said that he was looking forward to when I would start fighting for my wife. I had no idea what he was talking about at the time. But based on this, I think he wanted my wife and me to have the benefits of using anger productively. He may even have known that the absence of this was causing a deficit in our relationship."

"Yeah, you never know," Jim replied. "Whatever the case, he sounds like a good friend."

"He is—already," Mike said. "I've only known him on a personal level for a few months. He owns the café I go to on my way to work."

"It's great for your well-being to have somebody like that in your life."

Mike nodded, now understanding the benefits of having a friend like Isaiah. "My problem seems to have been that I thought of using my anger toward Sara, instead of aiming my anger toward correcting the problem."

"That's a common mistake," Jim said.

"It's hard to get past the fact that she's harsh and critical of me. But, I see the benefit of using the anger to be productive for our marriage as a whole."

"You know, it doesn't have to be just one or the other," Jim said. "You're anger is legitimate for how she treats you, and for how the state of affairs are in your marriage in general. I think that you've been angry for a long time about the state of your marriage, and you haven't known what to do about it. Now as a result, your anger pops up very easily and in different forms. I wouldn't be surprised if it comes out displaced onto other things. You may know the joke about displaced anger, that a man gets mad at his wife so he kicks the dog. It is important to keep your anger focused on the real issues."

Mike had a glimmer in his eye. "That's it! All I need to do is get a dog.... Nah. Are you kidding me? I could never do that. I'm too much of an animal lover. So I guess I'm forced to keep my anger focused on the real issues."

"What a great idea," Jim said sarcastically. "I wish I had come up with that."

"For years I've been ignoring the leaking faucet by not working on the communication breakdown between myself and Sara."

"Exactly. When your oil pressure light came on, you ignored it and went right on driving. Fortunately, you haven't grown so calloused to your emotion that you don't feel it anymore. Some people become so desensitized that they are almost unfeeling. It's similar to being exposed to a lot of violence on television. The first time people see someone get shot in a movie or stabbed with knife, it may disgust them. But if people watch a lot of action movies or horror shows, after a while they tend to have less of a reaction. Eventually, they could even see heads getting chopped off and it wouldn't phase them. Whether it's disgust, shock or anger, a person's heart can become hardened to it. That hasn't happened to you yet."

Things were getting a little too personal for Mike. He needed to lighten the mood. "You just don't know me well enough yet, Jim. I hate to say this, but your clinical judgment is a little off this time. You talk about desensitization, I'll show you desensitized!"

"Yeah, I bet you are," Jim said. "A regular Hannibal Lecter. Really, you're in good shape, Mike. You've got a lot going for you that will help you accomplish what you're after. And you're going to really like the benefits that come with raising your emotional intelligence."

"Is that so?" Mike asked. "What have I got to look forward to?"

"An outstanding education. It's free through your everyday life experiences with emotion. Well, free except for your co-pays to me." Jim smiled. "Emotions are so informative. I think you're going to glean a lot of wisdom from them that will help you in a variety of situations. Developing a higher EIQ, or Emotional Intelligence, enables people to make smarter decisions, communicate better, more easily resolve conflict and have enriched relationships. How does that sound?" asked Jim.

"Not bad at all," Mike said.

"Also, I don't know how much this would apply to you, Mike, but raising your EIQ also prevents addictions. Alcohol and drugs are used to block out uncomfortable emotions that people don't know how to deal with. When you know how to deal with uncomfortable emotions, it's no longer necessary to find ways of escaping them through abusing chemical substances.

"A final thought I'll share with you is that if you and Sara would like to have kids one day, you'll be able to teach your kids about Emotional Intelligence. This will raise their total level of health and will prevent them from developing addictions."

"Alright, I'm convinced. Jim, I think I'm going to implement my plan and talk to Sara this week. I have some ideas on how she and I can change some of our poor patterns in communication. We tend to quickly move into accusation mode, and from what I've been learning, that's using our anger against each other instead of against the problem."

"That's true," Jim said. "Plus, moving into accusation mode tends to escalate the situation and prevent you from accomplishing the actual goal of your anger."

"I am planning on telling her my side of the story, and as uncomfortable as it is, I need to tell her that I've been feeling hurt and angry. What I'm looking forward to is experiencing these emotions being productive for a change. I want to use them to launch a useful conversation about how we can treat each other in the future."

As they put the final touches on the plan, Mike was already feeling like his head was clearer. Feeling bold and nervous simultaneously, he was ready to fight for his wife.

SHOCKING SARA

"Sara, are you home?" Mike came through the door off of the garage. Sitting in front of the TV, Sara stared blankly at the news on the screen.

"There's food in the fridge. I saved some for you," she muttered. For the first few days after a fight, Sara was used to them acting in a cordial, self-protective manner.

Not wanting to lose his nerve, Mike jumped right in with the topic that he most feared. "Sara, I want to talk with you about Saturday."

Sara couldn't remember a time when Mike wanted to talk about a past fight. She used to bring up previous disagreements to try to finish working through the problems, but she had always been met with firm resistance. Weary from the futile attempts, she had long ago ceased her efforts. "Are you kidding me? You never want to talk about old fights."

"That 'never' just ended."

Sara folded her arms across her chest. "What do you want to talk about?"

Mike came and sat beside her on the couch and awkwardly began. "I was hoping that I could talk to you about how I've been feeling."

Sara choked out a laugh and accidentally sprayed Mike's face with saliva. Mike was startled, but was too nervous to react to the rainstorm. He grabbed a cloth to wipe his face. In spite of his disgust, he was glad for something to lighten the mood right before this conversation.

Even though this was new for Mike, he was a quick learner and could already apply the newly acquired information. First, he explained to Sara his conversation with their pastor and how Tony had challenged his beliefs about emotion. He told her that he now believed he should respond to his emotions, that they each had purpose. However, he still couldn't bring himself to tell her about his counseling appointment with Jim.

Sara was quiet, silenced by disbelief. A quizzical look appeared on her face as she speculated about why Mike would be meeting with their pastor. Had she not been utterly stunned by what she was hearing and still recovering from their previous fight, she would have been beaming about this change in her husband.

"I'm in the midst of changing from trying to ignore my emotion towards identifying my emotion and then using it for its intended purpose. I've seen that I've avoided it when I feel hurt or angry. By doing this, I've contributed to the problem of us not resolving our conflicts very well or even at all."

Sara was fearful of getting sucked in too easily. It sounded too good to be true, and she wasn't sure if she could trust what he was saying or not. Her face remained placid, but her body relaxed as she contemplated her husband's words. She still felt hurt over Mike's dismissal of her struggles to lose weight, but her anger was slowly dissipating.

Trying to convince her that he was sincere, Mike went to the heart of what he had been learning recently. "I'm very uncomfortable talking about this, but I felt hurt and then angry when we were talking about my work. I want us to have a relationship where we speak to each other more respectfully.

"You may not be aware of this," Mike continued, "But I set some limits at work, and I'm no longer covering for Travis. That's why I'm coming home earlier. He was pretty upset that I refused to help him do his work anymore, but I stood my ground. It was very difficult for me, because I like to please other people. You may have a hard time believing this, but I want to please you, too. I think that's why I was so angry when you commented on my working too much the other day. You weren't appreciating my efforts. I admit I hadn't told you about all of them yet, though."

As Mike told Sara the real reason that he was now getting home on time, her jaw dropped. "You mean to tell me that you didn't help Travis out even though he repeatedly requested it?" Sara asked.

While Mike relayed the story line by line, he and Sara could identify the patterns. Together, they could see how Travis had used various tactics to try to get Mike to cave in and help him. He had tried flattery, guilt trips, pressure and even insults to manipulate Mike.

"You know," Mike said, "I always thought that Travis was just inept and needed help. Now that I said no to him and saw how much of a hard time he gave me, I think there was more to it than just plain incompetence. I think he was deliberately taking advantage of me, and that makes me steamed."

Sara chimed in and said, "I'm proud of you. He was laying the guilt on pretty thick, and you didn't bite. Hey, whatever happened to Travis anyway?"

"Once I quit covering for him and people found out his inability to get his work done on his own, he got put on probation. He could see the writing on the wall and quit before he could get fired. I heard from someone that he switched careers and got into sales. I think he'll do better at that."

Sara noticed within herself a newfound respect for her husband.

It was nice for Mike to have some appreciation from Sara. He also noticed that they were both on the same side for a change. Instead of her demanding that he make changes, she was rooting for him. They were working together against the problem.

QUESTIONS FOR GROUP DISCUSSION OR INDIVIDUAL REFLECTION

1) What is something you learned from The Purpose of Our Emotions chart? Have you seen any of the emotions listed in the chart serve a clear purpose in your life? Describe this.

2) Take another look at the handout titled The Purpose of Our Emotions. Do you see in your life any of the effects of avoiding emotion that are summarized in the handout? In order to cement your learning, talk about your observations with a friend or your small group.

3) Often people do not get what they want in relationships because they do not ask for it. Think of a relationship in your life that is creating unpleasant, Change Indicator Feelings. Name one emotion that is being generated. What change do you think this emotion is trying to inform you is needed?

4) Identify an emotion you've been experiencing recently in your life. Determine what situation or circumstances this emotion is related to in your life. Fill out the blank worksheet in Appendix G titled Allowing Your Emotions To Succeed in accordance with this situation and the emotion it is generating. This worksheet will help you come up with a good plan to respond to your emotion properly. Appendix G also has some samples of completed worksheets to illustrate the concept and stimulate more ideas.

SKILL #6

CULTIVATING YOUR
SPIRITUAL LIFE

## CHAPTER FOURTEEN

Revolution of the Will

F airly good at singing, Mike bellowed in his best baritone: "Amazing love, how can it be that thou, O Lord, would die for me?" *Maybe I should be in the choir, since I'm too old to go on* American Idol. *I'm glad our church added the electric guitar and drums to the worship band. I know some people like the traditional services where they do things the same way it's been done for centuries. Me, I like the modern rock sound to worship and the images on the big screen that accompany the sermon.*

Church fascinated him. It somehow persevered throughout the centuries and still had a faithful following. *What keeps people coming? Why do I go? That's a good question, but I don't have time to think about it now since the chorus is coming up—my favorite part.*

Sara leaned over, put her arm around her husband and gently put her head on his shoulder. *Is she tired?* Mike thought. *Maybe she's pregnant.* Panic ensued for a moment, until he remembered that it was too early in the month for her to be pregnant. *Dodged another month—there are too many things to do before we get pregnant. This is not the time.*

Sara noticed his shoulder slightly pull away and she turned to look at him with a puzzled look. The song was ending, and they sat down to see the pastor moving up to the pulpit.

This was the first time that Mike had heard his pastor preach since he had met with him. From the pew it was much easier to be a critic than in a one-on-one conversation. He now saw his pastor in a new light. No longer was he a perfect man on a pedestal, but an individual with both strengths and weaknesses, relying on God to help him do his best. Putting himself in the place of his pastor for a moment,

Mike considered what it must be like week after week to stand up and speak to someone like himself, who for the most part listened and went on his merry way. Mike quickly decided that he would pay careful attention today and consider putting into practice whatever the pastor said. So far, all the conversations he'd had with his pastor were very helpful. He thought that maybe this sermon could be useful as well.

Looking at his church bulletin, Mike saw the sermon title, *Knowing Who You Are*. Mike smiled. *You gotta be kidding me—I am a spitting image of William Wilberforce*. Images came to mind of the British Member of Parliament standing his ground to combat the injustice of the slave trade. Mike and Sara had just watched the movie *Amazing Grace*, and Mike identified with Wilberforce's anger rising up to challenge the inhumane treatment of others.

The pastor had already started speaking, and Mike kicked himself for not paying attention. Drawing him out of his self-penitent behavior was the voice of the pastor saying, "…because that is who you are in God's eyes."

Who am I in God's eyes? Mike thought for a second of asking Sara what the pastor had said, but he thought that she would just tell him to pay attention, which would probably be a cover for the fact that she wasn't paying attention either. His attention was now riveted on the pastor.

"There is therefore no condemnation for those who are in Christ Jesus," the pastor continued. This turned Mike's thoughts back to eighteenth-century England. Wilberforce had endured slander and had been condemned by his opponents because of his stance against slavery. Insults were hurled at him as he promoted justice for all people groups. *What does that mean that there is no condemnation for those who are in Christ Jesus?*

"No matter what you have done, if you are in Christ, you are a friend of God," pastor Tony said.

Wilberforce's long-time friend Prime Minister William Pitt was his supporter in the midst of adversity. Does God see me as a friend in the same way? Mike wondered.

"See what love the Father has for us," the pastor said, "That we should be called children of God." Mike attention drifted once again. *What does that mean? I'm not a child. But that would mean God views me as a son. Can I really be as a son to God? Does he truly like me, or does He just tolerate me?*

"The love of God has transformed my own life," the pastor continued. "One of the things that God has been showing me is that I have been busy 'accomplishing for God' instead of 'relating with God.' There is a big difference. He wants my friendship more than my service.

"I once had a friend who asked me to imagine God in human form in the same room as me. This friend said, 'What is the expression on His face as He looks at you? What kind of body language does He have towards you?'

"The image that came to mind was God standing across the room from me with his arms crossed. He had an angry, critical stare. God slowly started shaking his head side to side in a disapproving manner. I felt that all the things that I had attempted to accomplish did not measure up to His expectations. Through this exercise, I realized that for a long time I had been feeling like I was letting God down. I had been trying hard to please Him but didn't really know what would make Him happy. At times, I gave up, thinking it was futile. How could I ever make God proud of me?

"What changed my life and faith wasn't seeing what I accomplished for God. It was understanding how God truly saw me, how He felt about me. I read the passage where Jesus said, 'I have called you friends, for everything that I learned from my Father I have made known to you' (John 15:15). My friends don't have that type of disapproving posture that I assumed that God had towards me. They are warm, accepting and loving. Why then if God is my friend did I have this image that God was condemning me? I have needed to develop a more accurate image of God and how He thinks of me, to see Him smiling at me, standing close and reaching out to shake my hand.

"It took me a while to see this was possible, that I could know God just like one of my friends. Could we have the same camaraderie? The acceptance? Could I know Him that well? The Bible describes people having a relationship with God that is that close."

Mike was attracted to this idea that God and he could be close friends, but he had definite doubts that it was possible. *That sort of thing is reserved for super spiritual people, not me. I'm no Moses.*

"You may be thinking that intimacy with God isn't possible for you," said the pastor, "That you're incapable of such a thing, or God doesn't desire that with you. It's second nature for most people to think only the Apostle Paul-type characters achieve closeness with God. But I'm telling you that God wants to be close to each one of us. Would God sacrifice His son Jesus on the cross for His casual acquaintances? Or would He only do such a thing for people whom He dearly loved? The apostle Paul tells us that through sending us Jesus as a Messiah, God was 'reconciling the world to himself' (2 Corinthians. 5:19). He was creating a way for there to be a close relationship between Him and every person."

Mike could relate to these questions. He believed in God, but he doubted if there could ever be a real personal connection. God had always been more of a concept, an intellectual premise. Contact with Him was superficial in nature; it went no deeper than the epidermal layer of his skin. If Mike was honest, it may have been because he preferred it that way. The distance was a safe barrier from the unknown, and it was helpful in maintaining autonomy and control. He thought that if he got too close to God then he would be forced to make changes that he would not want to make.

This new paradigm of being a friend to God took Mike back. Describing Christianity that way was not what he was used to. What he was used to was mainly a divinely ordered set of rules. This new paradigm was not a condescending relationship that induced guilt. Instead, the idea of a friendship indicated a choice— a voluntary decision to hang out.

Previously, Mike had a different view of God than his pastor. As he kept listening to the sermon, he came to understand that his view was distorted. *I had been viewing God as a teacher writing on the chalkboard with his back towards me. He would speak in a monotone voice and prattle on, covering subjects that had no relevance to what I wanted to do in life. His assignments were cumbersome and tedious. I knew that doing these things was good for me, but it was out of duty rather than passion that I did them. This image is not consistent with the God that Pastor Tony is describing.*

The pastor continued on, talking about the relationship between God and David described in the Old Testament. "The king at the time, Saul, had sent men out to find and kill David. Forced to live in isolation and hide in caves, David counted on his friendship with God more than ever. We see the intimate nature of their relationship in Psalm 61:1–8:

> Hear my cry, O God; listen to my prayer. From the ends of the earth I call to You, I call as my heart grows faint; lead me to the rock that is higher than I. For You have been my refuge, a strong tower against the foe. I long to dwell in Your tent forever and take refuge in the shelter of Your wings. For You have heard my vows, O God.... Then will I ever sing praise to Your name and fulfill my vows day after day.

"God and David related in a personal way. By how they communicated, clearly God was on David's side, a protector and encourager to him. David knew God was committed to the relationship, and he relied on it. There is no doubt in Psalm 61 that God was safe and trustworthy. David knew that if he messed up and disobeyed God, there would be consequences but his Lord would never abandon him or stop loving him. God promised to stay in relationship, and David longed to live in fellowship with Him forever."

The pastor returned to his own life story. "This was a very different God than the God I had imagined with a cold disapproving stare. I experienced this personally when I was in my pastoral training. Life was extremely busy, and I learned that God did not care so much about what I did for Him as much as He cared that I was in relationship with Him."

Pastor Tony described how he loved being a pastor and caring for people, but that it was hard work. Supporting people through difficult times in life could be wearying, he explained, and it was hard to deal with some people.

"Quite a while ago," Tony said, "I remember waking up one morning feeling disgruntled. It was strange because the night before I had been feeling energized, close to God and full of faith. The next morning I was ruminating on all of the difficult tasks that I needed to do that day. I clearly remember thinking, 'Why am I doing this job? How did I get myself in this line of work anyway? It seems like all I ever do is deal with problems.'"

Mike caught the pastor's faulty thinking pattern right away. *Aha! He's using Negative Filtering. See, even someone like Pastor Tony can get tripped up.* Amused, Mike felt like he had a leg up on his pastor for a moment.

The pastor continued with his story. "I wondered why I was so fickle. How could I be swayed and discouraged so easily?"

Mike identified with the pastor's struggles and appreciated that he was willing to talk about it. Mike's admiration for his pastor returned. *It is rare to have the confidence to publicly admit one's own problems.*

"Over the years, I realized that my faith and trust in God tends to seep out of me over time," Tony explained. "As a result, my confidence easily erodes. I learned that I need to frequently reconnect with God and let Him fill me with what I need for my daily challenges."

It's hard to believe that even Pastor Tony struggles with this. In a strange way, I find that comforting to know that I'm not alone, Mike thought.

Pastor Tony leaned up against the pulpit. "As I lay in bed that dreary morning, negative thoughts kept coming. I replayed a recent conversation in which I inadvertently insulted a member of the congregation. The man needed some help in his marriage, and in retrospect I think that I came across a bit too harshly. I could tell by his reaction that he didn't appreciate my conclusion that he was just as responsible for the disagreement as his wife was. My assessment of their conflict was correct, but I relayed it insensitively. I tortured myself for the manner in which I handled the conversation and mulled over all the ways that I could have said it better. I spent my energy berating myself instead of figuring out how to rectify the conversation and reconcile with this individual. Also, I compared myself to others, thinking how they would have handled the situation more carefully. This only made me feel worse. Ideas came to mind of all the things that I should be doing as a pastor but wasn't. As these thoughts accumulated, I became increasingly despondent. I felt like quitting and moving to a tropical island, spending my days snorkeling, sipping from a coconut shell and forgetting my worries."

Again, Mike was quick to diagnose the faulty thinking pattern in his pastor. It was second nature for him to do it now. As an onlooker, it was relatively easy to see how his pastor was Thinking in Extremes, Mind Reading, and being Ruled By Shoulds. *How gratifying it would be point that out right now. It would be a tad socially unacceptable, though, to interrupt a sermon and point out your pastor's faulty thinking patterns.*

Really, Mike appreciated how honest his pastor was in discussing the flaws in his own life. By discussing his own mistakes he set the tone for the congregation to have a level of honesty in relationships instead of trying to appear perfect. *If I were a pastor, I'd likely try to cover up my own mistakes.*

Pastor Tony carried on: "Initially, the thing that I wanted was for God to solve my problems, to give me advice or direction in what to do. But that's not what happened. In the midst of my angst, I did something that turned the whole thing around—I asked God to help me. This is what God did; He reminded me of His promise: 'I am with you always.' Immediately, I knew what He meant. God would be with me just like He was with David. I knew that in Scripture that phrase means that not only is God present with us, but it means He is looking out for us and blessing us. This snapped me out of my despondence. It broke my self-reliance and helped me to see that I am a partner with God. I could trust we were on track as a team. Recognizing my dependence on God helped me to break off from performance-oriented Christianity. No longer did I feel the burden of trying to earn God's love. Through telling me that He was with me, God expressed His unconditional acceptance, regardless of the number of good things I had done. He asked for my faithful friendship, not a guarantee of perpetual success.

"I am certain that the reminder of God being with me wasn't something that I thought up myself. I knew it had to be from God. He wanted me to know He was on my side and He cared. It was a pivotal moment for me—a transformation in my thinking. God loved me and cared for me because of me, because I was his child, his friend—not because of an action that I did for him. This reminded me of why

I became a Christian in the first place. Sure, I had to logically consider the evidence of Christianity, but that is not what made me long for a relationship with God. I followed God, because He showed me His kindness. I wanted a relationship with Him for who He was and how He loved me. In an instant it all came back to me."

This was a critical moment for Mike as well. All that he had been learning in the past few weeks about thinking patterns, setting limits, taking care of his body and the benefits of emotion came from Godly wisdom. His life had been changed for the better. At times, Mike could hardly believe how he used to live. It seemed distant, as if he had been under a fog that clouded his senses and discernment. *I think I've been missing something. There's a whole Person behind the wisdom of Christianity that I've not been connecting with. Could it be that God is always with me, too? Could He really be happy with me the way I am right now?* It seemed too hard to believe. Friendship with the God who created everything seemed highly attractive but unattainable.

Reveling in this concept, Mike started to question his notion of God being a cold teacher with his back turned away from him. A new picture emerged in which God approached him with a smile on His face and sat down on the seat beside him to talk. Mike felt surprisingly comfortable and at ease with this friend. He wanted to confide in Him free of any pretense.

The pastor declared, "The heaviness was gone."

A sensed of peace rushed over Mike. He noticed that his body felt uncharacteristically relaxed. He looked at Sara in an awkward glance to see if something was happening to her as well. She gave him a quizzical look as if she thought he was about to tell her something and then decided against it.

Something was changing. Mike wasn't sure what it would look like, but he knew that things would soon be different. He was already benefiting from what he had learned from Isaiah, his doctor, pastor and counselor. His life was more complete than he could remember it being in the past. How much the Bible was contributing practically to his life continued to surprise him. Mike sensed that there was another step to take right now. However, it was unclear exactly what it was that he was supposed to do.

The pastor paused. Lost in thought, Mike wasn't sure what Tony had just said. He tuned in as the pastor began to speak again: "It was the love of God that helped me through my difficult times. God quietly cheered me on. With the understanding that God approved of me despite my shortcomings, my need to appear perfect dissipated. It really wouldn't have been effective to put on a façade with God anyway, since He knew my true condition. Admitting my failures to God would not lead to condemnation. It's true that God desires for me to change and become more like Christ every day. But the thing that was revolutionary was realizing that God was thrilled about me where I was at the moment."

Mike knew he couldn't say the same thing for himself. He was his own worst critic. He was trained to think critically, which was very helpful in his line of work, but not so good for his own self-esteem and relationships. He thought God felt the same way about him that he did.

Pastor Tony spoke passionately. "It was by allowing myself to be receptive to the goodness of God that healing started to come. Being able to allow God in to the broken areas and hurts of my life is what started patching things up. God poured truth in my life and exposed the falsehoods I had been believing."

Yeah, like all of those faulty thinking patterns. And the inaccurate ways we all see ourselves, Mike thought.

"When I'm experiencing pain," Tony continued, "I allow God in and expect that God will transform me. I've learned to lean and depend on the goodness of God. Jesus, the son of God, desperately wants to be with me. It's hard for me to comprehend that. But if you take the Bible at its word, you see that before Jesus was crucified, He went to the garden of Gethsemane to spend time praying for us. He prayed that all of us would get to know God and choose to have a close relationship with Him. He wants us all to be with God for eternity. Compelled by His love for us, Jesus was willing to suffer tremendously on earth in order that we may be united with God."

Mike had heard this before, and even though he had been to church many times in the distant past the message was impacting him differently now. It was as if he was hearing with a different set of ears and gaining a new degree of insight. *I don't think that I've ever experienced God the way that Pastor Tony is talking about. How do I start to relate to God that way?*

"I've been a pastor for many years now, and I'm still learning about my dependence on God. When I get back in the habit of relying only on myself and doing things the way that I think is best, I find that I soon become miserable and exhausted. I have spoken to many people who, when it comes right down to it, will admit the same thing. Living life in connection with God is what brings deep fulfillment.

"God's kindness has transformed my life. He sent Jesus to earth to be our savior—to die on the cross to take the penalty for all of our wrongdoings. Our mistakes or sins are the things that separate us from a holy God. He is a gentleman though, not a dictator. He gives us the choice to accept Him as our savior or not.

He set it up that we have the free will to invite Him into our lives or not. To become a Christian, we must choose Him, be open to Him, learn from Him, and follow Him. This means not flagrantly continuing to do the things we know are wrong, but trying to live our lives the way God wants us to. Of course, we won't do that perfectly, but it is choosing to try."

This was something that appealed to Mike. His previous concept of Christianity was that he was supposed to be a nice, moral guy that went to church regularly. What a boring proposition, he thought. *This reality of an opportunity to have a life-giving relationship with a personal God is much more attractive than a religious set of rules for life.*

Looking back, Mike could see how God might have been looking out for him already. Thinking of the time when he barely escaped a high-speed car accident, he remembered how the police officer had said it was a miracle he hadn't died. *Maybe this was God protecting me, even though I wasn't following Him at the time. This sounds like the patient, loving God that Pastor Tony is describing. I've never before recognized how appealing God is as a person.*

Slowly grasping the magnitude of God's kindness towards him, Mike wanted more. This new paradigm was real, electrically palpable and unfamiliar—while at the same time it was the only rational way to move forward having experienced what he had been through the past few weeks. His previous constructs were blown out of the water. Mike had been clinging to a sea-soaked branch to keep him from drowning, only now to see an exploration vessel offering him a lift aboard to join the adventure.

QUESTIONS FOR GROUP DISCUSSION OR INDIVIDUAL REFLECTION

1) Have you ever realized you had a misunderstanding of God? Describe what helped you to have a more accurate understanding of Him.

2) Do you think that God cares more about friendship with you or how you perform? Please explain why you believe this.

3) Are there any ways your faulty thinking patterns influence your faith? For instance, do you bounce back and forth, thinking in extremes between the ideas of God loving you and rejecting you? Do you often feel guilty and shy away from God because you are being ruled by shoulds?

4) On a scale of one to ten, how much do you think that God accepts you and loves you as you are? (A zero means you feel completely rejected by Him, and a ten means you feel completely accepted by Him.) What factors influence how you think God sees you?

5) Close your eyes and imagine yourself in a room alone with God. Where is He in the room, and where are you? What is His body language and facial expression toward you? What might He say to you? Being aware of God in the room with you, how would you describe your posture and facial expression? What thoughts go through your head? Take a moment to think about how this exercise can help you to have a clearer understanding of how you view God and how you think He views you.

CHAPTER FIFTEEN

The Critical
Decision

Mike's paradigm was on the verge of a major shift. Pastor Tony was concluding his sermon and said, "This is the God that I know. I've described to you some of God's character as He's revealed Himself to me in my life. I've also explained to you how you can become a Christian. It's about responding to God's invitation to a relationship with Him. Do any of you feel God urging you to go deeper in your faith? Would you like to know God in a more intimate way and deliberately choose to follow where He leads you? I want you to realize that this will mean you sometimes do things you don't want to in order to keep your life in line with God's will for you. In certain instances, it may be really hard to surrender your agenda and instead follow God's plans, but usually you end up seeing the wisdom of it. Your life will be transformed in ways you would never have dreamt up on your own. I believe God is much better at enriching our lives and deepening our fulfillment than we are.

"Choosing to invite God into my life has been the best decision I've ever made. If you have never made this decision before and are ready to now, please raise your hand and join me in prayer."

In the past, Mike would have thought that he had already done this step and that it was not necessary to raise his hand. He believed all of the theological points the pastor had made. Intellectually, he believed that Jesus was the Son of God, sent to be our Redeemer. He knew that Jesus died a horrific death, which was so clearly seen in the movie that he had watched, *The Passion of the Christ*. *The reason that He died was to take the punishment for sin that belonged to me, so that I'm cleared, forgiven and free to enter a relationship with God.* Mike understood this and he believed it, but if he was honest he knew that his life had not changed—there was something missing. *I don't want to be one of those people who claim to be a Christian, but their lives show no evidence whatsoever. In fact, they live their life in opposition to what the Bible says. Hypocrites turn me off, and I don't want to be one of them.*

Mike now understood that what God had been teaching him over the past few months was that He was alive, relevant and vibrant just as He had been in the times of the Old and New Testament. God was not confined in history.

The transformation in Mike's life had occurred because he had listened to what God said. It was applicable to his life. It made sense. God was no longer just a construct, an image or an ideal. God was on his side and urging him to live a life of adventure, joy, passion, laughter, trials and hard work. *Come to think of it, I've never invited God into my life in such a relational way. I've never allowed God to be in charge of my life before. Certainly, I've not allowed him into areas of my life that I'm reluctant to change. Every way that I've recently allowed God to change my life has made it better. He's proven Himself to be trustworthy. All things considered, I am ready to make this step.*

Mike knew that it would be a life where he would not be calling all the shots. He would be listening to find out what God wanted for his life. This thought made him a bit nervous that things would be out of control, but Mike realized that when he was behind the steering wheel, his car could easily careen off the edge of a cliff. With God in the driver's seat, his life was actually much more in control. This had already been proven through what God had done over the past few weeks.

Sara looked over and saw her husband slowly raise his arm. She looked up at his face with a confused glare, but his eyes were focused on Pastor Tony. She was baffled about what he was doing. She thought he already was a Christian.

The pastor started a prayer for those who had raised their hands and asked them to say the words with him. "God, I see what you have done for me. Thank you so much for letting Jesus suffer on the cross for what I deserved. Forgive me for how I have wronged You and others. I want You to lead me throughout my life. I choose to follow Your will and welcome You to make changes in me and my life where You know is best. I trust that You have great things in store for me and that I can depend on You. Amen."

Contemplating what had just happened, Mike felt a wave of peace flow over him. He couldn't remember ever feeling like this before. Immediately, he had a new sense of God's pleasure in him. He had made a decision to commit himself to follow God, yet somehow he felt extraordinarily free. It was as if the shackles of a prisoner were loosed, and now he could stretch out and roam as was intended. *What does this mean for my life? Where will my life go from here? Am I becoming a radical?* He wanted to talk this over with Isaiah.

The service ended, and Mike and Sara filtered out of the pews and headed out to their car. *Can I tell her about what just happened?* Mike thought. *Would she understand what is going on in my life? The last time I left her out of the loop and didn't tell her about setting limits at work, it led to an argument. Plus, she's my wife; she needs to know what is going on.* Mike tried his best to explain how he was starting to see God in a new light and how he had a better understanding of how God viewed him as a son and as a friend.

Sara took a minute to digest what her husband was saying. "I appreciate that you are sharing this with me. I think I understand what you are talking about. You're committing to learn more about God—to read the Bible and pray more, right? I just don't think that it was necessary for you to raise your hand."

For Mike, there was a major distinction. "I already know a lot about God. It wasn't so much about knowing more about God, even though knowing more about God is important. Instead, it's desiring to know God, just like I want to know you."

Sara appreciated his desire to know her, and she smiled. "I see the difference. But is that really possible?"

This was a question that Mike had been wrestling with over the past several weeks. "I believe so. That's why I raised my hand."

"Hmm." Sara was pensive and knew that she would have to think some more about this before she would consider arriving at the same conclusion as her husband.

WHAT JUST HAPPENED?

"Let me guess—an Americano?" Isaiah couldn't help but notice that Mike appeared a little taller, or perhaps he was standing up straighter.

"Sounds good, but I'll stick with Italian soda," Mike replied and started to whistle as Isaiah went to work.

"Did you get some more sleep last night?"

"I feel great. But no, I got the usual amount of sleep. I gotta tell you what happened."

Isaiah paused in his finely tuned system of making the drink. "Tell me what?"

"I made a decision."

"Okay."

"And it has been turning around the way I see everything." Mike was beaming with exuberance. "My load feels lighter, and I see things more clearly now."

"Sounds like you've had quite an experience." Isaiah couldn't help but join in the infectious excitement.

"This may surprise you, but life is not all about me."

Isaiah laughed. "Oh come on. It is too."

"No, seriously. I'm not egocentric enough to think that life revolves around me. But I've come to the conclusion that my life is not my own to do as I please or as I wish."

"And you are excited about that?" Isaiah asked, knowing full well what Mike was now talking about. He just wanted to give Mike an opportunity to explain what God was doing in his life.

"I've decided to get to know God and partner up with Him in what He wants for my life."

Isaiah went Socratic for a moment. "Why does partnering up with God make you so excited?"

"I feel like I have a purpose and a calling that is far better than my previous expectations. I'm not sure what that purpose is, but the important thing is that I'm now willing."

Isaiah couldn't help himself. "If you want, I'd be very happy to direct your life for you." Isaiah turned around and brought Mike his drink. "But then again, you would end up having a mess on your hands."

"That's right! Last night I asked God what He wanted for my life, and I asked for help in being willing to follow Him. I'm not sure what this means, but after I prayed I kept having thoughts about work for some reason. It felt as if it's time for me to move on. It doesn't make any sense, because I'm finally starting to like work again. At last, things are getting better for me; why would I want to leave?"

"I don't know the answer to that," said Isaiah. "I've found that sometimes God has led me to do things that didn't make a whole lot of sense initially, yet afterwards I found out it was the best possible thing for me."

"That has been the case for me recently. I've been listening to what wise people have recommended that I do. They taught me Biblical principles, and my life has improved. Now I am willing to find out more of what God wants for me, but I'm not very good at it on my own yet."

"I do believe that God wants to speak to us," said Isaiah, "and that once He does, we get the benefit of knowing for certain what His will is for our lives. Personally, I find that God speaks to me in a variety of ways. Moreover, I've observed that's true for everyone. I bet you encountered one of those ways last night. It seems pretty common for God to direct people's thoughts during or after a time of prayer.

Often during times of prayer and worship, I find that God draws my mind to important matters. Also, I find that God confirms that the thoughts I had were inspired by Him. For example, He sometimes has another person tell me the same idea out of the blue. I'm not a big believer in coincidences, so I don't just chalk this up to fate or an accident. Other times God guides me through giving me a sense of peace about something, through a Bible verse striking me in a new way, or occasionally through a dream. God is creative. He can speak to us through anything."

"That's helpful. I'm discovering that the Christian life is much more exciting and unpredictable than I would have ever thought."

"No kidding," said Isaiah. "You don't know what it's like until you try it out. My life is rarely dull, living by faith following God. It's invigorating with the inherent tension between uncertainty and certainty."

"That fits with the way I have been coming to understand God," Mike replied. "It's been great to talk to you, Isaiah. I appreciate your input. It's nice to have someone who's been a Christian longer than I have to talk with. In you, I seem to have found a good friend and a mentor of sorts."

"You must like living on the edge. I hear ya, though. I have friends in my life whom I go to for advice and encouragement. Christianity is not defined by church attendance, but church fellowship can certainly be a marvelous gift from God. Spending time with other believers can help us in getting to know and experience God more fully."

"I could see that," Mike said, as he was preparing to head off to work. "Speaking of spiritual camaraderie, will you be praying for me about my job?"

"I've got you covered. Take care, Mike. I'll be curious to see what's around the next turn for you."

Questions for Group Discussion or Individual Reflection

Note: If you would like to complete a Spiritual Health Assessment, you can visit the authors' website at www.TheRestofHealth.com.

1) Have you ever felt God beckoning you to a closer relationship with Him? How so, or in what way?

2) What do you think is the difference between a religion versus a relationship with God?

3) Have you ever experienced God giving you direction or speaking to you somehow? Describe that experience.

4) How would you explain what it's like for you to live by faith? What's difficult about it for you? Are there any advantages to it?

## CHAPTER SIXTEEN

It Makes All the Difference

I feel stupid. Can I truly rely on this? Will God really speak to me? Mike was no longer at the height of his spiritual awakening. Back in the routine of work, doubts were creeping in. *How come my life is so different than the people in the Bible?*

Mike had started reading the Bible, and the words on the page had come alive. The people in Scripture were examples of how God could transform everyday folks into bold and courageous leaders and how they could then live adventurous lives of faith following God's lead. *Could I ever be like that? Do I have it in me to be a Paul or Moses?*

Mike then recalled events of Moses' and Paul's lives when their actions were less than heroic and lacked faith. In fact, Moses was filled with self-doubt and tried to get out of what God asked him to do. Mike could see that over time they had grown in their ability to trust God in difficult times. It was through communicating with God and taking small obedient steps that this transformation had taken place. Repeated faith-building experiences changed the way they responded to God.

That's encouraging that I'm not the only one that has doubts. I can start off floundering like Moses did and still end up not half bad in the end. For Moses to make progress, He needed to remain in communication with God.

What do I say to You, God? More importantly, God, what are you saying to me? I want to hear from You, and I do believe that doing what You want will be the best for me.

"Hi Mike." Sylvia rounded the corner and caught him off guard.

Mike turned around and saw that she was coming over to his desk for a brief social visit. "How are you doing?" she asked.

"Oh, hi Sylvia. I'm fine. How are you?"

"I'm doing well."

Ever since Mike had limited his time at work, he was focusing his time and energy on other areas of his life. It had been ages since he had caught up with what was going on in his co-worker's life. His physical attraction to her had been slowly fading as he worked on his relationship with Sara and his overall personal health was improving. Mike now saw her in a more platonic light.

"Did you hear about the new job opening in the marketing department, since Mitchell is moving to Montana?" she asked.

"No, when did you hear about that?" Mike queried.

"Last Friday was when he gave his notice. The position has already been posted. You should apply. I think you'd be perfect for the job. You're so good with people."

His first reaction was to immediately discard her idea as he cynically thought, *Yeah, if I could knock my habit of mind reading and needing to be right, then I'd be better at interacting with people*. He changed his tone as he responded to Sylvia. "That's nice of you to say, but I am quite happy with my job right now. We have a great team, don't you think?"

"Oh, I love the team we work with. It was just that when I heard about this job, the first thing that came to mind was that you would be the best person for the job. It would be sad, though, to no longer have you on our team."

This time, Mike allowed himself to consider what she was saying instead of instantly rejecting it as he had the first time. His thoughts shifted and focused on the question of God's will for his life. As he did, some of the pieces of his previous thoughts and discussion with Isaiah came together. He was gripped by this question: *Could this all be a coincidence that I was thinking about a job change the other day? God, do you want me to apply for this job?*

"What are you thinking about?" she asked with a look of uncertainty, noticing Mike appearing far away in thought.

"I was just thinking about something I've been learning lately. Sorry. Actually, on second thought, I'm starting to consider that job opening."

Thoughts of a job change had been far from Mike's mind since he had become more content with the recent improvement at his job. He considered the pros and the cons. A marketing position suited his personality and style, and now seemed like a good time in his career to make a switch. The position would give him great experience, and he had the technical background to support the move. The drawback was that he would be working with a different group of people where he might run into similar problems to those he had had with Travis. There was uncertainty in trying something new. On the other hand, Mike now had better developed skills for working through difficult relational problems. Even if there were interpersonal conflicts, he would be better equipped to handle them. He would miss the camaraderie that he enjoyed with the current team, though. There were benefits to both staying and leaving.

"I spoke with HR," said Sylvia, "And they've already had a few applicants since the position opened up. I'm not sure when they will begin the interviews."

Unintentionally, Mike began imagining what it would be like to be part of a marketing team. This was reverie, not pretension. *I wonder where they would put me?* He envisioned an office with a window where he could put his creative mind to use. He saw the team in action devising a marketing plan. The more he thought about it, the more it felt right. It didn't seem like a drastic move any longer. *Maybe this is how God speaks to me and gives me assurance. This may be God nudging me to change things up at work by having Sylvia bring this up. I do feel like I have new ideas to contribute to the organization.*

The uncertainty dissipated. Logic was not the only factor that made Mike feel at ease with the new idea. It went far deeper. Mike was getting his mind wrapped around the notion that God was answering his prayer and showing him where he was supposed to go. He suspected that this was God helping him to overcome the doubts that he'd been having and demonstrating that He really did want to communicate with him.

Sylvia, now sick of waiting for Mike to come back from his glazed stare impatiently asked, "Michael, are you with me?"

From their previous conversations, Mike knew that Sylvia was a Christian. He was sure that she would be interested to hear what had been happening in his spiritual life recently. *Should I really tell her that I am going to apply for this job because I feel like God wants me to? That would be ludicrous. She might think that I'm insane. Then again, she may know more about God's leading than I do. I wonder how many other people make decisions based on things such as this?*

"I'm sorry, Sylvia. I got distracted. You might think this is a bit strange, but I think that God wants me to apply for the job." He went on to explain what had been occurring in his life and how he wanted to follow God in a new way.

Sylvia replied, "I don't think what you're talking about is odd at all."

"Really?" Mike eyes widened and he leaned forward in surprise.

"If the Bible were written to give us specific answers to every question in our lives, it would fill many libraries with its countless volumes. God certainly speaks to us regularly through Scripture, but He's not limited to this. He also speaks to us through our circumstances, His Holy Spirit, songs, or whatever He wants. So, I don't think that this is odd at all. In my opinion, what you're experiencing is normal for Christians. I think we can expect to have supernatural events in our daily lives."

"I'm glad to hear that," Mike said. "Today I was feeling discouraged, because I was uncertain that God would speak to me. Right now I feel like God sent you to have this conversation with me."

"It's amazing how God works." At this, Sylvia paused and became lost in thought. "You know, I just came across an article in a magazine last month that introduced a good method for decision-making. I hadn't seen anything like it before, but I liked it and have a copy of it here at the office. Want to see it?"

"Sure," Mike replied.

"Okay, hang on a second." After a couple minutes Sylvia returned with the magazine and flipped it open to the article she had mentioned. "Here it is."

The Four-Point Model of Decision-Making

	Score of 0 or 1
Logic -	____
Emotion -	____
God's Will -	____
Wise Advice -	____
Total Score: # of factors that line up in agreement (0-4)	____

Steps To Making a Well-Thought-Out Decision

Each of the above components is a main factor in determining how to make a decision. For any decision you face, it can be smart to consider each of these.

1) Describe the dilemma about which you have to make a decision:

_____

_____

_____

2) Formulate the decision into a yes/no question. "Should I move to Chicago?" or "Should I take this volunteer position?" or "Should I buy a new car?"
    My question: _____

3) Logic: Looking at the circumstances of the situation, what does your logic tell you to do?

    _____

    _____

    _____

4) Emotion: Do you feel at peace or have other emotions that would reinforce answering "yes" to the question you formulated in number two? Or do you feel uneasy, hesitant or other emotions that could indicate you should answer "no" to this question or that other options would be better? Feelings that reinforce a "yes" answer to the question would score a point for emotion.

    _____

    _____

    _____

5) God's Will: If you're a praying person, ask God to guide you in the decision. Listen in prayer, and look for signs of His guidance in your life. As closely as you comprehend it, what do you think is God's will in this situation? (If you are a dedicated Christian, you may want to have God's will count for more than all of the rest, (i.e. weigh it as two or three potential points).

    _____

    _____

    _____

6) Wise Advice: Do the people you respect in your life support or oppose the option you are considering? What have they said?

_____

_____

_____

7) Tally up the score. How many aspects line up in agreement? Total: _____

8) Reflect, and finalize your decision. A score of four implies that this is likely a sound, reliable decision. You may feel comfortable saying "yes" to your question with a score of three or four. If you scored only one or two, it may be prudent to deliberate further, glean more information in order to make your decision, or say "no" to the question you're asking yourself.

My Decision: _____

_____

_____

_____

"Let's see how this would apply to my decision," Mike said. "As for questions number one and two, the question I am asking is, "Should I apply for this job?" After debating the pros and cons in my head, there are several positive features of the job that seem to suit me well. I'll mark one point for logic."

"That makes sense to me," Sylvia said, trying not to oversell her position on the matter.

"From an emotional perspective," Mike said, "I do have a sense of excitement with this prospective position, and I'm eager to share my new ideas with the company. I love doing that sort of thing. Those seem like emotions that reinforce a "yes" answer, so I'll give emotion a point, too.

"Regarding God's will, I am a novice at this." As far as Mike could tell, it was a direct answer to his recent prayers that Sylvia had asked him if he was going to apply for the job. Mike wondered if God was speaking through Sylvia. Overall, he believed that God was leading him to apply for the job. "But with all of the things we've been talking about, I'm going to give a point for God's will."

"So, what about wise advice, Mike?" Sylvia asked, knowing full well that she was the only person who knew he was considering the position and the only person he had talked to.

"Hmm…I'll have to find someone wise to talk to about this." Mike laughed as he playfully insulted his co-worker. *I need to be careful not to be too flirtatious*, he thought after the fact.

"Thanks a lot."

"Okay, okay, one point for the supportive advice from my very wise co-worker who thinks that I should apply for the job."

"That makes the score four out of four," Sylvia observed.

"And a solid decision indeed," quipped Mike.

"So what are you waiting for?" Sylvia asked, turning and heading back to her desk. "Keep me updated on things."

"Okay, I will. Talk to you later, Sylvia." Mike appreciated how God seemed to intentionally place Sylvia in his life at that moment to help him in this crucial decision. He marveled at how easy and simple it could be sometimes to follow God's lead.

But, while Mike had let his co-worker Sylvia know of his decision to apply for the new job, he neglected to mention it to his wife. That was a mistake.

QUESTIONS FOR GROUP DISCUSSION OR
INDIVIDUAL REFLECTION

1) Several spiritual resources have been mentioned in this chapter for how to make good decisions: prayer, meditation, journaling, Scripture, wise counsel from mentors or other trustworthy people, a person's sense of God's will or the leading of the Holy Spirit, etc. What resources do you tend to draw from to make your decisions? How has this been helpful to you in the past? Please describe one of your experiences.

2) Mike was questioning his ability to hear God and step out in faith and obedience. He was intimidated by the biblical examples of Moses and Paul, but recognized that their ability to trust God in difficult situations increased over time as they gained practice and confidence stepping out in faith. Can you see any ways your faith has grown over the years? Have you had any specific experiences that have increased your ability to trust in God? Is there anything that God could ask of you that you'd be willing and ready to do now that before you would have been unable to do?

3) The Four-Point Model of Decision-Making presented in this chapter can be easily applied to virtually any situation. Pick a dilemma that you are facing, and use the worksheet provided in Appendix H to assist you in making your decision. The appendix also includes a completed sample Decision-Making worksheet to further demonstrate how to use this model. If you are part of a small group reading this book, you could share with others your experience of using this model and the decision you reached.

SKILL #7

FINE-TUNING
RELATIONSHIPS

## CHAPTER SEVENTEEN

The Near-Fatal Mistake

Good intentions don't cut it. Mike had the best of intentions to tell Sara of his decision to apply for the new job. He realized she deserved to have her say in the matter and that he needed to include her in on the decision. Still, he was hesitant to discuss it with her because of the last conversation they had had after the church service. She had thought that he was foolish for raising his hand. *How would she react now if I told her that I think I'm sensing that God is advising me to apply for the job?*

Mike wanted to do the right thing by talking to her about it, but it was a bit complicated. He also hadn't mentioned it to Sara because he thought she would immediately reject the idea now that things had improved at work. She believed in the philosophy that if something wasn't broken, you shouldn't fix it.

Mike was aware that this was another instance of him talking about something to Sylvia more than to his wife. This had been a problem in the past. Sara and Mike had had a few fights about how he had spoken too personally with his co-worker Sylvia. He had admitted, to himself anyway, that it was true that he was allowing their relationship to be too close emotionally. This subject remained a sore spot for Sara, even though the relationship had changed between Mike and Sylvia. Driving home from work, Mike realized he had blown it again.

Mike thought to himself, *I should have told her about this a week ago when it first came up. Now I'm in a jam because as the application deadline came up, I felt compelled to submit my resume.* Mike could feel his pulse pounding in his temples. In the old days, this would have been the prime time for an anxiety attack. But Mike thwarted off his inclination to imagine a disaster. *My faulty thinking habits are hard to evict,*

Mike thought. *Like cockroaches in the basement, they like to linger in dark, hidden places for a while until they are completely extinguished.* This time Mike was able to hold back his worry and not agonize over a potential clash with his wife.

The relationship between Mike and Sara had grown much closer over the past several weeks. Despite his vacillation, Mike had finally decided that he would go ahead and tell her everything. He didn't want to disrupt the flow of their marital successes.

Mike entered the house and found Sara at the kitchen table, poring over the taxes. Approaching with hesitation in his step and uncertainty spread across his face, Mike was intimidated. Sara was dutifully working at her task and wouldn't stop until she was finished, so interruption was the only answer.

"So how's your date with Uncle Sam?" Mike inquired. He truly did appreciate the fact that she liked doing the taxes, since he would rather have a bout of poison ivy than add up all those receipts for deductions and find the right box in which to plug the numbers. Mike was not the best yet at appreciating his wife's efforts by giving verbal affirmation, but he was improving. *If I had developed this skill earlier, I'd be in the running for the husband-of-the-year contest. Sara loves hearing verbal appreciation.*

Sara laughed. "So far so good. I don't want to get audited, so I'm being careful. I saw what happened to Jerry Seinfeld when he got audited and he asked George's girlfriend to help him out."

"Oh yeah, just don't give our receipts away." Mike was pleased by how things were going so far. He desperately wanted their conversation to stay on amicable terms. *Do I bring it up now, or wait a bit?* He could sense a prompting from within to address the issue quickly. Looking back on this moment, he knew he should have taken the opportunity while he had it. But regrettably, he wasted time with quaint chitchat. By the time he got to what he really wanted to say, she was in a mood to finish doing the taxes. As a result, her side of the conversation was terse and bent on returning to her task. This put more pressure on Mike.

"I wanted to touch base with you about something. Can I have a minute?" he asked, now noticeably nervous.

"Sure, what's up?" Sara turned and faced him, giving him her full attention.

"Sylvia, I wanted to know if..." Mike caught himself mid-sentence, realizing his mistake. *Uh-oh. How could I do that? That's not what I was supposed to say. Of all the names to accidentally call her, that's the worst one. This'll set her off.* His old tendencies kicked in quickly. *I need to play this off and hopefully she won't notice that I just called her Sylvia.*

What could I say that would work here? What do Sara and Sylvia have in common?

"I wanted to know if you and Sylvia…" He wasn't very smooth in his cover-up, which made his mistake more obvious.

Sara jumped in, "Mike, did you just call me Sylvia?" She had correctly interpreted the odd behavior of her husband as a failed cover-up. Not only was she upset about the name slip-up, but she was now suspicious of the cover-up. Now she wondered what he could be hiding.

Mike was in a predicament. *Should I admit my mistake and hope that she understands, or should I try and lie my way out of this? Where is my integrity? If I get caught in a lie, that will be so much worse than if I just admit my mistake. She'd probably think that I was having an affair if she found out that I wasn't telling the truth. I'll be honest and keep it as simple as possible. God, please help me.*

"I am so sorry. I was in a conversation with Sylvia today at work, and I just slipped. It was an accident."

Recovering from the shock of being offended, Sara grew angry as she remembered their past conversations. They had already talked about Sara's suspicion of the relationship between her husband and Sylvia. Sara shook her head and spoke quietly, as if to herself: "I can't believe you just called me Sylvia."

Recurrent jealousy reared its aggressive head. Sara was seething. She had thought things were improving in their relationship. She considered that this might be the calm before the storm. Knowing that some couples started to have less conflict after one of the partners decided to separate, Sara wondered if that was the case in their marriage. Was he planning on leaving her for Sylvia? How could she trust him if he had been so close to Sylvia?

Mike's apology did not give her much relief from her fury, but she didn't feel like having a long conversation with him about it. She decided that she would give him the benefit of the doubt this time, and she had nothing more to say to him. Sara turned away from Mike and went back to doing the taxes.

After this, Mike squashed any consideration of talking about his job opportunity. This operation was blown. *If I had only followed the initial plan instead of delaying, I probably wouldn't be in this mess.* He regretted not listening to God's promptings to take care of the situation quickly. He was beginning to more clearly understand how important it was to act upon God's leading. *Following God's wisdom does prevent unnecessary difficulty.*

I'm sure that following God's lead doesn't make everything a cinch the first time around—but God certainly has a much better grasp of the whole situation than I do. Mike hoped that he and Sara could mend things soon and he could get around to telling her of his potential career change.

The Surprise Informant

Morning came, and Sara felt a little better. She was now definitely leaning towards clemency. She knew it would be helpful for her to collect her thoughts and get away for a short while. Shopping was a reprieve for her. It enabled her to have time alone, yet still be surrounded by others to stave off loneliness. Plus, there were family birthday presents to buy, so the excursion had more than one purpose.

Sara was unprepared for the shock of that early morning shopping run. It wasn't sticker shock. It was the person she coincidentally ran into—Sylvia. Coming down the aisle from opposite directions, their eyes met, and Sara knew it would be out of the question from a social standpoint not to acknowledge Sylvia. Sara prepared herself to be friendly, despite her longing to punch Sylvia in the nose.

The two had met several times before, usually briefly at company parties. Their relationship was that of acquaintances, with the bulk of what they heard about each other coming from Mike. Sara lacked an understanding of Sylvia's past, her values and interests, and frankly she was fine keeping it that way. Mrs. Forrester quickly noticed that Sylvia's blouse and skirt were not the most becoming for her figure. She crossed her arms and attempted to put on a smile.

Sylvia spoke first. "Hi, Sara. Good to see you—it's been too long." Sylvia wore a genuine smile and focused her attention unwaveringly on her visitor.

"Hi, Sylvia," Sara said, lacking enthusiasm. Succumbing to the appropriate social rules, she replied with words that were the exact opposite of how she felt. "It's good to see you, too."

Oblivious to the fact that Sara was harboring bitterness towards her, Sylvia continued the conversation casually and comfortably. Reflecting on her discussion with Mike, her eyes and mouth grew wide as she remembered Mike was seriously considering taking a new job. Her voice rose in pitch and she clasped her hands together as she exclaimed, "Oh yeah, did Mike decide to go for it? I think he should. What do you think?"

Clueless as to what Sylvia was talking about, but not wanting to be bested by her rival, Sara thought for a moment and replied, "I'm pretty sure he will go for it."

"I thought so. If he gets it, and I'm sure he will because he is so talented and will interview so well…"

Sylvia continued, but Sara tuned her out. Sara's fears caused her anger to return with a vengeance. Mike no longer had the benefit of the doubt. Clemency was gone. He was charged, tried and convicted, with Sylvia as his accomplice. All that was left was for him was to receive his sentence, and Sara was happy to let him have it.

Sylvia's words were still swirling through Sara's head, but unknowingly, Sylvia kept adding to the fire. "Mike thinks that it's God's will that he take the new job. I'm so excited for him. I'll miss working with him so closely, but I'm sure that he'll come by and visit. Better yet, the three of us could get together. That would be great," Sylvia said with a naïve enthusiasm.

A dagger struck Sara's heart. Her hopefulness that she and Mike were on their way to a better marriage was now obliterated. There'd be absolutely no getting together with Sylvia. She lied and said, "Yeah, maybe we could work that out some-time."

"Well, I should probably get going," Sylvia said. "I need to go pick up a few more things."

Sara was relieved that the conversation was nearly over. She tersely said, "Good-bye," twirled around and walked off.

"Goodbye, hope to see you soon," Sylvia said to Sara's back. Sara was already heading around the corner.

Sara no longer felt a need to follow social graces and left the items sitting in her cart by the headless mannequin. She stormed out of the store to the parking lot.

Hot Water

Sara slammed the car door and charged into the house. Where should she start? Sara was the type to come right out with it, and she had no desire to soften the question with tact. Immediately upon finding her husband in the living room, she challenged him with the question, "Are you having an affair with Sylvia?"

Mike knew that he was in trouble from the night before, but he thought things had mellowed out some. "Of course not! Like I told you last night, I just accidentally used her name, because I had been talking to her recently. Why won't you believe me? It's the truth."

She looked at him in disbelief. His excuse was worthless. To her, they were empty words. She wasn't naïve to his pattern of telling half-tales to make him look more innocent than he was. "I see. Then 'truthfully,'" her sarcasm mounted, "can you tell me why she knows about you applying for a new job and I don't?"

A look of alarm leapt on his face. "How did you find out about that?"

"I think the better question is, why are you hiding it from me? What's going on, Mike? What is this job anyway?" Sara desperately tried to fight off the tears.

Quickly inhaling, she went on, "You apologize and tell me not to worry about it, but I just ran into Sylvia at the department store and she gave me a very different impression. I feel like a fool. I thought things were getting better between us, and now it looks to me like you've been slinking around behind my back."

Mike let out a painful sigh of regret. There was no maneuvering out of this. Lying wasn't an option to him. *If I expect God to help me get through this, I should conduct myself in a way that would be pleasing to Him*, he thought.

It wouldn't be a quick fix. The truth wouldn't restore her faith in him instantly. But Mike didn't need to have a quick fix. He was willing to do what it took to make things right.

Feeling the discomfort of this emotionally charged conversation was worse than any physical pain that he had experienced. The perceived threat shook the core of their marriage. His natural inclination was to leave the scene, but a gentle reminder ran through his head informing him that anger could be useful. *Her anger is a good thing; it can help us get to the source of the problem. God gave us the capacity for anger to protect our marriage. The trouble is, my own stupidity has caused me to lose my credibility. I meant for things to go so much differently. How do I explain this?*

Drawing from his counseling sessions, Mike now had more tolerance for emotionally charged discussions. He wanted to work through the issue instead of running from it. "I don't expect you to believe me. I'm sorry how all this went. I meant to tell you last night that I was interested in this new marketing job. Actually, I felt like God urged me to apply for it, but I was hesitant to tell you, because I was worried what you'd think. I'm sorry that I didn't tell you about the job sooner."

She was not swayed. Something was missing. "What did you guess I would think? I can tell you what I think—I think that you're full of it. Why should I trust anything that you say?"

Tensions were mounting in the Forrester household. Out came the final blow. Sara asked Mike, "Are we going to stay together?"

Mike's heart sank. He wanted to explain everything to her. As he started to speak, he reached his arm out to gently touch her shoulder in a kind gesture.

Sara cut him off. "Don't touch me."

Mike snapped back his hand. He needed some help, and out of the chaos in his mind, a moment of clarity came to him. "Sara, I'm committed to work on our relationship. I'm not exactly sure how to do it at this point, but I value our marriage. I've been faithful to you, and I'm dedicated to you."

Sara softened, but the look on her face told Mike that she was not fully convinced. Inwardly, Sara had her doubts, but overall she thought she could believe Mike. She knew time would need to be a factor in the healing process, but something else was needed, too.

"There's something else I haven't told you about. I've started seeing a counselor," Mike said.

"Really? You've been meeting with our pastor and a counselor?" Sara was mystified. "What for? Is there something really wrong with you?" she asked with a note of concern.

"I don't think so. I mean, I do have a bunch of things to work on, but I'm not losing my mind or anything. Jim, the counselor that I have been seeing, has been helping me with areas that have been a challenge for some time. I couldn't get past them on my own, and I figured his training would help me in the remaining areas where I was stuck.

Sara thought for a minute. This shattered some firm assumptions she had of her husband. He seemed to be too headstrong to go to counseling. She had thought of them going to couple's counseling in the past but thought Mike would never go for it.

"The counseling is helping a lot, and I think it could help us, too. Would you be willing to come with me to the next appointment?" Mike asked.

Sara didn't know what to say. She was hesitant to join in halfway through, because she was worried that Jim might be on Mike's side. Then it would be two against one. She was torn, because she did see positive changes in Mike's life, which she now knew were partly attributed to going to counseling. Sara thought counseling could improve their chances of having a more satisfying marriage, but it would mean being very vulnerable with a stranger. She weighed her options and then made up her mind.

"Okay, Mike, I'll go with you to an appointment on a couple of conditions. I want the session to focus on the current problem about you, Sylvia and this new job. I don't want to get analyzed by Jim about things in my distant past. Secondly, if I don't like it, I won't go back. Can you agree to that?"

"Yes, I can. I think that's a good place to start. I would like you to be open to talking about other things later, though."

"I can't make any guarantees. I haven't even met the guy. If I think it will help, then yes, I'll talk about other things, too."

Mike was relieved that his wife was willing to go, and he readily agreed to her terms. Both of them were counting on counseling helping them, and glad to get some outside input on their situation. Until the scheduled appointment, however, the air in the Forrester home was filled with both anticipation and trepidation.

Questions for Group Discussion or Individual Reflection

1) As long as Mike kept information from his wife, there was an obstacle to intimacy and vibrancy in their relationship. Mike was afraid to talk to her, because he was afraid of her reaction. What tends to inhibit you from having tough conversations with people?

2) Think of the times you have risked being open with people. What positive results have come from being open and having those tough, honest conversations?

3) How do you act when you are in hot water in a relationship? How do you try to get out of the predicament or resolve the conflict?

4) Although the negative stigma associated with counseling is lessening, it still exists. Historically, counseling was primarily viewed as being only for people who were severely mentally ill, but it is now accessed by all sorts of people for a wide array of purposes. Would you ever consider going to counseling? What do you think you could get out of it? New insights, support, marriage enrichment, skills training, or assistance setting goals?

## CHAPTER EIGHTEEN

Steps on the Path to Reconciliation

S ara, it's nice to finally meet you," Jim said with a smile, reaching out to shake her hand. "Mike called to let me know that he wanted you to join us today. Thanks for coming."

Sara extended her hand to Jim and said, "I'm glad to meet you, too. Mike should be here any minute. I hope he hasn't made me into a complete monster." She thought Jim looked like a decent guy. He passed the first impression test.

"Not at all," Jim replied. "I try to put him to work on his own issues instead of having him focus on other people too much."

Sara was relieved. "That's good."

Usually Mike was in a jovial mood with Jim, but his solemn demeanor today reflected the change in circumstances. Today he was meeting Sara at the counseling office after work. As the connector between the two parties, Mike felt the pressure. What would it be like to have Sara at the appointment? Would Sara trust what Jim had to say?

Mike knocked on Jim's door. After some brief pleasantries, Jim set up the ground rules. "While you're here, I want you to focus on telling your own story and not the other person's story. Please stay away from assuming what the other person is thinking or feeling. I think we'll get further if you don't try to say what the motives were for each other's actions. Instead, I'd like you to say what is going on in your own head and heart. Lastly, please listen when the other person is talking, without interrupting. No matter how much you want to correct their story, you need to wait till it's your turn. Does that sound reasonable?"

Both Mike and Sara felt safer with those ground rules in place. Their arguments in the past would have been less likely to deteriorate if they had been following rules for fair fighting and proper communication. The couple agreed to the rules. The time to dive in had come.

Jim got down to business. "Let's begin by seeing if we can get a good idea of what the problem is from both of your perspectives. Who wants to go first?"

Sara, still hesitant about the process of counseling, shifted things over to her therapy veteran husband. "You start, Mike."

"Okay. Well, in the past we've had difficulty getting through conflict. We fight, but it seems like we never get to the point where things are fully resolved. I hope that we can improve in this area so that we don't keep rehashing the same things over and over again. I tend to avoid conflicts, and when Sara feels like I'm putting other priorities ahead of her she becomes angry and critical of me."

Sara was about to respond, and Jim quickly intervened. "Remember, Mike, you're supposed to stick to your side of the story. Let Sara talk about what she feels and why she does the things she does."

"Sorry, I didn't even realize that I was doing that," Mike said.

Jim added, "I understand. Most people don't realize when they are doing some mind reading or interpreting another's experience. But when we do this, the other person easily become defensive and wants to correct us. Speaking from your own perspective helps to minimize that defensiveness."

"I could see that happening," said Mike. "I don't like it when she tells me what I'm thinking either. Getting back on track, the way I see it, one of our main problems is that we don't seem to make any progress when we fight. I get frustrated when we argue and I want to reconcile, but I don't seem to be able to say or do the right things." Mike went on to describe some of their recent arguments, including the one about Sylvia.

"Thanks, Mike. What about you, Sara?" Jim inquired.

Sara was a quick learner and didn't repeat the same mistakes that Mike had made. "I felt wounded when you called me, 'Sylvia.' Then, after you apologized and assured me that it was just a simple slip of words and things were different now, I found out that you had confided in Sylvia about your possible job change. I felt injured, angry and jealous, because I'm your wife and you hadn't told me anything about your application for a new job. I agree that we have problems with conflict resolution. I want to be able to trust that when you apologize you mean it, and you aren't going to do the same thing again."

Mike and Sara both sighed and looked at the counselor.

Jim could tell that this couple was at a loss without the problem-solving skills to get out of their gridlock. He said to them, "A common starting place for what you're dealing with is to fine-tune the arts of apologizing and forgiving. These skills are not instinctive; everybody needs practice to be good at this. Once you can navigate conflict through quality apologies and genuine forgiveness, reconciliation is right around the corner. Here, take a look at these. These are a couple of handouts on reconciliation."

THE PATH TO FORGIVENESS, THE CHOICE OF RECONCILIATION

Live a life worthy of the calling you have received. Be completely humble and gentle; be patient, bearing with one another in love. Make every effort to keep the unity of the Spirit through the bond of peace.

EPHESIANS 4:1-3

Dealing With Conflict: Why Bother?

Relationships are a major aspect of anyone's life. They impact the quality of our life, our mood and our energy. Resolving conflict is foundational to healthy relationships. As long as we still have a propensity toward hurting each other, accidentally or intentionally, we need to be able to deal with conflict.

This requires us to try to address offenses and hurts in an open, direct and caring manner. It is imperative to maintain a clean slate with each other, to regularly clear the air and not be bogged down with old resentments. Indispensable to this process are the crucial skills of apologizing and forgiving.

Through the process of dealing with conflict, we discover how the people in our lives like to be loved. We learn how they like to be treated, spoken to and supported. In this way, conflict is incredibly valuable to relationships.

WHAT HAPPENS WITHOUT RECONCILIATION?

Above all, love each other deeply, because love covers over a multitude of sins.

1 PETER 4:8

It's tempting to avoid conflict and brush things under the carpet. In the short term it may seem like the easiest, best thing to do. In the long-term, it makes things a lot harder and a lot worse. When people are carrying resentment, they are inhibited from loving. When people harbor unforgiveness, they are so much less able to see a person's good traits. They forget why they used to love the person they are mad at. They don't remember why they committed themselves to them or how they became close friends in the first place. Resentment brings a relational blindness to the good things about the other person or the relationship itself.

Just like a car, without maintenance, a relationship will start to break down. What happens if you never do maintenance on a car? Rust spots grow into large gaping holes. Your timing belt breaks, and it ruins your engine. Continuing to ignore problems in your relationship or your car without making the needed repairs will result in more expensive and costly damage. If you don't maintain your car/relationship, you will turn to the car/relationship when you need it, and it won't be dependable. It won't come through for you when you need it the most.

Sara said, "That makes sense to me. But it's easier said than done. When I am upset, apologizing is one of the last things I want to do."

"I agree," Jim said. "It is very difficult, and often we need to ask God for help in order to have the humility and willingness to apologize. I also think that it is useful to develop a plan to help you apologize well. That way you are prepared when you have the opportunity to apologize to someone."

Sarcastically, Mike quipped, "I can hardly wait for opportunities to do that."

"Oh yeah, I bet you lie awake at night wondering, 'To whom can I apologize next?'"

"You counselors are so good at figuring people out. That is exactly what I do every night."

"That's great, Mike. Here's a guide you can use to do just that tonight."

Quality Apologies

If it is possible, as far as it depends on you, live at peace with everyone.

Romans 12:18

All of you, clothe yourselves with humility toward one another, because, "God opposes the proud but gives grace to the humble."

1 PETER 5:5

Unresolved conflict is a barrier to strong relationships. As most will concur, it is by far easier to forgive someone if they have apologized. Certainly one can forgive whether or not an apology has been given, yet it takes more determination, understanding and grace.

Whether you are the one who needs to give an apology or receive it, it may help you to know the ingredients of a Quality Apology. The following is a description of the elements and process that lead to a meaningful, effective apology.

Remember that the tone, timing and circumstances of an apology can make all the difference. Sincerity is a prerequisite. Humility is an aid. Evidence of remorse and the beginnings of change are your best assistants. Without these, you may not be taken seriously. Without these, you may not be ready to apologize.

Components of an Apology

1) Be respectful of the other person's choice to forgive or not. Do not demand forgiveness. Find a time to talk when you won't be rushed, and a location that is private (if both parties feel comfortable being alone together).

2) Admit your error, fault or sin.

   Examples: "I have wronged you by…" "I messed up by…" "I did something I shouldn't have when I…" "I made a mistake when I…"
   Your statement of error: _____

   _____

   _____

3) Acknowledge your responsibility in the matter. Don't make excuses. Don't tell the other person what he/she was responsible for.

   Examples: "It was my fault that…" "It was wrong of me to…" "I'm sorry that I…." "No one else made me…"

Admit your responsibility: _____

_____

_____

4) Humbly guess how you think you affected the other person. Express how you think you may have harmed them or impacted them negatively through your mistakes, actions or words. State this tentatively and not authoritatively.

   Examples: "My actions may have caused…" "I think that I made you feel…" "I may have made it hard for you to trust others by…"

   Your guess at how you affected them: _____

_____

_____ _____

5) State your hope for how you would like to conduct yourself differently in the future. Explain how you would like the situation to go next time, if it could/does arise again.

   Examples: "Next time…" "If I get in this situation again I plan on…" "In the future, I hope I…"

   Your hopes and plans for the future: _____

_____

_____

Ask the person to forgive you.

   Examples: "I'm so sorry. Will you forgive me?" "I regret what I've done to you. Will you try to forgive me?" "I know you may not be ready to now, but I'm willing to wait for you to forgive me. Will you try to prepare to forgive me?"

   Your request: _____

_____

Complete All Six Steps!

Many people stop the process of forgiveness or reconciliation after step five of the apology. The offender or perpetrator doesn't specifically ask the other person to forgive them. Do not stop there! It can mean a critical difference in the future of your relationship in two ways.

First, if you are the offender and you only say you're sorry and don't ask the person to forgive you, then the person may never truly make the choice in his or her heart to forgive you. You see, if you don't bring it up specifically, the person may never get to the point of decision. The other person may not ask himself or herself if they are actually going to forgive you. They may have listened to you and appreciated what you said, but not made the actual decision to forgive.

Consequently, they may go on harboring bitterness and resentment against you, even though you said you were sorry. If they are able to forgive you and say it out loud, then it somehow causes a change in their heart. It also holds them accountable to themselves and to you that they have pardoned you.

The second result of not actually asking the other person to forgive you is that you may never get to hear the wonderfully freeing words "I forgive you." Stopping the process prematurely by skipping step six may steal from you the joy and sense of cleansing that comes from being forgiven.

Giving an apology and working toward reconciliation is not complete without this step of directly asking for forgiveness.

Getting to the end of the handouts before Sara, Mike blurted out, "This is where we have our problem! We don't forgive each other for past hurts. I can't remember either of us saying, 'Will you forgive me?' or 'I forgive you.' I think we need to use the actual words to truly get past our fights and grievances."

Jim jumped in, "I think most couples don't go through that important step in the process. As a result, many couples accumulate relational injuries over time—they accrue a huge list of grievances against the other person. It can get to the point where they are so angry at the other person that they no longer feel love for them. When I do marriage counseling, I regularly hear people say 'We fell out of love.' I think it's usually because of this problem of unresolved conflict. Couples are left with gaping wounds that don't get healed."

"I believe it," said Sara. "I think I have a few of those wounds myself. But I sure don't want things to get to the point of our love dying because of it. What do we do to prevent that?" she looked to Jim earnestly, now invested in the counseling.

"Well, we've just seen the six steps of making a Quality Apology. Let's move on to the crucial steps to forgiving someone. Combined, these two skill sets will give you the key tasks to focus on in order to resolve your conflict and not have it accumulate."

Jim then handed them the handout on forgiveness.

WHAT IS TRUE FORGIVENESS?

Be kind and compassionate to one another, forgiving each other, just as in Christ God forgave you.

EPHESIANS 4:32

Defining What Forgiveness Is:

There are many ways of describing forgiveness:
- to let go of a grudge
- to choose to pardon
- to decide not to hold something against someone
- to excuse an offense without demanding punishment
- to acquit or set free from consequences or penalty
- to grant relief from payment or need for retribution
- to cease to feel resentment
- to let go of a desire for revenge
- to allow room for error or weakness in another

Some commonly used definitions of forgiveness are in fact unhealthy, unrealistic or even impossible. If a faulty definition of forgiveness has ever been imposed upon you, you may have felt frustrated, confused and guilty in response. You may have interpreted that you were a failure or that things were futile. Unrealistic expectations that are placed upon you, either by yourself or others, will render your attempts at forgiveness unsuccessful. Take a look at these erroneous definitions of forgiveness.

What Forgiveness Is Not:

- saying that the act, behavior or transgression was not wrong after all
- denying or nullifying responsibility

- forgetting the offense
- pretending it never happened
- minimizing the harm or damage
- giving permission for the wrongdoing or sin to be done again

The Difference Between Forgiveness and Reconciliation

Forgiveness is sometimes confused with trust. Just because you forgive someone does not mean you have to trust him or her again. This is the distinction between forgiveness and reconciliation. When you reconcile with people, it means you not only forgive them but you do what is needed to restore the relationship. Reconciliation involves rebuilding trust and intimacy.

There are situations where reconciliation may be unwise or dangerous. Simply said, some people can be in such dire condition that they are not safe to be around. Take, for instance, a person who is regularly under the influence of mind-altering drugs, or a person who is prone to violence. Reconciliation under those terms could be hazardous. The decision of whether to reconcile or not can be complicated and worthy of careful attention. At times, it is best to wait for the other person to show remorse, repentance or personal growth before you allow them back into your life. In other cases, it is wise to avoid certain situations with that person for a while, such as living together, working together or being financially involved.

Even if your intent is not to reconcile or renew a relationship, forgiveness is still a beneficial, therapeutic path to take. Forgiveness can open the way for healing, relief, letting go and moving on.

Of course, if reconciliation is possible, safe and sought after by both parties, it can be the most wonderful outcome! Forgiveness taken to this final stage allows for optimal cleansing, healing and repairing to be accomplished. Reconciliation can be the most complete and liberating of avenues to take. It provides the opportunity and means for fresh starts, new ways of relating and unexplored healthy potential.

Sara looked up and told Jim, "I don't feel in danger in our marriage. Mike isn't violent, and to my knowledge he isn't using drugs, either."

"Hey, definitely not!" Mike replied, a little insulted that she was not completely certain that he wasn't using drugs.

Jim jumped in. "Now that we've got that settled… I think you guys know that many people have a difficult time reaching the point of reconciliation for one reason or another. You two have fewer obstacles than some other couples. It also makes a big difference that both of you are here and are interested in the process. The majority of couples come to counseling only as a last resort before divorce. Often, one person has already made up their mind to divorce. Fortunately, it doesn't seem like you are that kind of couple. I think that you are smart to be addressing your issues earlier rather than later, and not letting things deteriorate so badly. Let's take a look at the next sheet that walks through the steps of forgiveness."

Steps to Forgiveness

Forgiveness is a choice. It is an act of the will, heart and mind. It is a decision that you make for your own good and also for the well-being of others. Forgiveness is something that can happen in a moment or as a process over time.

Oftentimes the deeper hurts and more serious offenses require us to keep choosing to forgive. It is natural for our feelings of anger to resurface or linger even after we have decided to forgive someone. Therefore we sometimes need to repeat a decision to forgive, or remind ourselves that we have chosen to forgive someone. The following are steps to forgiveness on the path that can lead to reconciliation:

1) Make sure you truly understand the offense. What wrongdoing was committed against you? What moral, spiritual or societal rules did the other person violate? Did the offender breach your trust?

   Name the specific offense(s): _____

   _____

   _____

2) Do not rush the decision to forgive. Yes, it is good to forgive readily. Yet, you need to allow yourself the time and permission to figure out how you were harmed, injured or affected. Let yourself identify the impact the other person's actions or words had on you. If you rush the decision without recognizing the impact of the other person's actions, you may need to

repeat the forgiveness process each time you realize more of the consequences of what they did to you.

How did this person affect you? _____

_____

_____

3) In your decision of whether you will forgive or not, honestly evaluate where you are and what you are capable of on your own, or with God's help. The other person(s) may or may not apologize to you and ask you for forgiveness. Either way, you still face the question of whether or not you will forgive. You may choose to respond any of the following ways:

   a)   I forgive you.

   b)   I will try to forgive you.

   c)   I'm not ready yet.

   d)   I will ask God to help me want to forgive you. I can't forgive you on my own. I need His help.

If the other person is talking with you about what happened, speak your answer out loud, directly to him or her. If the other person isn't talking to you about what happened, you may still want to speak your decision out loud since it can have a greater impact that way.

My choice is: _____

_____

_____

If you've answered (b), (c), or (d), go back to step one. It's also probably a good idea to reflect on what the benefits are of forgiving or reconciling versus the costs of holding a grudge.

Mike interrupted and said, "I thought we were supposed to quickly forgive and not stall. This seems to be saying that we should wait to forgive."

Jim clarified, "That's a common misunderstanding. It's not really saying that. Certainly, it is good to readily forgive. But what good does it do if you don't know what you're actually forgiving? People need to take a moment to realize the basics of what happened and how they were affected. Then, yes, by all means, forgive quickly.

"Mike and Sara, before you try to implement this, I want you to look at this next sheet. There are a few more points to understand before you put this into practice."

Say It Clearly, Out Loud

It may seem odd, but there is a distinct difference in our experience depending upon whether we say "I forgive you" out loud to someone, or we just think it in our heads. By declaring it to the other person, there can be a distinct change that occurs in our heart or mind by saying the words. It can bring great relief to us and to the person we are forgiving.

Do verbalize your words instead of just using body language. When the offender apologizes, it is ineffective for the offended person to shrug their shoulders, give a wave of their hand or just look away. The hurt person might be trying to be polite, or trying not to make too big of a deal of things, but don't settle for this. Body language is not as clear, beneficial or effective as words. Plus, it is can be misinterpreted.

Say it straight. Stick to specific words such as "I forgive you," and avoid using colloquial phrases. In other words, after someone has apologized to you, avoid saying things like "It's okay," or "It's alright." It is not okay or all right that you were hurt. Using a casual slang expression can minimize what happened. It's better to say the direct, clear words "I forgive you" or some other phrase that truly captures what you mean.

The Cost of Holding a Grudge

You may have heard the saying "Holding onto a grudge hurts *you* more than it hurts the other person." From a psychological perspective, this tends to be true. When you hold on to a grudge, it means you're holding on to the bitterness, pain, harsh memories, anger and frustration. It can also involve replaying and therefore reliving the hurtful incident over and over in your head.

This is apt to lead to irritability, depression, illness and difficulty trusting people or moving past the circumstance. Resentment and bitterness weigh people down and hold them back in life. By choosing not to forgive, you may be choosing to keep yourself frozen in the wounded past.

One thing many people don't realize is that when a victim refuses to forgive, he or she maintains a bond between himself or herself and the perpetrator. They are tied together emotionally in some ways. The victim may play a role in keeping the offender stuck in the past under condemnation and shame. Forgiveness can release both the victim and the perpetrator from each other and from the past.

Is It All Better?

Unfortunately, forgiving others does not make the effects of their transgression disappear. It would be great if the choice to forgive brought immediate, full healing to those who have been injured. Nevertheless, over time, forgiveness can indeed bring recovery and peace of mind.

Furthermore, people can't be fully assured that they won't ever get hurt again in the same way, or even by the same person. There may be a repeat scenario that will require you to decide again whether or not to forgive the same mistake, if not the same person. In these situations, let tomorrow worry about itself. You cannot predict the future. Nor should you hold off on forgiveness today for what might happen tomorrow.

One intelligent thing you can do is choose your company well. Surround yourself with respectful, kind people. Be smart about whom you trust. You may choose to gradually be more vulnerable with someone and see how they handle that trust. If they handle it respectfully and maturely, you could open up more.

"I'm ready," Mike said after finishing reading the handout. "I'll go first." He was prepared to give this method a try.

Mike thought about how his actions must have made his wife feel. Caring enough to risk failure, he was willing to attempt to describe it to her and apologize for it.

Now Mike felt nervous. He felt like he was in the spotlight during a dramatic play on Broadway. It was his character's turn to speak, but he needed a script. *I hope the fact that I need the handout to prompt me in my apology doesn't detract too much.* Mike queried, "Can I see that list of steps to make a good apology? I think it'll help." His wife didn't seem to mind. *Okay, here goes.*

"Sara, I realize that I have not been honest with you in the past. I've been selective in what I've told you and can see how it's been manipulative. I remember times when I was afraid of how you would react, so I purposely misled you. I even tried to get you mad at other people to distract you from being mad at me. I understand now that it was because I was afraid of strong emotion, and I felt like I needed to run from it. I avoided talking to you about difficult issues, because I was nervous about how you might respond. This was my problem, and it greatly affected how we related to one another.

"Jim and I have been working on this in our counseling sessions, and I know that I've made gains in this area. I can understand how the way I've acted may have made it hard for you to trust me. I could also see how you may not have felt loved by me because of how I disengaged and blocked you out when we had conflicts. If that was the case, you had every right to feel that way. I don't want this to be the pattern in the future. I want you to be able to trust me and feel confident in what I tell you. And most importantly, I want you to feel loved by me.

"Spending time with our pastor has made me care more about being a man of integrity, a man who lives up to his word. In the future, I want to be completely honest with you. I don't want you to have to worry that I'm just making something up so that I can get what I want. And I'll try to let you in on things in my life quickly so you don't hear news from a different source. That must have felt awful to hear about my job through Sylvia. I wish you hadn't had to go through that.

"Having said all this, I'm sure that it'll take some time to gain your confidence again. I'm very sorry for my part in these conflicts and how I've hindered things from getting resolved. Will you please forgive me?"

Sara couldn't believe it. She had never heard her husband talk like this before. He was being vulnerable, honest and speaking from the heart. He even sounded like he meant it. After a moment, she replied, "I'm sorry. I've been hurt too much in the past. I feel like too much has happened between us that I can't honestly forgive you for all of it right at this moment. I wonder if I'll need to forgive you in parts for specific things."

Mike had been holding his breath. His hope, like an air balloon floating over the ground, was slashed by a large blade and sank to the ground. Deflated, Mike stared at the floor.

The therapist had seen this before. He wanted the couple to experience genuine forgiveness, so he didn't want to force things or rush the couple.

Jim broke the silence. "That's perfectly alright, Sara. You're being honest, and that's important. Let's take a look at where to go from here."

Sara was relieved that she wasn't being criticized or pressured by the therapist.

"Sometimes people need to process things some more and prepare to forgive, especially when there's been a lot of hurts, or a major infraction. There are certain scenarios where it can seem impossible to forgive. Have you seen the movie *Hotel Rwanda*?"

"Yeah, about a year ago," said Mike.

"I can't believe the gruesome violence that took place there," said Sara.

"Yes, it's a hard thing to watch in a movie, never mind living through it," Jim said. "The events that some people live through are astonishing. It can be hard to comprehend how anyone could do such evil things to another human being. The victim's pain can run so deep that the crimes feel unforgivable.

"It's even harder to forgive if the person who wronged us shows no remorse or won't even admit that they did anything wrong. If the offenses happened over an extended time period, or a long time ago, people can become very accustomed to thinking about the perpetrator in a certain way. It can be difficult when approaching forgiveness to be able to see the perpetrator any differently."

"Well, it's not as if Mike did something to me that was as cruel as the things in that movie. But I can still see what you mean," said Sara. "The hard thing for me is that Mike has been hurting me for a long time. What he's saying now sounds really good, but I'm not sure if I can trust it—trust him. It's hard to imagine him being any different."

"Haven't you seen me already start to be different?" Mike asked.

"That's true, I guess," Sara said hesitantly.

"Obviously, you guys can relate to what I'm talking about," Jim said. "So where do we go from here? In these instances, many people have come to the conclusion that they cannot forgive on their own. It's hard to let go of things. It's human nature to want to take revenge or see people suffer for their wrongdoing. For people who look to the Bible for guidance, they uncover the truth in Psalm 73 and other places that God is just and will hold people responsible for what they've done. Knowing this helps some people to let go of their bitterness and pardon their offender.

"For people who are spiritually minded, there are some situations in which they know the only way they are going to be willing to reconcile is if they have help from God. The only way healing is going to happen in these instances is if people ask God to help them and rely on Him to change their hearts. They cannot find the strength or ability to do it on their own. Yet, God can change hearts and help people to become willing to forgive, even where they have no desire in their human strength. God is pleased to do this and is very capable of doing so.

"Furthermore, God is able to change the ways of the perpetrator. We don't know the changes that are going to take place in the person who hurt us. Maybe they will become remorseful, or maybe they'll become kinder. It's important not to judge them or rule out anything positive happening with them."

Mike responded, "I've been guilty of that. I had this good friend for a long time. We got into a fight one day, and we never recovered. He did and said some things I couldn't get over. Hearing what you've said makes me realize that I judged him and wrote him off. We haven't talked in years. I wonder what it would be like if I gave him a call and saw how he was today. Maybe things would be different."

"Yes, they might be," Jim said.

Sara was listening intently. A flicker of recognition flashed across her face as she identified that she had judged Mike in her heart. She had boxed him in by her judgment of his character. Her conclusion that he was a distracted, insensitive husband had led to a bad outcome. As long as she continued to relate to him according to her negative opinion of him, they would be locked into a pattern. She was not able to see the little changes in his behavior, because her judgment of him overruled her ability to see improvements or alterations. She inhibited change in their relationship because she was failing to adjust to the differences in her husband. In her counterpart role, Sara was keeping him in the box.

Allowing things to sink in, Jim paused a moment before continuing. "It is also helpful to remember how much God has forgiven us, because none of us are perfect. We've all hurt people we care about. In fairness, we can't expect others to be perfect and never wound us. If we hang out with others long enough, at least a couple of hours," Jim smiled, "we're bound to get hurt. It's a part of life.

"God's plan for us, though, is to try to heal the hurts as soon as possible. Forgiveness and reconciliation are major themes of the Bible. God spells it out in numerous places to show how we can reconcile with each other, and how we can be reconciled to Him.

"Back to the situation here," Jim said, turning to Sara, "I don't want you to feel pressured to forgive Mike right this moment. Think it over, pray about it if you want…"

Sara cut him off, "Oddly enough, I do feel ready now. I've realized that I was blinded to the changes Mike was making because of my attitude towards him. I'm more able to see now how he has been making great changes and prioritizing time with me more. That gives credibility to his apology, and I believe it was sincere."

Sara shifted her position and looked her husband in the eyes, "I forgive you, Mike." Sara meant it when she said it, too.

The bench press bar that had been weighing heavily on Mike's chest was suddenly lifted. "Thank you," he said, letting out a sigh of relief.

"I wasn't expecting that to happen today," Jim said.

"Nor was I," replied Sara. "But it was the right time, I think. After our conversation, I felt myself wanting it."

SARA'S TURN

Looking at the handouts, Sara realized how effectively Mike had used this resource to make amends. She was uncertain of how to proceed. Not having had the same amount of experience in counseling that Mike had, and not knowing Jim as well, she was feeling unsure of herself. But Sara was not a woman who was easily flustered. Even though she was new to counseling, she was a quick learner.

Sara began, "On my end, I admit that I've frequently made comments to you that were harsh and disrespectful. That was probably very hurtful. I'm responsible for what I say and how I say it. It must feel terrible to be on the receiving end of my criticisms. I can see how that must make it hard for you to talk to me about things sometimes. I think that I have high expectations and I can be impatient. I'm sorry for how this has affected you. I love you, and I don't want to keep treating you this way. Instead, I want to work on how I deal with my frustrations and learn how to manage them better. I admire how you've taken the initiative to work on things lately. I can't promise that I'm going to be perfect at it, but I'm committed to making it better.

"I've been thinking over your job opportunity, Mike, and I think you should go for it. I support you in your decision to apply for it. In the future, I want us to stop avoiding conflict and to resolve things quickly. I will try to respond calmly and patiently. Will you forgive me for how I've acted?"

Mike was ecstatic. It felt so good to have Sara acknowledge how she came across. Plus, he was especially relieved to hear her intentions for the future. "Of course I forgive you. Thanks for what you said. And thank you for coming to this appointment." Feelings of tenderness for Sara surfaced again—feelings Mike had experienced during their early dating days.

Yes, they still had things to figure out, but today was a major triumph. When Mike thought of his wife now, he didn't picture a nagging, disgruntled spouse. The image that came to mind was one of a caring partner who wanted the best for him and was pulling for him. They had gone from being opponents to allies. He had fought for his wife, and he had won her heart.

QUESTIONS FOR GROUP DISCUSSION OR INDIVIDUAL REFLECTION

1) What makes an apology meaningful to you?

2) What helps you or hinders you from forgiving someone?

3) Think about a relationship in which you've recently resolved conflict. What unpleasant Change Indicator Feelings did you have before you resolved the conflict? How did they serve you or motivate you to fix things?

4) What pleasant Reinforcer Feelings did you have after the conflict was resolved that confirmed your choice to reconcile?

5) What motivates you to deal with conflict instead of avoiding it?

6) Complete the worksheets on apologies and forgiveness, found in Appendices I and J. These appendices also include completed sample worksheets to provide you with more illustrations of how to apply these skills. When you're ready or feel prompted, deliver your apology or prepare to forgive. As much as you're comfortable, talk about these experiences with a friend or with your group members if you're studying this book in a small group.

## CHAPTER NINETEEN

Fit To Be Free

So what did you think of the NCAA basketball tourney?" Isaiah asked as they were driving up to see the opening game of baseball season.

Mike's eyes grew wide with passion. "Unpredictable as ever. Also, what an experience going to the Final Four. The only problem was that Duke lost in the sweet sixteen and didn't make it."

"Even better—you got to see my UNC Tar Heels," gloated Isaiah.

"How appalling," Mike shook his head in disgust.

"You gotta love the NCAA. Never a dull moment in March!"

"My main consolation is that I've had great workouts during the games."

"And it shows," Isaiah complimented him as he changed lanes on the freeway.

"Thanks for working out with me," Mike said. "Without you, I probably would have stopped weeks ago. My wife isn't into lifting weights, but you remember how she and I like to play sports together?"

"Sure."

"Well, we just found out that for the last two years there's been pick-up volley-ball in our church gym on Saturday afternoons. We started going, and as a bonus we're getting to know some cool people from our church. Between playing volley-ball and exercising at the YMCA, I dropped another four pounds over the past month. I thought I'd lose more, though."

"I bet you converted fat into muscle. Everybody knows that muscle weighs more than fat. You're starting to look like a lean marketing machine. Sure you look good, but how do you feel? That's more important..."

Mike interrupted, "Watch out!" An SUV suddenly cut them off, and Isaiah slammed on the brakes, barely avoiding a collision.

"That was close. Good thing I have lightning quick reflexes," Isaiah remarked.

"Yeah, not bad for an old guy," Mike quipped.

Isaiah laughed. "Hey—where's the appreciation for the person who just saved your life?"

"Hardly," Mike replied with jest, but then admitted, "Well, maybe you did prevent a fender bender and some whiplash. One thing is for sure, I'm not going to Imagine a Disaster of what could have happened. I've done plenty of that faulty thinking in the past."

"Nice work, Mike! Look at the improvements you've made."

"Now before you almost got us into an accident, weren't you asking me how I feel? Ironic, isn't it?"

"Ironic? I guess that depends on what you mean," Isaiah said.

"I was just about to tell you how relaxed I've been feeling lately," Mike said.

"Nothing like the threat of an accident to help you unwind."

"Actually, now that I have less stress in life overall, I feel like I can take things in stride better—even the close call of a crash."

"Your lifestyle has created a stress buffer. It seems like you have some energy in reserve to deal with the unexpected."

"Yeah, I think that's it. I was going full out before and didn't have any drive left for emergencies. Which reminds me, I haven't had an anxiety attack in ages."

"Glad to hear it. You know, I'm feeling better too." Isaiah was glad to have helped Mike, but the benefits went both ways. Being an exercise partner for Mike had been good for Isaiah as well. "Running my business over the last few years, I've been in a rut of all work and no play. This 'dull boy' has enjoyed taking time out to watch sports, work out and joke around." They had become good friends through it all.

"It's strange," Mike remarked. "In the beginning, I felt like I didn't have enough time to exercise. But even though I've added exercise to my schedule, I'm actually more productive overall. I find that I'm more efficient with my time now."

"Our fast-paced way of life is crazy, isn't it? A person needs to cut back on things just to have time to take care of their health," Isaiah said.

"I've been pleasantly surprised at how my workout already seems easier than it did a few weeks ago."

"You're getting into shape. It's probably also easier because it's become a habit. On my end, I don't need as much to spur me on to get to the gym, because it's part of my weekly routine now," Isaiah said.

"I hear ya."

"One of the best things that's come out of us meeting up at the YMCA is that I've had less back pain. I used to get really stiff but using the step machine makes my back stay more limber." Isaiah shifted in his seat, testing out his flexibility.

"I like the fact that I'm burning more calories. It gives me more freedom to eat my wife's homemade pies. That's reason alone to hit the gym."

"Wait a minute. Your wife makes homemade pies, and you've never invited me over for dessert? What's the deal? I thought we were friends."

Mike laughed, "Okay, okay. I'll share some with ya. Just don't tell anybody else."

"You know, over the years I've changed my diet considerably, but I'm not militant about it. There's no way I could give up chocolate mousse, and I don't do anything too radical. Just every now and again I'll add something into my diet that's healthy and drop something that isn't."

"Sounds like a good way to do it. Hey—did I tell you about my last visit with Dr. Chang? She told me that my blood pressure was lower and my fasting blood sugar was down to the normal range. No daily pin pricks for me. Thank God! I didn't want to have to be checking my blood sugar every day."

"Way to go!" Isaiah cheered. "Although, if you didn't want to give yourself insulin injections, I'd be happy to jab you myself. I used to work with the medics in the military. Don't worry, I wouldn't reuse any needles on you more than a dozen times."

"How kind of you. I think something my counselor Jim taught me could come in handy here. This would be a great time to use Filtering with the slight twist of filtering out everything you have to say."

"Oh, you're making me mad now," Isaiah said facetiously. "And if I recall correctly, that's something else Jim taught you about: anger for a good purpose. That purpose would be to rectify the injustice of your inappropriate comment," Isaiah joked. "My emotion would reach its goal once I socked you one. And then my anger would complete its purpose after you realized your mistake and gave me a Quality Apology."

"Okay, I'll give you an apology alright," quipped Mike. Hmm…let me remember the steps…ahhh yes."

Mike began his proclamation. "I admit that I was fully in the wrong by saying that I should filter out everything you say. Rather, I should go along with everything you tell me. When giving me injections, feel free to reuse needles as many times as you like, even if I don't need any insulin. In fact, use the oldest, most rusty needles you can find."

Mike went on, "I fear the impact of my comment may have been that I have destroyed your self-esteem forever. I wouldn't want to have come across like I was saying you had nothing good to say. In the future, I plan to listen to everything you have to say. Especially when you acknowledge that Duke is the best basketball team of all time.

"Most Revered Isaiah, I realize that you have the choice to forgive me or not. I humbly acknowledge that you may not. I will understand if you choose to harbor resentment for the rest of your days. I only ask that you please don't seek revenge by putting arsenic in my coffee. Old friend, and I sincerely mean old, will you forgive me?"

"Wow, you're really getting good at that apologizing," Isaiah said dryly. "Your only error was putting the word 'Duke' in the same sentence with 'best.' Other than that, it was perfect. I'd be happy to forgive you."

"Thank you. It was good for me to get some practice. Maybe I should insult you more often so I can become an expert apology maker. It takes a while to get it down to make it really good. But as you've experienced today, it's much more effective when you do all the steps."

"Yes, it felt incredible to receive such a heartfelt, well-thought-out confession. Your remorse was touching," Isaiah said.

"Glad you liked it. Anytime."

"I can see why your marriage is improving. Sara must be impressed," Isaiah said, now almost serious. "I see you have what it takes to deal with conflict."

"Yeah, joking aside, I do think she and I are better prepared to actually work *through* difficulties, instead of working *around* them. We still have a lot to learn, but I can tell you that one of our issues was significantly resolved. Sara forgave me for not telling her about the job offer, and we both agreed to talk to each other early in the process of making major decisions."

"It appears to me," said Isaiah, "That you figured out what was causing the conflict and came up with a solution to address the root issue. In my marriage, a nice thing about tackling conflicts head on and resolving them was that over time we eventually started have fewer conflicts. We had dealt with them and got past some. We had been getting sick of going in circles, but it took us a while to learn how to do it any differently. We never went to counseling like you, although that would have helped I'm sure. Instead, we found an older couple to mentor us."

"Good idea. Sara and I have the same hope, to find ways to overcome our repetitive problems. Fortunately, she isn't so worried about an attraction between my co-worker Sylvia and myself anymore. I'm sure it will take time to rebuild the trust and security in our relationship. I was open with her and told her about my previous attraction to Sylvia and how I was now avoiding things that would foster a physical or emotional relationship with her."

"How are you doing that?" Isaiah was curious.

"Part of it was making a mental resolution to honor Sara in my relationships with other women. I realized that I was letting Sylvia into my life too much and sharing more with her than I was with my wife. Sara had a right to be angry about it. Our marriage was threatened, and I needed to have higher boundaries with Sylvia. Even though I enjoyed Sylvia's company, I needed to prevent a possible inappropriate relationship by limiting my time and what I shared with her. What helped the most was for the attraction not to be a secret anymore. The secrecy was like gas to a flame. Once I talked with Sara about it, it wasn't nearly as tempting."

"Is Sara happy with that plan?"

"Yes, and she's even happier now that I've moved to the marketing team and have less contact with Sylvia. I've wondered if that was why she became such a fan of the job transfer."

"So how's the new job going?" asked Isaiah.

"It's great—more flexible hours, and it's right up my alley in terms of what I like to do. I feel like I was made for this."

"Well, what do you expect when you listen to what God wants for your life? He designed you, so He knows what will be fulfilling to you. It hasn't been an easy path, but it sure seems that this is where God wants you to be," Isaiah reflected.

"Thinking about all of the things that I have learned recently makes me aware of how far I have come in just a few short months. I can't remember a time of such rapid change and growth in my life," Mike said pensively.

Isaiah thought back to one of their conversations early on. "Remember when I said that you were halfway there by looking for some help? Look at what's been gained by you reaching out and being teachable. Being open to change makes such a difference. God loves an open and willing heart. When we invite Him to transform us, He is ready to make it happen."

"I believe it. When I was doing things on my own, the changes never seemed to be as big or lasting. Since I allowed God into my life more, He's altered the way that I think, the way I act, and how I relate to others and to Him. Naturally, I catch myself slipping back into old habits sometimes. I'm mostly susceptible to that when I am tired, frustrated or under stress. One way I've coped with that is I've asked God to help me to quickly recognize when I'm backsliding. I'm pretty sure He's helped me on several occasions to get back on track. One of the things He works through is the Bible. I have it on CD, and I listen to it in my car. It amazes me how hearing it changes my attitude and fixes my faulty thinking."

"From the sidelines, it's been fun to watch you," Isaiah said. "You're like those home renovation TV shows, except it's your very own core or self that's being renovated."

"It feels like that to me, too. I never want to go back to my old ways. I definitely don't miss how I used to be so stressed out over work, my marriage and my health. No wonder I had the chest pain. I did it to myself."

"If you want, I can give you something to stress about," Isaiah said tauntingly.

"Watch it, buddy. Don't make me angry. I know how to use it," Mike said in a mocking authoritarian tone.

"Okay, okay," Isaiah said, briefly lifting his hands off the steering wheel and holding them up as if he were getting arrested.

"I'm no longer afraid of the emotions that I once avoided. I'm still clueless about how to respond to them sometimes, but I trust they're there for a reason and I give myself time to figure them out. As a result, I'm finding that I don't get triggered so easily. What Sara used to do to get me fired up doesn't bother me so much. I'm sure it's partly because we're communicating better and don't have as many built-up resentments."

They had almost reached their destination. Driving into the parking garage at the baseball stadium, they began looking for an open spot to park.

"Life. You never know what's going to happen next, and it takes a while to find the space where you fit in."

"True."

Life for the Forresters wasn't perfect, but Mike now truly was the fun-loving, upbeat guy people saw him as. No longer was there a façade hiding worry and troubles. Mike could live in the present, his full self, enjoying the moment.

Getting out of the car, Mike turned to Isaiah and said, "Dinner is on me. I'm feeling generous. Buy as many hot dogs as you want."

"Great. Thanks, big spender. Pass me my baseball glove."

Tossing Isaiah his glove, Mike said, "Hey, I bet you twenty bucks he pitches a shut-out."

"You're on!"

Questions for Group Discussion or Individual Reflection

1) Of the seven skills illustrated in this book, which one did you learn from the most? (Refer to the Table of Contents for a list of them.) Have you seen any changes in the way you think, act, feel or relate to others based on what you have learned?

2) Which of these seven skills would you like to focus on more?

3) Which of the worksheets, guides or resources found in the chapters or appendices do you think you'd like to use in the future? (See a list of Appendices in the Table of Contents.)

4) Are there any ways your view of God, Christianity or Christian living has been altered as a result of reading about Mike's life and experience? Or, have your views changed through your involvement in the discussion, reflection or activities of this book?

APPENDICES

Appendix A

Thought Patterns Card

Feel free to photocopy this card or tear it out of this book so that you have a copy of it handy in your wallet or purse or on your night table. Review it once a week for a month. Think of some specific examples of what's been going through your head recently, both on the faulty and healthy side of things. This will deepen your learning and cement your skills.

Faulty Thinking Patterns vs. Healthy Thinking Patterns

Stop Faulty, Damaging Thoughts and
Put Accurate, Constructive Thoughts in Their Place

Negative Filtering	vs. Consider All the Facts
Thinking in Extremes	vs. Realize the Range of Experiences
Pessimistic Predictions	vs. Trust in a Good Future
Mind Reading	vs. Double-check Your Assumptions
Imagining a Disaster	vs. Stick to the Facts
Taking Things Too Personally	vs. You're Not the Center of the Universe
Confusing Responsibility	vs. Emphasize Personal Responsibility
Stuck on Fairness	vs. Accept That Life Is Not Always Fair
Ruled By Shoulds	vs. Freedom Within Structure
Assuming Emotion is Truth	vs. Consider Emotions as Indicators
Waiting on Others to Make You Happy	vs. Let People Live Their Own Lives
Making Fast Judgments	vs. Give It Some Time and a Chance
Living in the Wrong Time Zone	vs. Focus on the Present
Compare and Despair	vs. Be Your Personal Best
Need to be Right	vs. Foster an Attitude of Learning

Appendix B

How To Change Your Thoughts

How To Change Your Thoughts

1) If you'd like to, invite God into the process of repairing your thoughts.
2) Monitor your thoughts. Identify the Faulty Thinking Patterns. Observe mood changes, as this will help you to recognize when you've begun to think poorly.
3) Stop the flow of your thoughts when you notice they are flawed.
4) Reject inaccurate, troublesome thoughts and replace them with accurate, thruthful thoughts.
5) Develop these skills into a habit. Practice them until it gets easy and fast.

Faulty Thought Patten to Watch For: _____

Healthy Thought Pattern to Substitute:_____

Appendix C

Replacing Troublesome Thoughts

Completed Sample Worksheet
Replacing Troublesome Thoughts

For this worksheet, select your own top three Faulty Thinking Patterns that you'd like to fix. On the left side, give a personal example of a specific troublesome thought of that type that goes through your head. On the right side, write the new and improved thought with which you'd like to replace it. To assist you in this, you could use the Alternate Healthy Thinking Patterns guidelines located on the right side of the Healthy vs. Faulty Thinking Patterns chart in chapter four.

My #1: Name of Faulty Thinking Pattern:

MIND READING

Name of Corresponding Healthy Pattern:

DOUBLE-CHECK YOUR ASSUMPTIONS

My Personal Example: I tend to think that people are judging me or upset with me by how they look at me, how they talk or even their body language. For instance, I saw Sam give me a funny look at the office today. I interpreted his expression to mean that he hates me and he was dreaming up a way to steal my job from me.

My Healthy Replacement: I can't interpret things perfectly. I can't know for sure what people are thinking or what their opinion is of me. If I want to know, I can ask them. In this case, I saw Sam with an unusual expression on his face, looking in my general direction. I wonder what's going on with him. I may ask him, but it likely has nothing to do with me.

My #2: Name of Faulty Thinking Pattern:
IMAGINING A DISASTER

My Personal Example: My teenager said he'd be home by 10 pm. It's now almost 11 pm. What if he got into a car accident? Oh no! Maybe I should go for a drive to try to find him. Should I call the hospital or the police? I hope he hasn't got seriously hurt! When people I care about are late to come home or arrive somewhere else, I tend to worry that something horrible happened to them.

Name of Corresponding Healthy Pattern:
STICK TO THE FACTS

My Healthy Replacement: I'm not going to let myself get carried away by worry when I'm just guessing something could be wrong. I want to withhold my reaction until I know for sure. My son is late. As far as I know, he is likely fine, having fun with his friends and simply lost track of time. If he doesn't call me soon, I'll call the place he was going to. But I'm not going to get upset unless there's proof something bad happened.

My #3: Name of Faulty Thinking Pattern:
RULED BY SHOULDS

My Personal Example: I often worry that I'm letting people down too much or that I should do more to help others. I don't want to be a bad friend or a heartless person. My friend asked me to help her out on Saturday, and I said no. I'm pretty busy myself, but maybe I should have said yes.

Name of Corresponding Healthy Pattern:
FREEDOM WITHIN STRUCTURE

My Healthy Replacement: I do want to be a good friend, but I can't help everyone every time they ask me to. And I definitely can't please everybody. I want to change my "should" to a "could." I could help others when they ask, if it's not going to create a lot of stress for me or my family.

Reap the Benefits

Now that you have identified your top three troublesome thought patterns and came up with specific alternatives, it will make it so much easier for you to repair your thinking. You will notice the problematic ideas in your head much more quickly. Plus, you'll be ready with a positive, truthful thought to substitute in its place.

Well done! Over the next few days, re-read this worksheet a few times to rehearse for when you're going to need to swap thoughts. Once you memorize your own specific examples, it becomes easy to exchange them. You'll soon have the relief that comes from renewed thinking that's based on truth rather than on guesswork or worry.

Blank Worksheet

Replacing Troublesome Thoughts

For this worksheet, select your own top three Faulty Thinking Patterns that you'd like to fix. On the left side, give a personal example of a specific troublesome thought of that type that goes through your head. On the right side, write the new and improved thought with which you'd like to replace it. To assist you in this, you could use the Alternate Healthy Thinking Patterns guidelines located on the right side of the Healthy vs. Faulty Thinking Patterns chart in chapter four.

SAMPLE

SAMPLE

Name of Faulty Thinking Pattern:
MIND READING

Name of Corresponding Healthy Pattern:
DOUBLE-CHECK YOUR ASSUMPTIONS

Example: If I see someone look at me oddly, I think, "They must not like me." I tend to think that people are judging me or upset with me by how they look at me, how they talk or even by their body language.

Example: I can't know for sure what people are thinking or what their opinion is of me. If I want to know, I can ask them. I don't want to be upset over nothing.

My #1: Name of Faulty Thinking

Pattern:_____

_____

Name of Corresponding Healthy

Pattern:_____

_____

My Personal Example:_____

_____

_____

_____

My Healthy Replacement:

_____

_____

_____

My #2: Name of Faulty Thinking Pattern:_____

Name of Corresponding Healthy Pattern:_____

_____

_____

My Personal Example:_____

My Healthy Replacement: _____

_____

_____

_____

_____

_____

_____

My #3: Name of Faulty Thinking Pattern:_____

Name of Corresponding Healthy Pattern:_____

_____

_____

My Personal Example:_____

My Healthy Replacement:

_____

_____

_____

_____

_____

_____

Reap the Benefits

Now that you have identified your top three troublesome thought patterns and came up with specific alternatives, it will make it so much easier for you to repair your thinking. You will notice the problematic ideas in your head much more quickly. Plus, you'll be ready with a positive, truthful thought to substitute in its place.

Well done! Over the next few days, re-read this worksheet a few times to rehearse for when you're going to need to swap thoughts. Once you memorize your own specific examples, it becomes easy to exchange them. You'll soon have the relief that comes from renewed thinking that's based on truth rather than on guesswork or worry.

Appendix D

Create Your Own Personal Mission Statement

Mike's Completed Sample Worksheet
Create Your Own Personal Mission Statement

In today's fast-paced and media-saturated society, it is possible to go a long period of time without stopping to reflect on the big picture of our lives. It's easy to get distracted or overwhelmed. With the explosion of new technology, there are endless ways to waste your time under the seductive guise of entertainment.

Instead of losing sight of the big picture, take a moment to complete these sentences. In effect, you will synthesize your personal mission for each of these main areas of your life.

RELATIONSHIPS: I want to show the treasured people in my life that I care for them by *Providing for them with my job. Doing fun things together. Being affectionate and telling them that I love them.*

CHARACTER: I want to be remembered as a person who was *hardworking, responsible, caring, friendly and funny.*

BEING PRODUCTIVE: Before I die, I want to accomplish my goal(s) of *being the manager of the whole department I work in at my company. Retire by the age of sixty so that Sara and I can take that long trip we have dreamed about.*

ABILITIES: The main skill(s) I have to offer to others is *that I get along with others easily. I am intelligent and have a good education. I get the job done well and on time.*

SERVICE: In my own way, I'd like to make the world a better place for at least one person by *being a good husband, citizen and contributing to my field of business.*

Identify Your Passions

What things in life get you the most excited?
Sports, friendly competition and completing a project at work.

What activities cause you to lose track of time because you're so absorbed in what you're doing?
Working at my computer, watching sports, and seeing movies with Sara.

What things in life bother you the most, such that you wish you could obliterate them from the face of the earth?
Laziness, irresponsibility, the suffering of children, corrupt governments.

Is there a certain group of people that you feel drawn to assist (such as the poor, single parents, the disabled, political refugees, etc.)?
Friends, co-workers, veterans (since I have family who served in the military).

To live a life that revolves around your purpose or calling, it is essential to recognize what you are most passionately for and against. You can promote something that you believe in or you can oppose something you detest. For example, if you are an environmentalist, you could spend your time promoting green living by educating the public. Or, you could spend your time holding industrial companies legally accountable by opposing their wasteful and hazardous procedures.

Once you have identified your passions, you can narrow your focus, energy, talents, time and resources on what will be most satisfying to you. The rewards of your effort will become more obvious and happen at a faster rate.

Managing Your Time According To Your Mission Statement

Determining your priorities is a good way to start organizing how you manage your time. Use this worksheet to decide on an order to your priorities and to allot time accordingly. By clarifying what's most important to you in life, you'll have a springboard for making the best decisions.

You may have noticed that some of the things you value do not take a long time to fulfill. For instance, if one of your top values is honesty in relationships, you won't need to spend fifty percent of your time fulfilling this. For values such as this, the time component isn't as helpful to examine as the rank order.

Ranking Your Priorities

1) Fill in this chart by listing your core values in the first column.
2) In the second column, rank your core values as they actually are in current practice.
3) In the third column, rank your core values in the order you want to live them out.
4) Then put the percentage of time you currently spend on each core value in the fourth column.
5) Lastly, in the fifth column, write in the percentage of time you want to spend on each core value in the future.

My Core Values	Rank Order		% of Time I	% of Time I
	Actual	Desired	Now Spend on This	Want to Spend on This
1) My job(making $)	1	2	57%	40%
2) My wife	2	1	20%	30%
3) Extended family	3	4	5%	5%
4) God	5	3	3%	10%
5) Equality	4	6	10%	5%
6) My health	6	5	5%	10%
			100%	100%

Match Your Calendar with Your Priorities

The next step is to make sure these decisions are reflected in your weekly schedule. For the next three months, compare this list once every few weeks with your schedule book or calendar. See how well your rank list matches your time choices.

Leave this plan open to revision. You may get inspired later with fresh vision or take on a new role. Adapt this mission statement accordingly, as you feel led.

BLANK WORKSHEET

Create Your Own Personal Mission Statement

In today's fast-paced and media-saturated society, it is possible to go a long period of time without stopping to reflect on the big picture of our lives. It's easy to get distracted or overwhelmed. With the explosion of new technology, there are endless ways to waste your time under the seductive guise of entertainment.

Instead of losing sight of the big picture, take a moment to complete these sentences. In effect, you will synthesize your personal mission for each of these main areas of your life.

RELATIONSHIPS: I want to show the treasured people in my life that I care for them by _____

_____

_____

_____

CHARACTER: I want to be remembered as a person who was _____

_____

_____

_____

BEING PRODUCTIVE: Before I die, I want to accomplish my goal(s) of

_____

_____

_____

ABILITIES: The main skill(s) I have to offer to others is _____

_____

_____

_____

SERVICE: In my own way, I would like to make the world a better place for at least one person by _____

_____

_____

Identify your Passions

What things in life get you the most excited? _____

_____

What activities cause you to lose track of time, because you're so absorbed in what you're doing? _____

_____

What things in life bother you the most, such that you wish you could obliterate them from the face of the earth? _____

_____

Is there a certain group of people that you feel drawn to assist (such as the poor, single parents, the disabled, political refugees, etc.)? _____

_____

To live a life that revolves around your purpose or calling, it is essential to recognize what you are most passionately for and against. You can promote something that you believe in, or you can oppose something you detest. For example, if you are an environmentalist, you could spend your time promoting green living by educating the public. Or, you could spend your time holding industrial companies legally accountable by opposing their wasteful and hazardous procedures.

Once you have identified your passions, you can narrow your focus, energy, talents, time and resources on what will be most satisfying to you. The rewards of your effort will become more obvious and happen at a faster rate.

Managing Your Time According To Your Mission Statement

Determining your priorities is a good way to start organizing how you manage your time. Use this worksheet to decide on an order to your priorities and to allot time accordingly. By clarifying what's most important to you in life, you'll have a springboard for making the best decisions.

You may have noticed that some of the things you value do not take a long time to fulfill. For instance, if one of your top values is honesty in relationships, you won't need to spend fifty percent of your time fulfilling this. For values such as this, the time component isn't as helpful to examine as the rank order.

Ranking Your Priorities

1) Fill in this chart by listing your core values in the first column.
2) In the second column, rank your core values as they actually are in current practice.
3) In the third column, rank your core values in the order you want to live them out.
4) Then put the percentage of time you currently spend on each core value in the fourth column.
5) Lastly, in the fifth column, write in the percentage of time you want to spend on each core value in the future.

My Core Values	Rank Order		% of Time I	% of Time I
	Actual	Desired	Now Spend on This	Want to Spend on This
1) _____	___	___	___%	___%
2) _____	___	___	___%	___%
3) _____	___	___	___%	___%
4) _____	___	___	___%	___%
5) _____	___	___	___%	___%
6) _____	___	___	___%	___%
7) _____	___	___	___%	___%
8) _____	___	___	___%	___%
9) _____	___	___	___%	___%
10) _____	___	___	___%	___%
			100%	100%

Match Your Calendar with Your Priorities

The next step is to make sure these decisions are reflected in your weekly schedule. For the next three months, compare this list once every few weeks with your schedule book or calendar. See how well your rank list matches your time choices.

Leave this plan open to revision. You may get inspired later with fresh vision or take on a new role. Adapt this mission statement accordingly, as you feel led.

Appendix E

Steps To Implement a Boundary

Completed Sample Worksheet
Steps To Implement a Boundary

Think of a situation in your life in which you think you need to set a limit. Choose a situation that seems like it won't spiral out of control and won't surpass your current confidence level or skills. If you're feeling too unsure of yourself, narrow your focus or select a smaller limit to assert.

Describe the situation: *I (Jenny) confided in my brother Dylan that I've been smoking cigarettes with some of my friends, but I'm trying to quit. Dylan then proceeded to tell our parents, who told my aunt and uncle. Now I'm getting reprimanded by my family for picking up my smoking habit again.*

Step One: Identify a person involved in the situation who is basically respectful and kind. If there is no one in the situation that fits this description and you are new at setting boundaries, choose a different situation with other people. It's best to start setting boundaries with gentle and respectful people first. Avoid starting with those people who are the biggest manipulators and bullies you know. Practice your skills and gain more confidence before you attempt to set limits with rude or irresponsible people.

My 1st Step: The person in this situation that I'd like to talk with is *my brother Dylan for not keeping what I told him private. I'll eventually need to deal with my other family members too, but I first need to talk to Dylan.*

Step Two: What do you want to be different in the situation? What would need to change in order for this to occur? Are there certain things you want to take responsibility for and other things for which you want the other person to be responsible?

My 2nd Step: The things in this situation that I want to be different are *I don't want our family to be gossiping about each other. I want to be able to trust that what I tell one person won't get spread around to others. I want us to use discretion in what we share.*

STEP THREE: Practice what you will say to this person. Focus on being calm, direct and respectful. A basic outline is to state:

a)   how you see things.

b)   what is happening that you don't like.

c)   how it affects you negatively.

d)   what you want to happen in the future instead.

You could practice this out loud or in writing. If it's a sensitive issue, consult a wise and supportive person in your life. Let him/her know your plans, get feedback and explain how he/she can support you.

MY 3RD STEP: An outline of what I'd like to say is *Dylan, I'm upset with you for telling Mom and Dad about me smoking again sometimes. I shared that with you confidentially and thought I could trust you. Now I'm getting heat from the rest of the family. I want us to be able to tell each other private things and not have to worry about it being spread to others. Will you agree to this, or should I just be more careful in what I tell you?*

STEP FOUR: Find a good time to talk to the person with whom you want to set a limit. It shouldn't be a rushed or hectic time. It should be in a private setting, as long as you'll be safe. Make sure you've had adequate sleep and food so that your thoughts are clear and your mood is stable.

MY 4TH STEP: The setting and time period in which I will attempt to speak to this person is *I will talk with him about it in the car while we're driving to John's house.*

STEP FIVE: Expect to feel unsure of yourself right before and after you set the boundary. You may doubt whether it is worth it or whether it will do any good. Remember that there is a healthy balance between considering both your needs and others' needs. Healthy limits are protective of both parties' needs and interests.

Stand Your Ground

Be prepared to stand your ground. Some people will challenge your decision and try to deter you from enforcing your boundary. In an effort to get you to recant, people may try to:

- pressure you to change your mind.
- gain more sympathy from you to so that you will do more for them.
- try to make you feel guilty.
- be pushy and demanding.
- be verbally, physically or emotionally abusive.
- disregard your boundary or violate your limits and see how you react.

You shouldn't have to justify your decision or make excuses. If you get resistance, calmly restate your boundary and end the conversation. In order to be successful at maximizing your life through setting limits, you will need to be assertive and persistent at maintaining your boundaries.

My 5TH STEP: What will help me to stick to my decision and maintain my boundary is *If Dylan won't promise me that he'll keep things private, then I am pretty motivated to stop confiding in him. Deterring family gossip will help me stick to my decision.*

Benefits of Clear Boundaries

- Protects the well-being of you and others
- Keeps you from being too busy and overwhelmed with responsibilities
- Frees you from needless pressure and obligation
- Improves mental health
- Ensures time for rest and relaxation
- Allows you to be healthy enough to effectively minister to others
- Prevents you from being taken advantage of or manipulated by others
- Releases you from anger, bitterness, and resentment that comes from having poor boundaries
- Prevents burnout
- Provides clear understanding in your relationships of where you each stand, what you both expect and want. This leads to greater satisfaction in relationships.

BLANK WORKSHEET

Steps To Implement a Boundary

Think of a situation in your life in which you think you need to set a limit. Choose a situation that seems like it won't spiral out of control and won't surpass your current confidence level or skills. If you're feeling too unsure of yourself, narrow your focus or select a smaller limit to assert.

Describe the situation: _____

_____

_____

STEP ONE: Identify a person involved in the situation who is basically respectful and kind. If there is no one in the situation that fits this description and you are new at setting boundaries, choose a different situation with other people. It's best to start setting boundaries with gentle and respectful people first. Avoid starting with those people who are the biggest manipulators and bullies you know. Practice your skills and gain more confidence before you attempt to set limits with rude or irresponsible people.

MY 1ST STEP: The person in this situation that I'd like to talk with is

_____

_____

STEP TWO: What do you want to be different in the situation? What would need to change in order for this to occur? Are there certain things you want to take responsibility for and other things for which you want the other person to be responsible?

MY 2ND STEP: The things in this situation that I want to be different are

_____

_____

_____

STEP THREE: Practice what you will say to this person. Focus on being calm, direct and respectful. A basic outline is to state:

a)   how you see things.

b)   what is happening that you don't like.

c)   how it affects you negatively.

d)   what you want to happen in the future instead.

You could practice this out loud or in writing. If it's a sensitive issue, consult a wise and supportive person in your life. Let him/her know your plans, get feedback and explain how he/she can support you.

My 3rd Step: An outline of what I'd like to say is _____

_____

_____

STEP FOUR: Find a good time to talk to the person with whom you want to set a limit. It shouldn't be a rushed or hectic time. It should be in a private setting, as long as you'll be safe. Make sure you've had adequate sleep and food so that your thoughts are clear and your mood is stable.

My 4th Step: The setting and time period in which I will attempt to speak to this person is _____

_____

_____

STEP FIVE: Expect to feel unsure of yourself right before and after you set the boundary. You may doubt whether it is worth it or whether it will do any good. Remember that there is a healthy balance between considering both your needs and others' needs. Healthy limits are protective of both parties' needs and interests.

Stand Your Ground

Be prepared to stand your ground. Some people will challenge your decision and try to deter you from enforcing your boundary. In an effort to get you to recant, people may try to:

- pressure you to change your mind.
- gain more sympathy from you to so that you will do more for them.
- try to make you feel guilty.
- be pushy and demanding.
- be verbally, physically or emotionally abusive.
- disregard your boundary or violate your limits and see how you react.

You shouldn't have to justify your decision or make excuses. If you get resistance, calmly restate your boundary and end the conversation. In order to be successful at maximizing your life through setting limits, you will need to be assertive and persistent at maintaining your boundaries.

My 5th Step: What will help me to stick to my decision and maintain my boundary is _____

_____

_____

Benefits of Clear Boundaries

- Protects the well-being of you and others
- Keeps you from being too busy and overwhelmed with responsibilities
- Frees you from needless pressure and obligation
- Improves mental health
- Ensures time for rest and relaxation
- Allows you to be healthy enough to effectively minister to others
- Prevents you from being taken advantage of or manipulated by others
- Releases you from anger, bitterness and resentment that comes from having poor boundaries
- Prevents burnout
- Provides clear understanding in your relationships of where you each stand, what you both expect and want. This leads to greater satisfaction in relationships.

Appendix F

Quick Health Tips
Good Fats, Bad Fats

Believe it or not, there is such a thing as good fats. The type of fat is more important than the total amount of fat consumed.

The Good

Monosaturated and polyunsaturated fats (this includes omega-3 and omega-6 fatty acids in fish, canola oil, olive oil, many nuts, flaxseeds and avocados). Several studies report decreased risk of heart disease and heart attack with increased intake of these fats.

The Bad

Trans fatty acids (in products such as some margarines, store-bought cakes, cookies, muffins, chips and oils used for fast foods). Higher intake is linked to increased risk of heart attack. Avoid foods with the label "partially hydrogenated" or "hydrogenated oil."

Saturated fatty acids (in red meat, dairy products). Associated with increase risk of heart attack. There is some evidence that decreased intake leads to decrease in prostate and colon cancer.

Take Home Points: Try to replace trans and saturated fatty acids with monounsaturated and polyunsaturated fats. Eat fish once or twice a week. Remove skin from chicken and excess fat off of meats. Use lean cuts of meat. Try soybean products. Bake, broil and grill rather than fry. Slim down the dairy. Switch from whole or 2% milk to fat-free. Ditch the butter. Instead, cook with olive oil and canola oil. Limit margarines, packaged foods, and fast food which tend to contain high amounts of saturated and trans fatty acids.

Fiber

What is fiber anyway? Fiber is the part of the food that you can't digest (includes wheat, brown rice, oats, fruits and vegetables).

- High fiber intake significantly decreases the risk of heart attack and stroke compared with low intake of fiber.
- Increased fiber intake decreases the risk of developing diabetes.
- Increased intake, particularly in fruits and vegetables, improves the blood sugar control in diabetics.

Take Home Points: Eat whole wheat and grain breads instead of white bread. Replace white rice with brown rice. Add oatmeal to your menu. Eat whole grain cereals.

Benefits of Fruits and Vegetables (F/V)

For people eating five or more servings of fruits and vegetables a day, there is a decreased risk of stroke compared to those who eat less than three servings a day. Each serving of F/V a day decreased the risk of stroke by 6% (up to six servings a day).

Those eating a high intake of F/V had a 15% decrease in heart attack compared with those eating less of F/V.

Five to six servings a day of F/V gives the most benefit.

What is a serving? A yogurt, eight ounces of milk, one slice of bread, a cup of chopped broccoli, a medium apple. Read labels.

Take Home Points: Eat your fruits and veggies! Aim for at least five servings a day. Make sure to have fruit or vegetables easily available and already prepared so that they can be eaten as snacks as well as with meals.

Health Benefits from Exercise and Physical Activity

- Those who exercise regularly live longer.
- Decreases risk of heart attack and stroke.
- Exercise increases metabolism. This is essential for weight control.
- Maintains and/or improves muscle strength.

- Improves blood sugar control in diabetes.
- Decreases blood pressure.
- Improves cholesterol levels.
- Decreases anxiety and depression.
- Improves insomnia.
- Prevents osteoporosis.
- Improves fibromyalgia and chronic pain syndromes.
- Protects against certain types of cancer.
- Can help you to quit smoking.

What Can Help You Get Started?

- Start low and go slow.
- Set a goal of thirty minutes of exercise, four to six times a week.
- Look for things that you like to do. It can be as simple as walking, gardening, playing basketball, dancing, swimming (particularly good for people with arthritis, fibromyalgia, or other pain problems), bicycling, rollerblading etc.
- A habit takes ninety days to stick. So hang in there.
- It's best to have a partner to keep you on track.

Appendix G

Allowing Your Emotions To Succeed

Completed Sample Worksheet #1

Allowing Your Emotions To Succeed:

How can they help you? Will you let them?

Frequently, people view their emotion as the main problem. A woman may think, "I'm feeling so sad. I wish this feeling would go away." A man may think that he is a terrible person, because he is full of anger all of the time. A third person may say, "I'm fearful of this situation in my life. I wish I weren't so anxious." They're blaming themselves or their emotion for their suffering.

Many people simply want their uncomfortable feelings to quietly slip away, as quickly as possible. They want to get back to feeling "normal" so that they can get on with their tasks. In this manner, it is the emotion that is mistakenly being seen as the obstacle or hindrance.

This worksheet is a tool for evaluating the good purpose of a certain emotion that you're feeling. You can be guaranteed that emotion is there for a reason. It's not there to make you suffer but to assist you—to teach you and guide you. Emotions are meant to serve a wide variety of purposes in your life. This exercise allows you to consciously and deliberately determine how you can benefit from what you're feeling right now and to develop a plan of action.

Identifying The Emotion and Its Role

1) What emotion have you been feeling lately? (Just pick one.) *Fear*.

2) Can you identify which situation, circumstance or person this feeling seems to be related to? *I've been stressed over money*.

3) Based on The Two Categories of Emotion, this emotion belongs in which category?

    ◯ A "Reinforcer" Feeling   ⊗   A "Change-Indicator" Feeling

4) The general functions of emotions are listed below. Which general functions do you think this specific emotion typically performs?

⊗ Focuses our attention   ⊗ Guides and instructs us
⊗ Motivates us   ⊗ Helps us to adjust
⊗ Supplies us with energy   ⊗ Protects us or what we value
  and strength   ⊗ Protects us or what we value
⊗ Gives us new information   ⊗ Prepares and equips us
⊗ Aids us in decision-making   ○ Brings enjoyment to life

What Is Your Emotion Trying To Accomplish?

1) What could this emotion be attempting to get you to understand about your situation, yourself or what's important to you?

EXAMPLE: I'm feeling lonely. Maybe I need to spend more time with friends.
EXAMPLE: I'm feeling unsatisfied at work. Perhaps I'm not being challenged enough.

MY EMOTION COULD BE TELLING ME: *I don't want to live under this amount of stress. I need to find a way to make more money or to be assured that I can make ends meet every month. Plus, the debt I have is wearing me down.*

2) What could this emotion be showing you that you want/need for yourself, for your situation or your future?

EXAMPLE: I need to go out with my friends more or else I'll be lonely and bored.
EXAMPLE: I need to find a job that suits my abilities better.

I WANT/NEED: *I need more stability in my finances and to have a better idea of my budget. I don't really know what all my expenses are or how I could get out of debt the fastest.*

3) What might this emotion be guiding you to do? What action might it be urging you to take?

EXAMPLE: I'm going to make plans ahead of time for the weekend, so that I can count on getting together with friends regularly.

EXAMPLE: I want to research job openings in my field or see if a transfer to a different department in my company is available.

WHAT I MAY DO IS: *I need to write down a complete budget that lists all my expenses and income. I think getting it on paper will help me to not be so worried every time I spend money. I could also look at going back to school to get a higher paying job.*

4) What might it be leading you to say, and to whom?

EXAMPLE: To the friend I lost touch with, I could say, "I'm sorry I dropped the ball on our friendship. I miss getting together. Do you have any free time this week?"
EXAMPLE: To the human resources department at work, I want to say, "Are there any new job postings this week? I like my job now, but I'm open to other possibilities, too."

I COULD SAY: *I could ask my boss for a raise. I could call up the college nearby and get some information on their programs. Maybe I could talk to my cousin, who is an accountant, for some help with my budget and financial planning.*

5) Now that you've put together this plan, you probably have a better idea of some of the good that this emotion is trying to do for you. What do you think you may gain by completing the plan you just made?

EXAMPLE: Our relationship will be a lot better, and we'd both likely be happier.
EXAMPLE: I could get a job that's more fulfilling and satisfying.

WHAT I COULD GAIN IS: *If I did these things, I could know for sure how much money I had to spend each month on certain items. Plus, I could come up with a plan to get out of debt and begin to save up a bit of money for emergencies. That would alleviate a lot of stress. I think I'd sleep better at night and not be so grouchy sometimes.*

It's Your Choice: Friend or Foe?

You are free to choose to what extent you allow your emotions to serve you in your life. You can choose to make them the enemy or your servant, your friend or foe.

If you ignore how you're feeling, your emotion will not go away. This is because you will be blocking it from bringing the solution and positive changes to your life that are needed. Your feelings will linger until you respond to them.

If you choose to accept your feelings and work with them to accomplish their purpose, you stand to gain great benefit. The good news is that once an uncomfortable emotion has achieved its purpose, it goes away rapidly.

So what will it be? Will you partner with your emotion and let it accomplish its purposes? Will you opt to let your emotions work for you or consider them your opponent?

COMPLETED SAMPLE WORKSHEET #2

Allowing Your Emotions To Succeed:
How can they help you? Will you let them?

Frequently, people view their emotion as the main problem. A woman may think, "I'm feeling so sad. I wish this feeling would go away." A man may think that he is a terrible person, because he is full of anger all of the time. A third person may say, "I'm fearful of this situation in my life. I wish I weren't so anxious." They're blaming themselves or their emotion for their suffering.

Many people simply want their uncomfortable feelings to quietly slip away, as quickly as possible. They want to get back to feeling "normal" so that they can get on with their tasks. In this manner, it is the emotion that is mistakenly being seen as the obstacle or hindrance.

This worksheet is a tool for evaluating the good purpose of a certain emotion that you're feeling. You can be guaranteed that emotion is there for a reason. It's not there to make you suffer but to assist you—to teach you and guide you. Emotions are meant to serve a wide variety of purposes in your life. This exercise allows you to consciously and deliberately determine how you can benefit from what you're feeling right now and to develop a plan of action.

Identifying The Emotion and Its Role

1) What emotion have you been feeling lately? (Just pick one.) *Sadness*

2) Can you identify which situation, circumstance or person this feeling seems to be related to? *I've lost touch with a good friend of mine. We have not talked or seen each other in months.*

3) Based on The Two Categories of Emotion, this emotion belongs in which category?

   ◯ A "Reinforcer" Feeling   ⊗ A "Change-Indicator" Feeling

4) The general functions of emotions are listed below. Which general functions do you think this specific emotion typically performs?

⊗ Focuses our attention   ⊗ Guides and instructs us
⊗ Motivates us   ⊗ Helps us to adjust
○ Supplies us with energy   ○ Protects us or what we value
   and strength
⊗ Gives us new information   ⊗ Prepares and equips us
⊗ Aids us in decision-making   ○ Brings enjoyment to life

What Is Your Emotion Trying To Accomplish?

1) What could this emotion be attempting to get you to understand about your situation, yourself or what's important to you?

EXAMPLE: I'm feeling lonely. Maybe I need to spend more time with friends.
EXAMPLE: I'm feeling unsatisfied at work. Perhaps I'm not being challenged enough.

MY EMOTION COULD BE TELLING ME: *I don't think I realized how much our friendship meant to me. I miss it.*

2) What could this emotion be showing you that you want/need for yourself, for your situation or your future?

EXAMPLE: I need to go out with my friends more or else I'll be lonely and bored.
EXAMPLE: I need to find a job that suits my abilities better.

I WANT/NEED: *I need to have good friends like that in my life. I want to try to get back in contact again.*

3) What might this emotion be guiding you to do? What action might it be urging you to take?

EXAMPLE: I'm going to make plans ahead of time for the weekend, so that I can count on getting together with friends regularly.

EXAMPLE: I want to research job openings in my field or see if a transfer to a different department in my company is available.

WHAT I MAY DO IS: *I will call and see if we can get together. If it's not going to work out, then I think I need to find some other people to hang out with whom I can be open and have a great time.*

4) What might it be leading you to say, and to whom?

EXAMPLE: To the friend I lost touch with, I could say, "I'm sorry I dropped the ball on our friendship. I miss getting together. Do you have any free time this week?"
EXAMPLE: To the human resources department at work, I want to say, "Are there any new job postings this week? I like my job now, but I'm open to other possibilities, too."

I COULD SAY: *I think I might tell this friend what they mean to me and how I value our friendship. If they're too busy to get together regularly, then I will call up some other people.*

5) Now that you've put together this plan, you probably have a better idea of some of the good that this emotion is trying to do for you. What do you think you may gain by completing the plan you just made?

EXAMPLE: Our relationship will be a lot better, and we'd both likely be happier.
EXAMPLE: I could get a job that's more fulfilling and satisfying.

WHAT I COULD GAIN IS: *I think that it would help me to not be lonely anymore. I think I'd be happier and enjoy day-to-day life more if I had more good friends and went through life with them.*

It's Your Choice: Friend or Foe?

You are free to choose to what extent you allow your emotions to serve you in your life. You can choose to make them the enemy or your servant, your friend or foe.

If you ignore how you're feeling, your emotion will not go away. This is because you will be blocking it from bringing the solution and positive changes to your life that are needed. Your feelings will linger until you respond to them.

If you choose to accept your feelings and work with them to accomplish their purpose, you stand to gain great benefit. The good news is that once an uncomfortable emotion has achieved its purpose, it goes away rapidly.

So what will it be? Will you partner with your emotion and let it accomplish its purposes? Will you opt to let your emotions work for you or consider them your opponent?

Blank Worksheet

Allowing Your Emotions To Succeed:
How can they help you? Will you let them?

Frequently, people view their emotion as the main problem. A woman may think, "I'm feeling so sad. I wish this feeling would go away." A man may think that he is a terrible person, because he is full of anger all of the time. A third person may say, "I'm fearful of this situation in my life. I wish I weren't so anxious." They're blaming themselves or their emotion for their suffering.

Many people simply want their uncomfortable feelings to quietly slip away, as quickly as possible. They want to get back to feeling "normal" so that they can get on with their tasks. In this manner, it is the emotion that is mistakenly being seen as the obstacle or hindrance.

This worksheet is a tool for evaluating the good purpose of a certain emotion that you're feeling. You can be guaranteed that emotion is there for a reason. It's not there to make you suffer but to assist you—to teach you and guide you. Emotions are meant to serve a wide variety of purposes in your life. This exercise allows you to consciously and deliberately determine how you can benefit from what you're feeling right now and to develop a plan of action.

Identifying The Emotion and Its Role

1) What emotion have you been feeling lately? (Just pick one.) _____

2) Can you identify which situation, circumstance or person this feeling seems to be related to? _____

_____

3) Based on The Two Categories of Emotion, this emotion belongs in which category?

   ☐ A "Reinforcer" Feeling   ☐   A "Change-Indicator" Feeling

4) The general functions of emotions are listed below. Which general functions do you think this specific emotion typically performs?

□ Focuses our attention   □ Guides and instructs us
□ Motivates us   □ Helps us to adjust
□ Supplies us with energy   □ Protects us or what we value
   and strength
□ Gives us new information   □ Prepares and equips us
□ Aids us in decision-making   □ Brings enjoyment to life

What Is Your Emotion Trying To Accomplish?

1) What could this emotion be attempting to get you to understand about your situation, yourself or what's important to you?

Example: I'm feeling lonely. Maybe I need to spend more time with friends.
Example: I'm feeling unsatisfied at work. Perhaps I'm not being challenged enough.

My emotion could be telling me: _____

_____

_____

2) What could this emotion be showing you that you want/need for yourself, for your situation or your future?

Example: I need to go out with my friends more or else I'll be lonely and bored.
Example: I need to find a job that suits my abilities better.

I want/need: _____

_____

_____

3) What might this emotion be guiding you to do? What action might it be urging you to take?

Example: I'm going to make plans ahead of time for the weekend, so that I can count on getting together with friends regularly.

Example: I want to research job openings in my field or see if a transfer to a different department in my company is available.

What I may do is: _____

_____

_____

4) What might it be leading you to say, and to whom?

Example: To the friend I lost touch with, I could say, "I'm sorry I dropped the ball on our friendship. I miss getting together. Do you have any free time this week?"

Example: To the human resources department at work, I want to say, "Are there any new job postings this week? I like my job now, but I'm open to other possibilities, too."

I could say: _____

_____

_____

5) Now that you've put together this plan, you probably have a better idea of some of the good that this emotion is trying to do for you. What do you think you may gain by following through on the plan you just made?

Example: Our relationship will be a lot better, and we'd both likely be happier.

Example: I could get a job that's more fulfilling and satisfying.

What I could gain is: _____

_____

_____

It's Your Choice: Friend or Foe?

You are free to choose to what extent you allow your emotions to serve you in your life. You can choose to make them the enemy or your servant, your friend or foe.

If you ignore how you're feeling, your emotion will not go away. This is because you will be blocking it from bringing the solution and positive changes to your life that are needed. Your feelings will linger until you respond to them.

If you choose to accept your feelings and work with them to accomplish their purpose, you stand to gain great benefit. The good news is that once an uncomfortable emotion has achieved its purpose, it goes away rapidly.

So what will it be? Will you partner with your emotion and let it accomplish its purposes? Will you opt to let your emotions work for you or consider them your opponent?

Appendix H

The Four-Point Model of Decision-Making

Completed Sample Worksheet
The Four-Point Model of Decision-Making

	Score of 0 or 1
Logic -	1
Emotion -	1
God's Will -	1
Wise Advice -	0
Total Score: # of factors that line up in agreement (0–4)	3

Steps To Making a Well-Thought-Out Decision

Each of the above components is a main factor in determining how to make a decision. For any decision you face, it can be smart to consider each of these.

1) Describe the dilemma about which you have to make a decision: *I (Rebecca) need to make a decision whether or not to marry Frank.*

2) Formulate the decision into a yes/no question. "Should I move to Chicago," or "Should I take this volunteer position," or "Should I buy a new car." My question: *Should I marry Frank?*

3) Logic: Looking at the circumstances of the situation, what does your logic tell you to do? *My logic says that I respect his character, we have shared values, our friendship is strong and we enjoy each other's company a lot. Logic scores one point.*

4) Emotion: Do you feel at peace or have other emotions that would reinforce answering "yes" to the question you formulated in number two? Or do you feel uneasy, hesitant or other emotions that could indicate you should answer "no" to this question or that other options would be better? Feelings that reinforce a "yes" answer to the question would score a point for emotion. *My emotion in response to the question is that I love him and feel*

excited about the idea of spending our lives together. These are "Reinforcer" emotions. Emotion scores one point.

5) GOD'S WILL: If you're a praying person, ask God to guide you in the decision. Listen in prayer, and look for signs of His guidance in your life. As closely as you comprehend it, what do you think is God's will in this situation? (If you are a dedicated Christian, you may want to have God's will count for more than all of the rest, (i.e. weigh it as two or three potential points). *I think that it may be God's will for us to get married. I haven't sensed Him telling me not to marry Frank. Add one point for God's will.*

6) WISE ADVICE: Do the people you respect in your life support or oppose the option you are considering? What have they said? *I sought advice from Dorothy, my wise, caring aunt. Dorothy suggested that I am too young to get married and haven't known Frank long enough. She advised me to wait a year before committing to marriage. Wise advice scores zero points.*

7) Tally up the score. How many aspects line up in agreement? Total: _3_

8) Reflect, and finalize your decision. A score of four implies that this is likely a sound, reliable decision. You may feel comfortable saying "yes" to your question with a score of three or four. If you scored only one or two, it may be prudent to deliberate further, glean more information in order to make your decision, or say "no" to the question you're asking yourself.

MY DECISION: *I'm not sure if this score is high enough to get engaged. Because this is such a major decision, maybe I should wait until all these main components are in harmony and score a four before I go through with it.*

BLANK WORKSHEET

The Four-Point Model of Decision-Making

> Score of 0 or 1
>
> Logic -   ____
>
> Emotion -   ____
>
> God's Will -   ____
>
> Wise Advice -   ____
>
> Total Score: # of factors that line up in agreement (0–4)   ____

Steps To Making a Well-Thought-Out Decision

Each of the above components is a main factor in determining how to make a decision. For any decision you face, it can be smart to consider each of these.

1) Describe the dilemma about which you have to make a decision:

   _____

   _____

   _____

2) Formulate the decision into a yes/no question. "Should I move to Chicago?" or "Should I take this volunteer position?" or "Should I buy a new car?"
   My question: _____

   _____

3) LOGIC: Looking at the circumstances of the situation, what does your logic tell you to do? _____

   _____

   _____

4) EMOTION: Do you feel at peace or have other emotions that would reinforce answering "yes" to the question you formulated in number two? Or do

you feel uneasy, hesitant or other emotions that could indicate you should answer "no" to this question or that other options would be better? Feelings that reinforce a "yes" answer to the question would score a point for emotion. _____

_____

_____

5) GOD'S WILL: If you're a praying person, ask God to guide you in the decision. Listen in prayer, and look for signs of His guidance in your life. As closely as you comprehend it, what do you think is God's will in this situation? (If you are a dedicated Christian, you may want to have God's will count for more than all of the rest, (i.e. weigh it as two or three potential points). _____

_____

_____

6) WISE ADVICE: Do the people you respect in your life support or oppose the option you are considering? What have they said? _____

_____

_____

7) TALLY UP THE SCORE. How many aspects line up in agreement? Total: ____

8) REFLECT, AND FINALIZE YOUR DECISION. A score of four implies that this is likely a sound, reliable decision. You may feel comfortable saying "yes" to your question with a score of three or four. If you scored only one or two, it may be prudent to deliberate further, glean more information in order to make your decision, or say "no" to the question you're asking yourself. My Decision: _____

_____

_____

Appendix I

Quality Apologies

Completed Sample Worksheet
Quality Apologies

If it is possible, as far as it depends on you, live at peace with everyone.

Romans 12:18

All of you, clothe yourselves with humility toward one another, because,
"God opposes the proud but gives grace to the humble."

1 Peter 5:5

Unresolved conflict is a barrier to strong relationships. As most will concur, it is by far easier to forgive someone if they have apologized. Certainly one can forgive whether or not an apology has been given, yet it takes more determination, understanding and grace.

Whether you are the one who needs to give an apology or receive it, it may help you to know the ingredients of a Quality Apology. The following is a description of the elements and process that lead to a meaningful, effective apology.

Remember that the tone, timing and circumstances of an apology can make all the difference. Sincerity is a prerequisite. Humility is an aid. Evidence of remorse and the beginnings of change are your best assistants. Without these, you may not be taken seriously. Without these, you may not be ready to apologize.

Components of an Apology

1) Be respectful of the other person's choice to forgive or not. Do not demand forgiveness. Find a time to talk when you won't be rushed, and a location that is private (if both parties feel comfortable being alone together).

2) Admit your error, fault or sin.

EXAMPLES: "I have wronged you by…" "I messed up by…" "I did something I shouldn't have when I…" "I made a mistake when I…"

YOUR STATEMENT OF ERROR: *I (Spencer) messed up when I promised to help you move, Derek, and then I didn't show up. What makes it worse is that I lied about why I didn't come. I wasn't really sick. I got a last-minute invitation to go skiing, and I went because there was so much new snow.*

3) Acknowledge your responsibility in the matter. Don't make excuses. Don't tell the other person what he/she was responsible for.

EXAMPLES: "It was my fault that…" "It was wrong of me to…" "I'm sorry that I…." "No one else made me…"

ADMIT YOUR RESPONSIBILITY: *I'm sorry that I left you in a jam. It was wrong of me to commit to help you move and then break my promise. I'm embarrassed to admit it, but I was being selfish and I intentionally deceived you when I lied about my excuse.*

4) Humbly guess how you think you affected the other person. Express how you think you may have harmed them or impacted them negatively through your mistakes, actions or words. State this tentatively and not authoritatively.

EXAMPLES: "My actions may have caused…" "I think that I made you feel…" "I may have made it hard for you to trust others by…"

YOUR GUESS AT HOW YOU AFFECTED THEM: *My actions probably made your moving day a lot harder. It must have been brutal to lift all of the heavy furniture. I think that my actions must be hurtful, and you have every right to be mad at me. You probably will have a hard time trusting me in the future because of my actions.*

5) State your hope for how you would like to conduct yourself differently in the future. Explain how you would like the situation to go next time, if it could/does arise again.

EXAMPLES: "Next time…" "If I get in this situation again I plan on…" "In the future, I hope I…"

YOUR HOPES AND PLANS FOR THE FUTURE: *Next time I make a promise to you, I am not going to break it. If there is an unavoidable conflict or problem that comes up, I plan on being honest with you and not deceitful like I was this past time.*

6) Ask the person to forgive you.

EXAMPLES: "I'm so sorry. Will you forgive me?" "I regret what I've done to you. Will you try to forgive me?" "I know you may not be ready to now, but I'm willing to wait for you to forgive me. Will you try to prepare to forgive me?"

YOUR REQUEST: *You're one of my best friends. I feel terrible for lying to you and breaking a promise. Will you forgive me?*

Complete All Six Steps!

Many people stop the process of forgiveness or reconciliation after step five of the apology. The offender or perpetrator doesn't specifically ask the other person to forgive them. Do not stop there! It can mean a critical difference in the future of your relationship in two ways.

First, if you are the offender and you only say you're sorry and don't ask the person to forgive you, then the person may never truly make the choice in his or her heart to forgive you. You see, if you don't bring it up specifically, the person may never get to the point of decision. The other person may not ask himself or herself if they are actually going to forgive you. They may have listened to you and appreciated what you said, but not made the actual decision to forgive.

Consequently, they may go on harboring bitterness and resentment against you, even though you said you were sorry. If they are able to forgive you and say it out loud, then it somehow causes a change in their heart. It also holds them accountable to themselves and to you that they have pardoned you.

The second result of not actually asking the other person to forgive you is that you may never get to hear the wonderfully freeing words "I forgive you." Stopping the process prematurely by skipping step six may steal from you the joy and sense of cleansing that comes from being forgiven.

Giving an apology and working toward reconciliation is not complete without this step of directly asking for forgiveness.

Blank Worksheet

Quality Apologies

If it is possible, as far as it depends on you, live at peace with everyone.

Romans 12:18

All of you, clothe yourselves with humility toward one another, because,
"God opposes the proud but gives grace to the humble."

1 Peter 5:5

Unresolved conflict is a barrier to strong relationships. As most will concur, it is by far easier to forgive someone if they have apologized. Certainly one can forgive whether or not an apology has been given, yet it takes more determination, understanding and grace.

Whether you are the one who needs to give an apology or receive it, it may help you to know the ingredients of a Quality Apology. The following is a description of the elements and process that lead to a meaningful, effective apology.

Remember that the tone, timing and circumstances of an apology can make all the difference. Sincerity is a prerequisite. Humility is an aid. Evidence of remorse and the beginnings of change are your best assistants. Without these, you may not be taken seriously. Without these, you may not be ready to apologize.

Components of an Apology

1) Be respectful of the other person's choice to forgive or not. Do not demand forgiveness. Find a time to talk when you won't be rushed, and a location that is private (if both parties feel comfortable being alone together).

2) Admit your error, fault or sin.

   Examples: "I have wronged you by…" "I messed up by…" "I did something I shouldn't have when I…" "I made a mistake when I…"

Your statement of error: _____

_____

_____

3) Acknowledge your responsibility in the matter. Don't make excuses. Don't tell the other person what he/she was responsible for.

   Examples: "It was my fault that..." "It was wrong of me to..." "I'm sorry that I...." "No one else made me..."

   Admit your responsibility: _____

   _____

   _____

4) Humbly guess how you think you affected the other person. Express how you think you may have harmed them or impacted them negatively through your mistakes, actions or words. State this tentatively and not authoritatively.

   Examples: "My actions may have caused..." "I think that I made you feel..." "I may have made it hard for you to trust others by..."

   Your guess at how you affected them: _____

   _____

   _____

5) State your hope for how you would like to conduct yourself differently in the future. Explain how you would like the situation to go next time, if it could/does arise again.

   Examples: "Next time..." "If I get in this situation again I plan on..." "In the future, I hope I..."

Your hopes and plans for the future: _____

_____

_____

6)   Ask the person to forgive you.

Examples: "I'm so sorry. Will you forgive me?" "I regret what I've done to you. Will you try to forgive me?" "I know you may not be ready to now, but I'm willing to wait for you to forgive me. Will you try to prepare to forgive me?"

Your request: _____

_____

_____

Complete All Six Steps!

Many people stop the process of forgiveness or reconciliation after step five of the apology. The offender or perpetrator doesn't specifically ask the other person to forgive them. Do not stop there! It can mean a critical difference in the future of your relationship in two ways.

First, if you are the offender and you only say you're sorry and don't ask the person to forgive you, then the person may never truly make the choice in his or her heart to forgive you. You see, if you don't bring it up specifically, the person may never get to the point of decision. The other person may not ask himself or herself if they are actually going to forgive you. They may have listened to you and appreciated what you said, but not made the actual decision to forgive.

Consequently, they may go on harboring bitterness and resentment against you, even though you said you were sorry. If they are able to forgive you and say it out loud, then it somehow causes a change in their heart. It also holds them accountable to themselves and to you that they have pardoned you.

The second result of not actually asking the other person to forgive you is that you may never get to hear the wonderfully freeing words "I forgive you." Stopping the process prematurely by skipping step six may steal from you the joy and sense of cleansing that comes from being forgiven.

Giving an apology and working toward reconciliation is not complete without this step of directly asking for forgiveness.

APPENDIX J

STEPS TO FORGIVENESS

Completed Sample Worksheet
Steps to Forgiveness

Forgiveness is a choice. It is an act of the will, heart and mind. It is a decision that you make for your own good and also for the well-being of others. Forgiveness is something that can happen in a moment or as a process over time.

Oftentimes the deeper hurts and more serious offenses require us to keep choosing to forgive. It is natural for our feelings of anger to resurface or linger even after we have decided to forgive someone. Therefore we sometimes need to repeat a decision to forgive, or remind ourselves that we have chosen to forgive someone. The following are steps to forgiveness on the path that can lead to reconciliation:

1) Make sure you truly understand the offense. What wrong was committed against you? What moral, spiritual or societal rules did the other person violate? Did the offender breach your trust?

   NAME THE SPECIFIC OFFENSE(s): *Spencer promised to help me (Derek) move. Then he cancelled at the last minute, saying he was sick. I found out that he lied about it and he really went skiing that day. He let me down and violated my trust.*

2) Do not rush the decision to forgive. Yes, it is good to forgive readily. Yet, you need to allow yourself the time and permission to figure out how you were harmed, injured or affected. Let yourself identify the impact the other person's actions or words had on you. If you rush the decision without recognizing the impact of the other person's actions, you may need to repeat the forgiveness process each time you realize more of the consequences of what they did to you.

HOW DID THIS PERSON AFFECT YOU? *I was left in the lurch, because I only had one other person helping me move. My back was in rough shape for days after moving. Plus, it took us much longer to move, and I had to pay a late fee for the moving truck. I felt hurt and angry when I found out that he wasn't really sick, but he went skiing instead.*

3) In your decision of whether you will forgive or not, honestly evaluate where you are and what you are capable of on your own, or with God's help. The other person(s) may or may not apologize to you and ask you for forgiveness. Either way, you still face the question of whether or not you will forgive. You may choose to respond any of the following ways:
   a) I forgive you.
   b) I will try to forgive you.
   c) I'm not ready yet.
   d) I will ask God to help me want to forgive you. I can't forgive you on my own. I need His help.

If the other person is talking with you about what happened, speak your answer out loud, directly to him or her. If the other person isn't talking to you about what happened, you may still want to speak your decision out loud since it can have a greater impact that way.

MY CHOICE IS: *Spencer seemed to be sincere in his apology. I value his friendship. I plan to say, "I forgive you."*

If you've answered (b), (c), or (d), go back to step one. It's also probably a good idea to reflect on what the benefits are of forgiving or reconciling versus the costs of holding a grudge.

Blank Worksheet

Steps to Forgiveness

Forgiveness is a choice. It is an act of the will, heart and mind. It is a decision that you make for your own good and also for the well-being of others. Forgiveness is something that can happen in a moment or as a process over time.

Oftentimes the deeper hurts and more serious offenses require us to keep choosing to forgive. It is natural for our feelings of anger to resurface or linger even after we have decided to forgive someone. Therefore we sometimes need to repeat a decision to forgive, or remind ourselves that we have chosen to forgive someone. The following are steps to forgiveness on the path that can lead to reconciliation:

1) Make sure you truly understand the offense. What wrong was committed against you? What moral, spiritual or societal rules did the other person violate? Did the offender breach your trust?

    Name the specific offense(s): _____

    _____

    _____

2) Do not rush the decision to forgive. Yes, it is good to forgive readily. Yet, you need to allow yourself the time and permission to figure out how you were harmed, injured or affected. Let yourself identify the impact the other person's actions or words had on you. If you rush the decision without recognizing the impact of the other person's actions, you may need to repeat the forgiveness process each time you realize more of the consequences of what they did to you.

    How did this person affect you? _____

    _____

    _____

3) In your decision of whether you will forgive or not, honestly evaluate where you are and what you are capable of on your own, or with God's help. The other person(s) may or may not apologize to you and ask you for forgiveness. Either way, you still face the question of whether or not you will forgive. You may choose to respond any of the following ways:
   a) I forgive you.
   b) I will try to forgive you.
   c) I'm not ready yet.
   d) I will ask God to help me want to forgive you. I can't forgive you on my own. I need His help.

If the other person is talking with you about what happened, speak your answer out loud, directly to him or her. If the other person isn't talking to you about what happened, you may still want to speak your decision out loud since it can have a greater impact that way.

My choice is: _____

_____

_____

If you've answered (b), (c), or (d), go back to step one. It's also probably a good idea to reflect on what the benefits are of forgiving or reconciling versus the costs of holding a grudge.